Eisenstein
Yon Barna

CinemaTwo

Eisenstein (right) with Léon Moussinac at a festival of independent cinema at La Sarraz, near Lausanne, September 1929

EISENSTEIN

by Yon Barna
with a Foreword by Jay Leydas

Indiana University Press
Bloomington

Eisenstein by Yon Barna
First published in 1966 by Editura Tineretului, Bucarest.
This English-language edition, substantially revised
by the author, translated by Lise Hunter,
and edited by Oliver Stallybrass,
Published in 1973 by Secker & Warburg Limited
in Great Britain and by Indiana University Press
in the U.S.A.
Copyright © 1973 Indiana University Press

Library of Congress catalog card number: 73-81159
ISBN: 0·253-12135-3 (U.S.A.)

Printed in Great Britain

Contents

Foreword
by Jay Leyda   page   7

Introduction   9

  1. Sketch for a Portrait   11

  2. The Path towards Art   20

  3. Through Theatre to Film   46

  4. *Strike*   73

  5. *Battleship Potemkin*   90

  6. Searchings: from *October* to *The General Line* 114

  7. Abroad   138

  8. *Que Viva Mexico!*   163

  9. 'Polemics Rage Around Me'   186

10. Pedagogic Respite   202

11. *Alexander Nevsky*   206

12. The Path towards *Ivan*   222

13. *Ivan the Terrible*   234

14. Years of Meditation   264

15. Requiem   271

Notes and References   274

Bibliographical Note   279

Index   282

Acknowledgments   288

The first outline scenario that I ever wrote – for a pantomime – tells the story of an unhappy young man wandering, among others like himself, along a predestined, fixed and unchangeable trajectory.

Then comes the dreadful moment when the hero, proud till then of the straight line he has been keeping, that cuts through the meandering paths of his fellows, suddenly realizes that his own path is not a freely chosen one, but that his 'straight line' is in fact the circumference of a circle, which, though distant from the centre, is nonetheless just as surely predestined as those of the other characters.

The pantomime ends with a general cortège of intercut geometrical trajectories, which little by little drives the hero out of his mind.

EISENSTEIN

6

Foreword

Since the surprising appearance in 1939 of Vsevolod Vishnevsky's brochure, there has not been such an understanding and honest account of Sergei Eisenstein's life as this book by Yon Barna. Both Vishnevsky (on a small scale) and Barna (on a grand scale) show Eisenstein's career as one of constant struggle and constant victories, even though we have not directly benefited by all the films he wished to make. His victories are within the never-ending process of growth that can inspire us in the life of every great and stubborn artist – whether his name is Musorgsky or Bach, Daumier or Rembrandt, Balzac or Joyce – and it is this creative process that is the proper theme of Barna's biography.

Such a process is so powerful that it cannot be ended by death: it continues in the growth of other artists learning from the works and ideas of their predecessors. Most biographers of artists show no awareness of this continuity of creation, and the reader thus feels only regret when the hero dies at the end of the book; it is rare – perhaps the biographer has to be an artist, too – for the force of the hero's creation to be shown as stronger than any obstacle, any frustration, any self-doubt, so that the reader is as excited by the hero's aims as by his completed, public works.

This is why Yon Barna has given more attention than any other commentator or critic of Eisenstein to the large number of *unrealized* ideas in a career that gave us only seven finished films. This part of Eisenstein's creative life, obscured but essential – for these ideas also grew and flourished in Eisenstein's theoretical work and teaching – is for the first time shown to us here in relation to the more visible oeuvre, the films and film projects. One might be tempted to compare his work with the iceberg, only a fraction of which shows above the water, except that this would reinforce the legend of an ice-cold, cerebral Eisenstein. Intellectual he certainly was, but in him the workings of the intellect were the expression of a passion, one that heats his films to such a degree that we cannot forget them – the book discusses many such moments and passages. This emotional basis for his work is kept in mind by Barna throughout his book, which is written with a sympathy too seldom found in such a work of research. Though he has aimed at objectivity, Barna loves his subject.

It is amazing how, in the short time since Eisenstein's death, attitudes towards him and his art have frozen so quickly that one is instantly aware of Barna's book as altering what has already become the traditional portrait of this artist. Of course this 'traditional' way of looking at Eisenstein began right at the beginning of his career, when he astounded and often alarmed his colleagues and supervisors with his intellectual sharpness and the breadth of his aims. Yet his vision of the film as a synthesis of all the arts and sciences, instead of convincing his colleagues of his determination and devotion to his art, had the effect of dividing him from them; and it is from the other side of this barrier that the Eisenstein portrait formed and hardened. Of the traditional attitudes which it expressed Eisenstein would have said contemptuously, echoing Mahler: 'Tradition ist Schlamperei!' (tradition is slovenliness). Sometimes several generations have to pass before the accuracy of such traditional portraits is challenged. We are lucky in that Barna has gone to work so soon.

What would Eisenstein have thought of this account of his too-short life? Sympathy and the wish to understand he regarded as important virtues in the people around him: his fellow workers, his students, his friends and even a few of his critics, at home and abroad, were first measured by this criterion before they were trusted to enter the deeper levels of this artist's mind and heart – and reason. I wish that Eisenstein could have known Yon Barna and read his book.

JAY LEYDA

Introduction

A biographical study of Sergei Eisenstein, film director and theoretician, and a genius in both these fields, is timely now, because, paradoxically, although the specialized literature on Eisenstein is very rich, even a well-documented – though subjective – biography like Marie Seton's* is already obsolete and in many ways contradicted by the immense amount of biographical material made available in recent years, or still unpublished. Both the recently published and the unpublished material that I have used in my research change in many respects the traditional image of Eisenstein. It is in this vast amount of varied material – probably more varied than in the case of any other artist – that the biographer must seek the truth.

The material includes:

1. His films, of course;
2. The scripts of his films, sometimes with
3. Variants of these, and often also
4. The preparatory material (drafts, annotated documents relating to the plans, sketches, comments more or less systematically arranged by him, etc.);
5. Numerous drawings and sketches which embody in concrete form his intentions and ideas;

* Marie Seton: *Sergei M. Eisenstein*, London, 1952.

9

6. Notes and theoretical articles, written *while* the films were being made, reflecting from the viewpoint of aesthetic analysis the artist's intentions and different stages in the crystallization of his work;

7. Lucid, profound and detailed analyses of his own films, made after their completion, as well as studies embodying the general theoretic and aesthetic conclusions deriving from these analyses;

8. Stenographic records of his lectures on directing which are still waiting for a complete transcription;

9. Miscellaneous recollections, sometimes recorded initially as *aides-mémoire*, sometimes introduced, apparently at random, in the most diverse articles or lectures;

10. Drawings (other than the sketches for films), which have an obvious biographical value in suggesting preoccupations, reactions to specific events, moods during a given period, etc.;

11. Last but not least, an unusual document – the study-film made by Jay Leyda out of unsold parts of the original negative left over from Eisenstein's unfinished film *Que Viva Mexico!*, which gives an exact idea of the way in which the director worked and thought during shooting.

Unlike other biographies, this one does not attempt to analyse Eisenstein's work as an artist – such investigation awaits another occasion – but only to investigate its emotional sources, the circumstances in which it was born, that special concurrence of sensory and social events that determines the conditions for the appearance of a work. The biographer has used the published and unpublished material at his disposal – much of it not previously exploited – in order to trace, less the events or the facts than that exciting 'inner adventure', the biography of Eisenstein's creation. 'Probably no artist surveys the plan of his life in advance,' writes Thomas Mann, 'and knows the materials which he will utilize in the course of time. But frequently he can see a connection between each of his productions, can observe that germs of his newest work were already present in the preceding one; and he grows more and more aware that each element comes out of a personal centre so that a natural unity forms of its own accord.'[1] Eisenstein's biography is, in fact, an attempt to discover this unique personal centre and to trace its evolution.

Professor Eisenstein once asked his students what they would most like him to speak about during his lectures. One of them answered: 'Don't tell us about cutting, or about film production, or even about film direction. Tell us how somebody becomes Eisenstein.' This biography is an attempt to answer that question.

1. Sketch for a Portrait

They [the Impressionists] wanted to present the world as they
saw it. This is not my way. I want to portray my inner eye's
image of the world.
PICASSO

For Beethoven, as Czerny once wrote, 'sound or movement of any kind
becomes music and rhythm', while Romain Rolland commented that
Leonardo da Vinci 'reacted in a similar way when he saw in the cracks of a
wall or the flames in the hearth smiling and grimacing faces'. So, too, it might
be said of Eisenstein that all his ideas and perceptual experiences were
projected into his films. This is not to imply narrow-mindedness or a single,
obsessive interest. Far from it: Eisenstein's field of interests was exceptionally
vast, encompassing mathematics, painting, physiology, philology, ethnology
and literary history. It was rather that everything in his surroundings
impinged on his artistic consciousness, was distilled in the process and absorbed into his own unique vision of life. His artistic reaction to event or
landscape was on a level of heightened consciousness in which he instantaneously recognized their potentialities for the camera lens (just as Leonardo
saw faces in the cracks of the wall, without making a conscious effort to
conjure them up).

Eisenstein had this amazing capacity for seeing things around him in a
different light from other people. As he himself described it:

Whatever I read or think about appears to me in an exceptionally vivid mental
picture. It is probably a combination of a vast storehouse of visual images, an acute
visual memory and long, intensive practice at day-dreaming – day-dreaming of the

11

Four faces of Eisenstein

sort where you force yourself to follow your thoughts or memories in pictorial images, as on a strip of film. Even now, as I write, I am doing nothing more, in fact, than 'outlining' by hand the pictures of things that are flowing before my eyes in an uninterrupted succession of visual images and events. These impressions, which are first and foremost acutely visual, demand with painful intensity to be reproduced. At one time, I myself was the sole means, subject and object of such 'reproductions'. Now I have some three thousand 'human units' to help me in this way, bridges that rise up, squadrons, herds of horses, and fires. But very often, even now, it is quite enough for me to reproduce (not necessarily in every detail) a particular visual image that obsesses me to feel satisfied. There is no doubt that this practice is largely responsible for the exceptional visual intensity of my *mises-en-scène* or my frame compositions.

Nor shall we ever now know the precise inner intricacies of this visual gift that Eisenstein possessed. The biographer can only attempt to convey some of its aspects. But, before probing into the more complex regions of Eisenstein's mind, let us first make our acquaintance with the man himself.

Opinions about Eisenstein differ widely, even to the point of outright contradiction. He is sometimes spoken of almost with veneration, in the extremest of eulogistic terms, as embodying every ideal quality ever possessed by man; sometimes just the opposite. Eisenstein, clearly, was equally capable of arousing feelings of love and hatred. He could be cutting to people he despised, taking an almost childish delight in provoking their enmity. In the course of his life there were times when this provocative attitude boomeranged painfully: the tragedy of his unfinished Mexican film is to some extent a case in point. On the other hand, he was charming towards anyone he respected, and the biographer following in his tracks is inundated with spontaneous tributes – always more valuable than the eulogies of apologists – from a whole host of people who succumbed to his charm. (An amusing tribute is provided by Eisenstein's expulsion order from France in 1930, made out by the Paris Prefect of Police, Chiappe, whose specific charge was that 'M. Eisenstein, par son charme personnel', was winning over friends for the Soviet Union.)

The Great Eisenstein – or His Majesty (*Seine Majestät*) Eisenstein, as the Germans nicknamed him from his initials – retained to the end of his life something of the defenceless child. As he himself acknowledged in an autobiographical note published several years after his death:

Everyone sees himself in a different light. One person believes himself to be a d'Artagnan, another Alfred de Musset. Another Byron's Cain. Others are modestly satisfied to be a Louis XIV in their own little kingdom, their studio. I see myself as most like David Copperfield – delicate, thin, small, defenceless. And extremely timid.

And towards the end of his life he admitted that he had remained the same small boy as in his childhood, adding:

It is this that accounts for my bitterness. But also, in all probability, for my happiness.

He was, indeed, extraordinarily timid. This timidity was implicit in some of his self-caricatures, while he explicitly acknowledged that he was petrified of appearing in public. Paradoxically, and probably to cover this very timidity, he sometimes adopted an apparently aggressive attitude. Jay Leyda has recalled his first impression of Eisenstein: 'I was terrified. Eisenstein was like Jupiter, like an angry god. He always tried to impress you. . . . But this attitude of his was only a mask.'

It was his physical characteristics that struck some people most – the disproportionately large head, or the unusually soft voice. Others remember the almost hypnotic power he exerted. Léon Moussinac, for instance, describes being 'overwhelmed' by Eisenstein's personality when they first met. His dominance

was both physical and intellectual. Physical because of the mobility of his face and hands, the strength of the shoulders on which the powerful form of his head was set, the energy and intelligence radiating from his whole person.[1]

Yet these same characteristics evoked diametrically opposite opinions about him: that he was swollen-headed, for instance. He was certainly not modest. Nor was he the most amiable of men. Then, again, he had his idiosyncrasies; but it cannot detract from the universal respect he won for his intellect and extraordinarily logical and lucid mind if we learn that he was also a ready prey to superstitions of every kind. He was terrified of black cats, of walking under ladders, of Fridays (he would never film on a Friday) and of the number thirteen, and was deeply impressed by a fortune-teller's prediction, made when he was still a young man, that he would die at the age of fifty. (He did, in fact, die only eighteen days after his fiftieth birthday.) Similarly he tended to look on the black side of things and was sometimes given to bizarre forms of behaviour: for the whole of one winter he worked only at night, never changing out of his dressing-gown and drinking endless cups of coffee, purely because his imagination had been fired by learning that this was the way Balzac had once worked.

Only when all these contradictory facts are known can this complex artistic personality begin to be appreciated.

A person's home is often a good guide to his tastes and intellectual pursuits. Eisenstein's was no exception. While living in a single, book-filled room in Moscow on Chysti Prudi, he painted concentric circles in red and black on the ceiling to give an illusion of extra height. Sometimes they seemed to him to be revolving, giving additional breadth to the room. It was all part of his craving for space – of that interest in vast expanses and the monumental which permeated all his work.

Self-caricature

His later home at Potylika, on the outskirts of Moscow near the Mosfilm studios, was more spacious and had an unbroken view into the distance over a cherry orchard, reputedly dating from the time of Ivan the Terrible. The arrangement of his bedroom was a striking reflection of his taste for the extravagant, the eccentric and the humorous – that taste that came out in his requests to friends abroad to send him loud ties and pyjamas in clashing colours which he often wore during the day. In the centre stood an unusually wide divan (beside which he kept a pencil and paper for jotting down any ideas that came to him in the night), covered, normally, with a Mexican rug of weird design. Similar woven tapestries from Mexico, along with black-beaded Georgian and Ukrainian embroideries, gave the room a predominant effect of harsh, strident colours. The walls were hung with a variety of masks from Japan, Hawaii and Mexico, while a carved and gilded frame contained a globe. A second globe hung, in lieu of a chandelier, from the ceiling, with a moon for company. There was a carved figure from Africa, statues of Buddha in silver and porcelain on a narrow shelf along the wall, carvings of heathen gods, a wooden angel with outspread wings in one corner, while other corners contained life-sized wooden statues of the apostles, and a huge, seven-branched silver candelabrum, on which he hung the multi-coloured ties, in the window. Eisenstein loved showing these prized objects to his friends –

fondling them lovingly as he did so — and rousing their wonder at some rare piece brought back from his or his friends' foreign travels. But, thanks to the general disorder, there was nothing museum-like about the room; rather it exuded a warm, human presence and a generally lived-in air.

His study, like the rest of the flat, was full of colour. The furniture was of pale, light-weight metal, that contrasted with an old, raspberry-upholstered armchair and a piano covered with a gold-lamé Chinese brocade. And everywhere there were the familiar oddments — an antique, black-faced porcelain Madonna and Child dressed in white and gold, various other statuettes, and Russian, Mexican and African toys.

Here at Potylika one room was set aside as a library, the walls of which were dotted with signed photographs from Chaplin, Paul Robeson, Jean Epstein, Abel Gance, Walt Disney, Asta Nielsen and others. Its dark blue walls harmonized with a warm red carpet. There was a round table covered in a green and gold brocade, and armchairs and a couch in an old-fashioned English style, the couch draped with yet another woven Mexican blanket. The surrounding bookshelves — of plain wood, painted white — were crammed with several thousand books. In fact the library could not begin to house them all and they spilled over into the other rooms — under beds, on the floor, on the piano and in boxes — virtually taking over the whole flat and enclosing Eisenstein, as he put it, 'in their magic circle'. He often confided to his friend Esther Shub that his books were the most precious thing in his life: he could feel isolated even among people close to him, he told her, but never among his books.*

By the age of twenty-five he had a vast and astonishingly varied collection; but one of his favourites still remained the first book of his 'own free choice' — a monograph on Daumier, bought when he was ten years old with money wheedled out of his governess. He was constantly buying more books and always asking friends to send them from abroad; as late as 1944 we find him writing to an English friend that he is 'crazy about modern english and american plays (and *good* detective stories as well)', and asking him to send 'something of this kind'. Such was his passion for books that once, when a second-hand bookshop was to open in Gorky Street, he went to great lengths

---

* When the apartment on Potylika was demolished, Eisenstein's wife, Pera Attasheva, moved some of his furniture, books and personal belongings to her own flat. Later they were moved to another apartment where now Naum Kleiman, a highly respected Eisenstein scholar, has shown great piety in reconstructing, as far as possible, their former arrangement in Eisenstein's home. Admirers of Eisenstein now receive a friendly welcome in this apartment, and an inkling of the original, as they drink tea from Eisenstein's cups, sit on his chairs, and browse in his books. Other items of his furniture, which were not taken over by Attasheva, have been secured by Eisenstein's friends; Ilya Weisfeld, for example, showed me the metal chairs and the desk which he keeps carefully in his own apartment.

16

to get in early before the opening day, and thus make sure of first pick. Assistants at all the bookshops knew him and often telephoned about new finds, offering to keep them back for him. His book-buying sprees were special occasions, marked by the ritual ceremony on his return home of making huge quantities of tea to last him through endless hours buried in the new books, imbibing their contents into that prodigious memory that astounded his acquaintances. Many were annotated with marginal jottings (a full study of which has yet to be undertaken) in Russian and other languages. He could dig out at a moment's notice specialized works on the most varied and unlikely subjects. When the director, Mikhail Romm, once sought his advice about a projected screen version of Maupassant's *Boule de Suif*, he immediately produced a whole range of books – from critical works on Maupassant's stories to a history of French hair-styles. And to a painter who visited him he was able to boast: 'If you're interested in Daumier, you can find here anything that's been written about this artist anywhere in the world.'

This readiness to help others was one of his outstanding characteristics. His generosity – not only with money but with ideas, too – was a legend. Several of his colleagues, among them Dovzhenko, as we shall see, owed much to the weight of his personal prestige that he lent unstintingly on their behalf at crucial points in their careers. Erich von Stroheim recalls the prompt response to the despairing telegram asking Eisenstein's help in finding work in Moscow that he sent in 1935: 'Eisenstein did his best to get me to Russia. But my family was the problem; I could not send a penny out of Russia and my family did not want to go there.' Confident in his own talent and in the high professional esteem he enjoyed, he never exhibited those feelings of envy and fear of competition that dogged many of his contemporaries. On the contrary, he took genuine pride and pleasure in the successes of his colleagues, and particularly of his former students.

Friends were welcome at his house – though he disliked having more than a few at a time – and he always put himself out for new acquaintances, 'bewitching' them, as Esther Shub used to tease him, with his charm. Yet, though he hated making conversation in a crowd, he paradoxically loved large, rowdy gatherings at the homes of friends such as Vishnevsky, or Roshal and Stroyeva, particularly on festive occasions when Christmas trees blazed with lighted candles. At these times he was the life and soul of the party, amusing everyone with jokes and witticisms characteristic of that sense of humour that exploded in his caricatures. Usually he joined in the dancing with zest, sometimes launching into exaggerated, clownish antics, making fun of the latest modern dance – and simultaneously of himself.

When it came to classical ballet, however, he would sit entranced through performance after performance by Ulanova, whose art he considered little short of miraculous. He was similarly fascinated by the theatre, by concerts

Playing the fool

(despite his professed ignorance of music) – in short, by every aspect of Russian artistic and cultural life. When the new buildings at Nalchik, Khabardina, were going up, he took time off from his lectures to visit them and inspected the architecture with a deeply interested and acutely critical eye. The feudal Florentine style used for the Houses and Palaces of Culture struck him as outrageously anachronistic: 'Why do we need fortified palaces? Who are we going to defend ourselves from in our Palaces of Art?' Largely at his insistence, two leading architects were called in to reappraise the city's building plans.

This supreme confidence in his aesthetic judgement, and the general apparent self-confidence underlying his forceful and enterprising spirit, alternated perpetually with equally extreme bouts of self-doubt and fear reminiscent of the insecurity of his childhood. Similarly the strange contrast between his hypersensitive revulsion from violence of any kind and the cruelty that figured so prominently in his films may have owed something to a childish element in his psychological makeup, as also may his intuitive appreciation of Chaplin's works, the essence of which he saw as a combination of innocence and brutality, specific to the psychology of children. Meyerhold once analysed the similarities and differences between these two genii of cinematographic art:

In Eisenstein the predominant element is tragedy; in Chaplin it is pathos. Pushkin called laughter, pity and terror the three strings of our imagination which the magic of the drama sets vibrating. In Chaplin laughter and pity take precedence, while terror remains muted. In Eisenstein pity and terror predominate over laughter.[2]

The element of cruelty that was fundamental to Eisenstein's films had deep biographical roots reaching back into his childhood – as did, incidentally, his fear of becoming addicted to games of chance:

Sometimes you are terrified of being frightened. This used to happen to me in my childhood. I was afraid, not of the dark, but of being frightened if I woke up in the dark. For the same reason I avoid playing games of chance. I am afraid that if I once started playing I would become addicted.

And it was not without good reason, he claimed, that he tried (vainly, as it turned out) to avoid writers whose works were permeated with cruelty.

I encountered the disquieting chord of cruelty at a very early age. Curious though it may seem, it was through an impression on the screen, but a very vivid impression.

Many of his childhood experiences, as we shall see, had a profound and lasting influence on his later life and work. But they formed only a part of the mysterious depths lying beneath the personality and behaviour that he presented to the outside world. These deeper mysteries of which Eisenstein's inner existence was compounded will be our chief concern in this biography.

2. The Path towards Art

I must Create a System, or be enslav'd by another Man's.
BLAKE

Eisenstein's childhood and youth are unusually deceptive as pointers to his eventual artistic destiny. Until the age of twenty, he was, thanks to forceful parental persuasion and his own acquiescence, firmly set on the path for a career in civil engineering. Nonetheless, certain factors in his childhood, and notably those early experiences which helped to mould his sensitive nature, shed a revealing light on Eisenstein's mature years as an artist.

The training period

Sergei Mikhailovich Eisenstein was born in Riga, Latvia, on 23 January 1898.

In many respects his family was typical of any Russian middle-class family of those days. His father, Mikhail Osipovich Eisenstein, came from a family of German Jewish origin which had been baptized and assimilated into Russian society. After completing his studies at the Institute of Civil Engineering in Saint Petersburg, Mikhail Osipovich moved to Riga, where he worked for the district road construction department until his later appointment as the city's chief architect – being responsible, incidentally, for many buildings still standing today. He was, according to Eisenstein, a staunch representative and admirer of the Russian bureaucratic classes. His mother, Julia Ivanovna, came from a *parvenu* middle-class Russian family, her father, a raftsman in his youth, having tramped penniless to Saint Petersburg before establishing a flourishing barge-haulage firm. Virtually all Sergei Eisenstein could remember of his maternal grandmother was a 'strange Vassa Zheleznova [the harsh heroine of a play of that title by Gorky], the proprietress of a string of cargo boats that plied the Maria Canal and the Neva'.

Mikhail Osipovich was a powerful, stocky man, jovial but authoritarian, with a Kaiser Wilhelm moustache. Most surviving photographs show him posing in an attitude of pronounced self-assurance, verging on conceit – characteristics which the meagre facts known about him tend to bear out. They are worth examining, since the young Sergei, a very good and obedient child, was deeply influenced by his father, modelling himself on him throughout his childhood; and his subsequent revolt against everything that his father stood for played an important part in his spiritual development.

Mikhail Osipovich's vanity, love of flattery, and self-opinionated assurance were to some extent passed on to his son, who in later years was to refer to his vanity as 'a heavy inheritance'. Similarly, also, Sergei's tendency to pedantry was probably inherited from his father, who at times carried it to extremes verging on the pathological: over his numerous pairs of patent leather boots, for instance, which he kept in a 'boot garage' in strictly designated rows – 'new', 'old', 'scratched' and so on – and subjected to regular, minute inspection. His authoritarianism was exercised over the whole household with a tyranny which his son later compared with that of Père Grandet (and also signalized as being largely responsible for his own opposition to all forms of social tyranny and for his sympathy with the revolutionary cause). On social occasions it was tempered by a broad, somewhat coarse humour, illustrated by his behaviour whenever *Die Fledermaus* was performed in Riga: installing himself and his friends in the front row of the theatre, he would join the chorus in his own full-throated rendering of 'Eisenstein has gone to quod'. Maxim Strauch recalls how, many years later, Eisenstein invited him to a performance of *Die Fledermaus* and impatiently awaited the moment for the chorus to begin, starting to laugh and nudging his friend with his elbow as soon as it did.

In his work as a civil engineer, Mikhail Eisenstein had a positive obsession about the so-called 'modern style', in which he once had a whole street constructed, decorating the façade of one of the buildings with gigantic figures of naked females cast in iron. Their vulgarity was not lost on his young son, who one day plucked up courage to ask his father whether he was not ashamed of building such houses. When the statues were later taken down and used for sewage pipes, the memory remained imprinted on Sergei's mind, to reappear years later as a recurrent theme in his works: in his stage production of *Listen Moscow*; in *October*, where the statue of the Tsar is dismantled and pulled down, symbolizing the overthrow of tsardom ('there is no doubt that

Childhood

the beginning of this film, so reminiscent of the destruction of Daddy's work, was bound up for me personally, through the toppling of the Tsar, with my release from Daddy's authority'); and finally in *Ivan the Terrible*, when Malyuta finds the empty suit of armour in the tent of the traitor Prince Kurbsky, and later when the helmets of the Livonian knights resound hollowly to blows from the Russian soldiers' swords.

About Eisenstein's mother very little is known, partly because he himself was never able to forgive her for divorcing his father and generally evaded the subject.* Yet she seems to have taken a much warmer interest in his education than did her husband, whose only concern – probably motivated by vanity – was that his son should have a conspicuously successful academic record. His father's attitude is epitomized in the ritual conversation that marked every social occasion:

'Seriozha, come here!'

'Yes, father.'

'Aren't you going to tell our friends where you came in class?'

---

* Much of the correspondence between Eisenstein and his parents (464 letters, 362 of them written by Eisenstein) survives in the Eisenstein archive in Moscow, but permission to consult it is refused.

22

Parents

'I came first, and I got a prize, father.'

'Fine, you can go' – whereupon his father looked round triumphantly for his guests' approval.*

His mother, however, seems to have gone to considerable lengths to inculcate into her son a certain cultural refinement – though probably from a vengeful hope that he would thus outshine her husband, whose vulgarity she despised. Whatever her motives, it was probably thanks to her that by the age of ten young Sergei was fluent in English, French and German and had begun reading the classics of those languages in the original. She dreamed of sending him on a long study trip round the world – taking in Greece and Rome, Egypt and Mesopotamia – when his schooling was completed. The trip remained a dream, but in 1906, when he was eight, the child visited Paris – probably with his father. It left him with a series of vivid impressions, including that of his 'first cinema venture' to see one of Méliès's films, which many years later he could still recall in detail. His other memories were rather hazy ones: of the Métro, of the first lift he ever saw, of the hotel where he stayed, and of Napoleon's tomb and Notre Dame, which – as he later realized with some

---

* Eisenstein recalled some years later that he had been 'a sickeningly exemplary child, who learned in a sickeningly exemplary manner'.

bitterness – he visited in an unappreciative state of total ignorance. One other outing, to the Musée Grévin, stuck in his memory – not for the amusing incident when his cousin Modest tugged at the skirt of a woman, mistaking her for a waxwork model, but rather for the tableau of the Paris Commune. The scene of the *Grandes dames* from Versailles gouging out the eyes of *communards* with their umbrellas haunted him for years after; it was finally exorcized only when, 'against all better judgement', he reproduced it in *October* in the incident where the young worker is beaten up during the events of July 1917.

The Eisensteins' marital conflicts – which their son later put down to sexual incompatibility – came to a climax in 1905 when Julia Ivanovna left her husband and moved to Saint Petersburg. Finally, after a brief period of reconciliation which resulted in her husband's settling in the capital, she broke up the household for good, abandoning custody of her son and leaving for Paris.

For the young Eisenstein, witnessing the events that culminated in his parents' divorce was a long and painful experience. In his bedroom next to theirs, the violent quarrels that flared up night after night were clearly audible. Unable to bear these scenes, he would run in tears to his nurse's room and bury his head in the pillow until both parents arrived and tried vainly to console him. His mother's departure did not affect him too noticeably to begin with, especially as one immediate consequence – the removal of the piano – happily released him from the tedium of music lessons. There is abundant evidence, however, that all the upheavals of this time made a powerful impact on him inwardly, the full implications of which will probably be revealed only by his unpublished writings, rich as they are in details of the intimate side of his life.

Throughout his parents' first period of separation, Sergei lived with his father in Riga, attending the *Realschule* there, but regularly spent Christmas with his mother in Saint Petersburg. Summer holidays were passed at seaside boardinghouses, mostly near Riga where he became friendly with Maxim Strauch (the future actor), who remained his lifelong friend. During this period he joined with other children in all the usual games and pastimes: 'cowboys and Indians' (made popular by the novels of Fenimore Cooper), cycling, skating, tennis and so on. Although he enjoyed games such as 'cops and robbers' which involved a physical effort, in early childhood he had 'cried for hours on end before going unwillingly (and how unwillingly!) to the gymnastics lessons given by Herr Engels, a bald-headed, bespectacled German with a game leg'.

Even as a very young child Eisenstein was unusually perspicacious – and unconsciously ironic – in his judgement of people. The description of Herr Engels continues on the same ironic note:

My only bright memory of Herr Engels is that it was from him, apparently, that I learned two examples of palindromes in German, at a time when my interest in word games was just beginning to awake. . . . These were the christian name and surname: Relief Pfeiler, and the phrase, 'Ein Neger mit Gazelle zagt im Regen nie'.

Another recollection connected with a play on words – 'l'autrichienne' and 'l'autre chienne' – dates from the time of his Paris trip: that is, when he was only eight years old. This interest in the association of words at such an early age is particularly interesting in connection with his later discovery and elaboration of the concept of intellectual montage.

Another interesting point is Eisenstein's hearty dislike of his piano lessons and his later insistence that he had 'never had an ear for music' and could rarely remember or hum a familiar tune. Yet he was the first to discover in creative practice the idea of audio-musical montage and subsequently to elaborate with incredible precision and finesse the theory of combining visual images with music and sound – thus demonstrating a deep understanding of musical structure.

The person who, after his parents, played the most important role in Eisenstein's childhood was probably his nurse. He had an unbounded love for this warmhearted, illiterate woman of simple tastes, who later remained with him as his housekeeper. It was she who introduced him to the wonder world of fairy tales and legends, and took him to the cinema in Riga when his parents refused on the grounds that it was unbecoming for a respectable family to be seen there.

This, then, was the family background against which Eisenstein passed his first, formative years. It only remains to sort out from the events of his childhood and adolescence those which were significant for his later development.

The pattern of his daily life remained more or less unchanged until his father finally moved to Saint Petersburg. Soon afterwards the outbreak of the First World War found him, now aged sixteen, visiting local hospitals and entertaining the wounded soldiers with his sketches. Sketching had always been one of his pastimes as a child. Maxim Strauch's recollection of their summer holidays in the boardinghouse garden is of the small boy of ten absorbed in this activity, filling whole exercise books with imaginative and caustically humorous drawings.* Sketchbooks of his childhood drawings have been preserved but not, so far, published; of the drawings I was permitted to

---

* He used to copy the designs on his mother's cushions, or pictures from illustrated magazines or postcards. The latter, collections of which were often made at that time, usually depicted some melodramatic scene or other: a consumptive girl toiling at back-breaking work, lovers chained together, etc. Eisenstein later wondered whether it was these postcards that turned him against 'the subject' and 'the plot' when he came to begin his filming activity.

see in the Eisenstein archive, the majority take the form of a sort of comic strip and are extremely amusing, with a mordant irony unusual in a child. (He had come early under the spell of Daumier and other caricaturists.) Sketching remained a lifelong passion which Eisenstein often looked upon as his second profession. Curiously enough, in his school report his marks were excellent for every subject except one – drawing! But this was doubtless a set-style calligraphy that ran counter to his nature.

In addition to his sketching, several impressions from his earliest childhood were to play a clearly defined and important role in his subsequent creative work. One such impression, standing out clearly from the mist that usually shrouds early experiences, throws a revealing light on the origins of his interest in the close-up, and composition in depth. It was the impression made by a two-pronged branch of white lilac in full leaf hanging against his bedroom window and visible from his bed:

My first conscious memory is of this close-up. Beneath this bough of white lilac my conscious awareness was first aroused. Then, many years later, a similar bough again roused my senses. Only this was not a real, but a painted, lilac bough. Half painted, half embroidered in silk and gold thread. And it did not decorate a live bush, but a Japanese screen in three sections. For years on end I used to gaze at this bough whenever I woke up. When it was first put by my bed, I don't know. I remember it as though it had always been there. A luxuriant bough, weighted down under its burden of flowers. On it – birds. And somewhere, far off in the distance – just glimpsed between the flowers – a traditional Japanese landscape. . . . This branch was not merely a close-up, it was a typical piece of Japanese work: the close-up, and the distant background beyond. Through this I became familiarized with the beauty of composition in depth long before coming across Hokusai or Degas. . . . Then, one day, the screen was torn in two places by a chair. I remember the two holes; then the screen was taken away somewhere. Probably those two lilac boughs fused for me into a single, unique and vivid sensation of the two ideas: the idea of the close-up and that of composition in depth, which are organically bound up with one another. And when, many years later, I began to delve into the historical antecedents of the close-up, I did not look for them in portraiture, nor in landscapes, but, for no conscious reason, I analysed the exciting development of that process whereby, from the overall structure of a picture, one of its elements progressively advances into the foreground. From the general composition of the picture, in which you can sometimes only just make out Icarus crashing down, or Daphnis and Chloe, the figures come forward towards the foreground, gradually growing larger and larger until in the end they are so close to the spectator that they even shatter the picture frame, as happens with El Greco's *Esplojo*.

Another experience from his earliest childhood years was significant as the first of a chain of experiences which impressed him deeply and subsequently found an echo in all his films. It occurred when his mother once terrified him by denying that she was his mother.

As she said it, her face became set, her eyes glassy and staring. Then she came slowly towards me. There you have all the characteristic elements: a fixed, stony expression; a mask with ice-cold eyes; a face devoid of life.[1]

This terrifying first impression of some faceless alien force — together with another particularly vivid one from Eisenstein's Civil War days, which we shall come to later — turns up in one form or another as a key image in every film, symbolizing the inexorability of fate: the soldiers in the Odessa steps massacre — or rather the line of their descending jackboots, their heads remaining invisible (*Battleship Potemkin*), the death masks worn by the Mexicans on Death Day (*Que Viva Mexico!*), the sinister, face-concealing helmets of the Teutonic knights (*Alexander Nevsky*), the black-hooded members of the procession from the cathedral where the Tsar's death is being plotted (*Ivan the Terrible*). These obsessively persistent metaphoric themes had their roots in that early childhood memory.

Finally, the origins of yet another characteristic feature of Eisenstein's films — what he himself called 'the ocean of cruelty' permeating them — lay partly in one of the first films he saw as a very young child. In his own films barbaric killings are commonplace: in *Strike* workers are killed off like oxen in a slaughterhouse and children hurled from the rooftops; in *Potemkin* the crowd is massacred wholesale and children trampled underfoot on the steps; men and children are thrown to the flames in *Nevsky*, poisoned or stabbed to death in *Ivan the Terrible*, while in *Bezhin Meadow* a child is murdered by his own father — to mention only a few of the horrific events.

The film which foreshadowed these sequences contained a scene in which a blacksmith surprises his wife with her sergeant lover and wreaks his vengeance by branding the lover's shoulder with a red-hot iron.

I remember it as though it were yesterday: the bared shoulder, the branding iron in the blacksmith's muscular hand, his black sideburns, and the white smoke (or steam) hissing from the scorched flesh.

Though Eisenstein's memory of the film was hazy, the details of this particular scene remained 'stamped' on his memory for ever after:

In my childhood it gave me nightmares. It used to come to me at night. Sometimes I became the sergeant, sometimes the branding iron. I would grab hold of the shoulder. Sometimes it seemed to be my own shoulder. At other times it was someone else's. I no longer knew who was branding whom. For years on end, blonde side-whiskers (the sergeant was fair) or black ones . . . evoked this scene for me. Until the time when . . . the ocean of cruelty in my own films swamped the impressions produced by this 'fateful' film, to which, nonetheless, the cruelties were in certain respects indebted.

Eisenstein went on to emphasize, however, the effect on him of the 'infinitely more terrifying and shocking events' that he witnessed during his childhood

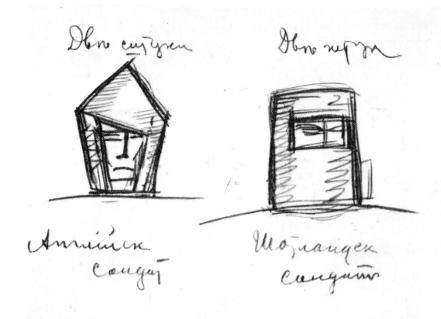

Sketches for a youthful theatrical project (top), and (below) the Odessa steps from *Potemkin*

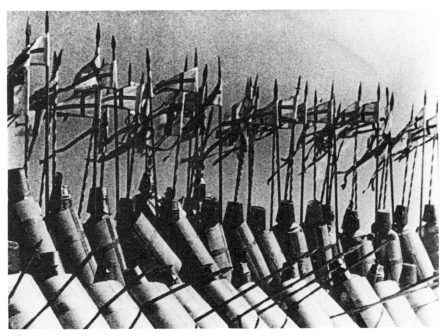

Alexander Nevsky

Ivan the Terrible: design and execution

days in Riga 'in the thick of the turmoil of 1905–6'. The particular relevance of these events to the cruelty in his films was, he maintained, that it was always 'interwoven with the theme of social injustice and the revolt against it'.

In addition to these indelible childhood experiences, Eisenstein's voracious childhood reading also influenced him profoundly and had a lasting effect on his later work.

The reason for his all-absorbing interest in books as a child is not difficult to trace. Loneliness, hypersensitivity inherited from his mother and nourished on his nurse's fairy tales, and, above all, the lack of parental warmth or a stable family life – all these helped to make him a withdrawn and introspective child, who sought refuge in reading. This escape world of books became a substitute for the world of the family circle which his parents had so signally failed to provide.

The astonishing extent of Eisenstein's childhood reading laid a solid foundation for his later encyclopaedic knowledge and for the development of his artistic and aesthetic ideas. Years after, when he had won recognition as the maker of dramatic composition of unique perfection in film art, he was to write:

Miracles of composition – this is merely a question of persistence and the expenditure of time during the 'training period' of one's autobiography.[2]

He read not only his own books, but his mother's and father's, and anything else in sight: magazines, newspapers, prospectuses, catalogues. (The catalogue of one of the *Expositions Universelles* he knew inside out, including the examples of photo-montage which particularly fascinated him, showing people in a variety of surroundings; but Eisenstein's supposition that it was these that triggered off his interest in montage seems somewhat far-fetched.)

One effect of this childhood reading was to prepare his sympathies for the ideas that later swept Russia. First there were the novels of Dumas, which initially roused his interest in the French Revolution. Then one Christmas saw the twelve-year-old boy gazing at the brilliantly lit Christmas tree laden with his presents. Yet it was not the tennis racket, the skis or bicycle that caught his eye, but two yellow books which he had long dreamed of possessing. Oblivious of the other presents, he made straight for these and buried himself in them till late at night. They were the two volumes of Mignet's *History of the French Revolution*. This was his first direct contact with the Revolution, and the second step – following Dumas's novels – towards his understanding of revolutionary ideas. From that point on his thirst for knowledge was insatiable. His imagination was fired by the symbol of the guillotine – which he vividly recalled in 1917 – by the clash of arms, the executions and the clanging bells which resounded in his ears. Next came Victor Hugo's *Les Misérables*, which brought to life for him both the romantic side of revolution and the realities of social injustice. Presently he came to Napoleon, his father's idol, of whom, at the age of seventeen, he was to comment:

Napoleon did not do what he did because he was talented or a genius. He became talented in order to achieve what he did.

Beyond the naïveté of Eisenstein's observation can be glimpsed something of the future artist's profession of faith. Yet more reading: the Paris Commune, Napoleon III, and on, in his adolescent years, to Zola's *Rougon-Macquart* cycle, and books on Marat and Robespierre, and the novels of Dickens, which he devoured avidly, sharing in the sufferings of his beloved heroes. All these impressions and ideas crystallized little by little, with the predictable result that the advent of the Russian Revolution found the young student Eisenstein, despite his upbringing in conditions of material plenty, ready to enlist whole-heartedly in the revolutionary army. His adherence to the Revolution was, however, a rationally determined, intellectual act.

To return to the 'training period' of his childhood, however, his reading was to contribute in other ways to his later development as an artist. A story by Edgar Allan Poe, for example, had a powerful effect on the young Eisenstein: Poe describes how, looking out of a window, he saw a gigantic prehistoric monster dragging itself slowly to a mountain top – only to discover that the supposed monster was a tiny insect battling its way up the window pane. It was, as Eisenstein explained on recalling the story, a composition in depth which no human eye could capture with the same objective effectiveness as the film camera. 'I suspect that my own most powerful and effective close-up compositions in depth – the skull and the pilgrims . . . from *Que Viva Mexico!* bear the seal of the white lilac and Poe's fantastic story.'

His reading was not only rich and varied, but often quite beyond the level of his years. On one occasion, discovering that he was to meet Dostoyevsky's widow, he read *The Brothers Karamazov*, so as to have a suitable topic of conversation in readiness. Not surprisingly, the learned discussion did not materialize, and the young boy alleviated his chagrin with a huge piece of bilberry pie.

What were the origins of that passion for the monumental and for hieratic spectacle that is evident in all Eisenstein's work? These, too, should probably be sought in his childhood. In the first place it should be remembered that he was the son of an architect, whose everyday concern was with massive construction projects. He was, moreover, exposed to the more or less persistent pressures of his father to follow in his footsteps as a civil engineer. Another powerful influence seems to have been the fables and legends told him by his nurse, and the impression made by their imagery and symbolic significance. In the majority of Eisenstein's films the dramatic construction follows an epic or legendary form, in which reality is projected larger than life

Que Viva Mexico!: close-up and composition in depth

through hieratic symbols. *Strike* is not just any strike but a legendary presentation of this particular form of industrial protest, just as *The General Line* is a fable about the collectivization of agriculture. Likewise *Que Viva Mexico!* is a legend, as also is *Alexander Nevsky*. Moreover, one particular fairy story from his childhood, the story of Sohrab and Rustum (to use the versions of the names most familiar to English readers), turns up recurrently both in his theatrical work and, many years later, in his preparatory work for the projected mammoth film (which never, in fact, got beyond the project stage) about the Ferghana Canal. Two young people were to have figured in the film.

And what associations this young pair evoked for me! It was impossible to get away from Rustum and Zabora [Sohrab], for whom I wept as a small boy. A father and son conflict with a happy ending that would make up, as it were, for all the tears shed as a child over the unhappy ending of this ancient poem – there was a time when I used to dream of bringing about some such compensation.[3]

Similarly, the origins of his passion for dramatic spectacle should be sought in his childhood period. First and foremost there was the circus, which quite simply infatuated him. He went to it at every possible opportunity and played at circuses with his friends in the garden, acting out the whole programme down to the last wild animal. His father also liked the circus, especially the *haute école*, and often took Sergei there. But while, to please his father, the young boy pretended to be watching the horses, it was really the clowns that fascinated him most of all. 'From my cradle I loved the "red-faced" clowns, but was always a bit ashamed of the fact. . . . In 1922 I inundated my show with them' – a reference to his spectacular stage adaptation of Ostrovsky's *Even a Wise Man Stumbles*. In 1930, according to a list in the Eisenstein archive, he planned a circus performance with the curious title *Moscow's Hand*. And when in 1934 he looked back over his period in the theatre he acknowledged the influence exerted on his stagecraft by the circus – 'which I loved passionately from childhood'. Even near the end of his life, when he was making *Ivan the Terrible*, the memory of the clowns was suddenly to rush in upon him, and he sketched a whole series of them, nostalgically labelling them 'Those anonymous friends', 'Souvenir d'enfance', 'Georges, maître de mes pensées' and so on.

In addition to Eisenstein's passion for the circus, Maxim Strauch recalls how he used to stage different war games, sketching the costumes for them, improvising the décor and directing everyone's movements. His inventiveness seemed inexhaustible. Once he built on the huge table in the garden an amazingly intricate structure out of sand, stones and twigs that had all the adults gathered round in fascinated curiosity at the child's imagination. The fascination that play-acting held for him deepened with his discovery of the theatre. This happened while he was still a young boy at Riga, when Strauch described a performance of Maeterlinck's *Blue Bird* he had seen at the Moscow Art Theatre. Eisenstein was so impressed that he decided then and there, on the beach, to improvise their own production of it. Strauch directed, while Eisenstein strained his ingenuity to the utmost playing the Fire. Later they changed roles, Eisenstein directing Strauch in their version of Gogol's *The Marriage*. After this Eisenstein went regularly to the theatre and opera in Riga, soon becoming familiar with the entire repertoire of plays and operettas, from *Hansel and Gretel*, *Götz von Berlichingen* and *Wallenstein* to *Madame Sans-Gêne*. Later in his youth he apparently attempted to stage two acts of Hebbel's *Die Nibelungen* for an amateur performance. During 1913 he saw the touring Nezlobin Theatre's production of *Turandot*, which came as a revelation to him: 'From then onwards the theatre became the object of my intense interest and unrestrained enthusiasm.' Yet for all that he continued undeflected on the path chosen by his father towards a career in engineering.

His artistic interests, however, were by no means relegated to the role of mere hobbies.

I was studying engineering. But a subconscious and unformulated inclination to work in the field of art induced me to pick a course within engineering that led, not to mechanical, technical fields, but to one closely allied to art – to architecture.[4]

Eisenstein may well have been embellishing the facts here, since the family precedent was more probably the basic reason for his turning to architecture; and he later admitted that

at that time . . . I had no intention of going on the stage and was quite content with following in my father's footsteps – with becoming a civil engineer.[5]

In any case, however strong the appeal of art may have been, in the autumn of 1915 Eisenstein enrolled at the Petrograd Institute of Civil Engineering, where his father had studied before him, and continued there until the Revolution forced him to make the break.

The Revolution

Eisenstein's period as a student was, until the Revolution, uneventful. It was, however, to influence him long after he had abandoned engineering, since it was during this time that he developed his 'leaning towards disciplined thinking' and his love of 'mathematical precision'.

There appears at first sight to be a puzzling incongruity between Eisenstein's mathematical training – which presupposes the development of deductive reasoning powers – and the strictly inductive approach in his film analyses and creative work (one of his major artistic discoveries was how to give metaphoric expression to inductive methods). But the key to this enigma lies in the system of mathematics teaching then practised in Russian higher technical education, which followed the traditions of the national school of applied mathematics with its emphasis on the inductive method.* Thanks to his engineering training, Eisenstein later 'eagerly delved', as he put it,

deeper and deeper into the fundamentals of creative art, instinctively seeking the same sphere of exact knowledge as had succeeded in captivating me during my short experience in engineering.[6]

The Institute's course in bridge-building, in its early, most rudimentary stages, struck him in retrospect as being essentially a course in the art of *mise-en-scène*. He was to be particularly fascinated by the assembling of a pontoon bridge, which he saw as a rhythmic, collective dance, a unique symphony of human activity, involving a precise time–space relationship and a fusion of man with nature – factors that he later identified as basic to film montage. From his knowledge of explosives, also gained from the engineering course, Eisenstein was able to draw the conclusion years later, after analysing the

---

* His mathematics professor at the engineering institute was Professor Sokhotsky, whom he was later to describe as 'one of those flaming old fanatics . . . who could by the hour and with the same fire of enthusiasm discourse on integral calculus and analyse in infinite detail how Camille Desmoulins, Danton, Gambetta or Volodarsky thundered against the enemies of the people and the revolution. The temperament of the lecturer absorbs you completely. . . . And suddenly the mathematical abstraction has become flesh and blood.'

35

sequences in *Battleship Potemkin*, that an ' "explosion" in art, and especially an emotional explosion, is produced by exactly the same formula'.

Throughout Eisenstein's engineering studies, the theatre continued to exert its attraction. On one occasion he queued all night to make sure of a ticket for Chaliapin's performance in *Boris Godunov*, while Strauch remembers him spending hours of his free time after lectures in planning various stage settings. Most of Eisenstein's biographers – probably misled by an ambiguous statement in his own writings – date his decision to abandon engineering for the theatre after his return from the Civil War, attributing it to a fortuitous set of circumstances then obtaining. But it was, in fact, much earlier than this – just after passing his examinations in advanced mathematics in February 1917 – that he experienced the 'shock' of seeing Meyerhold's productions of Lermontov's *Masquerade*, Molière's *Don Juan* and Calderón's *The Constant Prince* at the Alexandrinsky Theatre, which, following *Turandot*, provided 'a second overwhelming and decisive eye-opener' and clinched his 'unexpressed resolve to give up engineering' and 'dedicate' himself to art. The conditions created by the Revolution merely made it possible to put the decision into effect:

If it had not been for the Revolution, I should never have broken with the tradition passed down from father to son of becoming an engineer. The germ was there, but only the Revolution gave me . . . the freedom to take my fate into my own hands.[7]

This then was his 'first debt to the Revolution' – his enrolment in the Red Army being less a politically motivated action than a means of breaking with engineering, as his actions from February 1917 until his departure for the Civil War front bear out.

The February Revolution dragged Eisenstein, willy-nilly, into its toils. During the first few days the Institute was converted into a centre, under the Izmailovsky regiment, for the maintenance of law and order, and Eisenstein began wearing a militia armband; in March he was issued with a service card. It was about this time, while he was still at the Institute, that his artist's interest in the fermenting public events was first aroused. With his characteristic keen-eyed and caustic powers of observation, he started sketching the scenes around him – catching the atmosphere in the streets with uncanny accuracy and psychological insight. He decided to try cashing in on his sketching ability by offering something for publication, and he not unnaturally picked on a topical theme that he assumed would find a ready market. His first attempt was with a caricature. It was the time when Kerensky was fulminating against the general clamour for a guillotine to be set up in Petrograd, and Eisenstein – drawn probably less by what he described as 'a consuming desire to play a part in the forging of history' than by that peculiar attraction of his towards acts of cruelty – drew his sketch. It depicted the haloed head of Louis XVI above the bed of Nicholas II and carried the caption: 'He got off lightly!' This he took along to the editorial offices of the *Satirikhon* review, only to have it rejected by the editor, the writer Arkady Averchenko, with a scathing 'anyone could produce that'. Eisenstein refused, however, to take this rejection as an aspersion on the quality of his work; attributing it instead to the particular genre he had chosen, he resolved to tackle another subject.

His next effort depicted a fracas between a group of housewives and militiamen above the caption: ' "What's going on – looting?" – "No, it's the militia keeping order." ' For this he chose the *Petersburgskaya Gazeta*, a paper taken by his father and familiar to him since childhood, whose sensational legal columns and 'chronicle of events' he followed avidly. Now he was actually in the paper's editorial offices, seeing its staff reporters for the first time. Eventually he was summoned to the holy of holies, to the presence of Khudekhov himself. Khudekhov scrutinized his sketch, nodded, and tossed it into the in-tray on his desk. Presently it appeared in the paper, and Eisenstein received his first payment as an artist – ten roubles.

Meanwhile the months were passing and, as Eisenstein approached the Nevsky Prospekt one summer's day, he suddenly came face to face with pandemonium breaking loose: it was the demonstration of 3 July in that historic year 1917. Without hesitating, he skirted round the Sadovaya, hastily taking cover in the hotel archway when the shooting began. From this vantage point he watched the events which, ten years later, he was to reconstruct on the same spot for his film *October*. Meanwhile his record of the shootings took the form of sketches, among them a series of four, the last of which, featuring a man with a shell protruding from his back, carried the laconic caption: ' "Look out, citizen, you've been hit!" – "What are you talking about? Really?" ' These sketches appeared also in the *Petersburgskaya Gazeta* under the pseudonym 'Sir Gay'. Eisenstein's fee this time was twenty-five roubles.

For the moment, it seems, the Revolution meant little more to Eisenstein than a source of subjects for sketches. By this time he was attending courses at the Officers' Engineering School, to which he had meanwhile transferred,* and for some time was fully occupied with the hastily arranged examinations. As soon as examination tensions were over, his thoughts turned once more to the theatre, and specifically to getting hold of a particular historical work on the subject. Priced at forty roubles, however, it was quite beyond his pocket, even with the payments for his two drawings. But he had immediate plans for expanding his source of income and therefore borrowed the money. The plans

---

* Eisenstein's application to transfer to the School was accepted in April 1917; but a longish illness had subsequently delayed his entry.

involved a whole series of sketches bitingly critical of Kerensky, which he presented to Propper, the editor of the weekly *Ogonyokh*. Though unenthusiastic about the theme, Propper was impressed by Eisenstein and promised to commission some work from him in the next day or two. Elated at this arrangement, Eisenstein set off home, too much engrossed in his thoughts, evidently, to pay much attention to the firing clearly audible from the direction of the Winter Palace. Back at home he wrote up some notes on the younger Moreau, the eighteenth-century engraver, that he had taken at the public library shortly before:

For about an hour I put my notes . . . in order. Then I went to bed. Somewhere in the town there was the distant sound of firing, but somewhat more violently than usual. . . . Before getting into bed, I jotted down on my notes the date of completing them: 25 October 1917.*

It was the beginning of the October Revolution – the event that was to transform the destiny of Sergei Eisenstein.

But the change did not come about immediately – not, in fact, until 1918, Eisenstein's third and crucial year at the Institute, when he abandoned his almost completed engineering studies to enlist in the Red Army. Even then the decision seems not to have been his own, but a collective one taken by the students *en bloc*, the Institute closing down as a result. For the first time in his life Eisenstein savoured the freedom of deciding his own destiny. Although it was as an engineer that he left for the front, he was never to resume his prematurely abandoned studies: 'Being swept up in the whirlpool of the Civil War and free for a while of the Institute of Civil Engineering was enough to make me break all my links with the past without a moment's hesitation.'

The Civil War

Eisenstein's movements during the Civil War are difficult to trace with accuracy, since the scant records available, including Eisenstein's own, are full of contradictions. But the precise chronological order of his postings is of less importance than their significance for his development as a creative artist. From this point of view, Eisenstein's two years on the shifting Civil War fronts provided a variety of experiences that were to prove vital for his future work. The 'cauldron of Civil War' inevitably cast him headlong into an intense, high-pitched existence in which everything took on larger-than-life proportions; to the sensitive youth, history was being made before his very eyes, and its events were of 'epic significance' – all of which was to incline him towards the monumental when it came to film-making. In the course of his various postings from Petrograd to Kholm, Veliky Luky to Vitebsk,

* *Sic*; but by the Gregorian calendar, which the Soviet Union adopted in 1918, the October Revolution began on 7 November.

Polotsk to Smolensk and Minsk, serving in a variety of capacities ranging from telephonist to adjutant to the chief of works, he amassed a vast storehouse of visual and perceptual impressions that were to turn up again and again in his creative work. Of more immediate consequence, however, the Civil War involved him in his first serious stage venture, which determined his choice of the theatre as a career.

Eisenstein's first posting – on the strength of his uncompleted engineering training – was to a military site on the outskirts of Petrograd where the city's ring defence system was under construction. There, at the Izhorsk camp, he adapted good-humouredly to the 'profusion of pamphlets and buckwheat porridge', making light of the tedious instruction as 'enjoyable' and of night patrols in the rain as 'romantic'. During patrol duty he invariably kept a copy of some travel notes by Dürer in one of his greatcoat pockets – the other held his pistol – snatching a glance at them by the dim light in one of the huts whenever he went to thaw out.

One of the camp's tasks was to construct a pontoon bridge across the Neva – an operation which re-aroused Eisenstein's earlier interest and again set him pondering on the aesthetic implications.

The young recruits, like a throng of ants swarming along symmetrically laid-out paths, worked with precision and disciplined movements, endlessly assembling the bridge, which edged forward hungrily across the river. Somewhere in the midst of the ants, I, too, was moving about. . . . Everything fused into an amazing contrapuntal orchestration in all its varied harmonies. And the bridge grew longer and longer. . . . Men scrambled about. The minute hand raced round. Hell, how splendid it all was! . . . As it crept forward over the immeasurably vast breadth of the Neva the pontoon bridge opened up to me for the first time the fascination of a passion that never left me! The irresistible force of its impression on me is easily explained; it impinged upon my consciousness at exactly the moment when my passion for art was beginning to take a step forward – the serious step forward from an all-absorbing appreciation of art to a vague hankering . . . after actually creating it.

Occurring as it did at a chaotic period of the Civil War, when Eisenstein felt 'a natural craving for order and harmony', the impact of 'this rhythmic, collective activity, carried out to a strict time schedule, was an unforgettable one'.

In the midst of directing the operations, his shouted instructions peppered with oaths, Eisenstein snatched odd moments to read a play by Maeterlinck. Back in camp at night he excitedly explored the works of Jacques Callot, Dürer, Goya, Hogarth and the Japanese woodcut artists. It was at this time that he discovered Kleist's and Immermann's ideas on the theatre – all of which acted as an incentive to strike out himself 'in a new direction'.

Next came a posting to a military work site close to Kholm, 70 kilometres from the nearest railway in one direction and 95 kilometres in the other, where more fortifications were being built. Here Eisenstein appears to have acted as adjutant to the chief of works. Rigged out in his battle dress, bare-headed and shod in a pair of well-worn, reddish boots several sizes too large for him, he was unfailingly good-humoured and full of life and energy.

Among Eisenstein's experiences from this period, one that stuck in his memory was a 'trifling, ephemeral incident', involving 'a narrow bench seat, a peasant accordion and a pair of legs'. It is worth examining for its bearing on the original artistic effects he later achieved in *Potemkin* and *The General Line* and subsequently expounded in his theoretical works. It happened when a rich kulak family named Pudov, who lived in the vicinity of Kholm, invited him to dinner one night with the aim of getting into his good books and thus ensuring that their only son – a section leader at Eisenstein's site – would not be posted away. They put on an unusually lavish spread and plied him throughout with drinks. After the meal, which was capped by a sort of hot toddy, the daughter persuaded him to cross the river with her in an old and leaky boat to see the village dancing. On the opposite bank Eisenstein watched the girl's bare legs, still wet from the boat, as she danced with her companions to the strains of a peasant accordion. It was dusk and cool. From his narrow seat Eisenstein watched the dancers and listened to the music, just audible above the monotonous clanking of the boats and the rhythmic tramp of the feet on the well-trodden ground. In this hypnotic atmosphere he soon began to doze off, and everything started to float before his eyes in a succession of strange images. It was not like seeing by day, when 'things appear live and fresh', when a harmony exists between part and whole, but only the very practised eye can pick out 'the islets of close-up from this overall harmony'. Nor was it like our perception of things by night, when 'we see them as if in a dream'. It was no dream, when 'both whole and part are in harmonious equilibrium, but in such a way that each remains equally vivid'. He was experiencing that peculiar state of semi-somnolence which precedes sleep, when 'sensations and the fragmented impressions left by these sensations leap out at random like dice and become jumbled up like playing-cards in a shuffler's hands'. Different images whirled before his eyes: an immense, purple-veined nose; a peaked cap, seemingly with an existence of its own; a group of dancing figures; a gigantic moustache; a remote village about to be engulfed in darkness; a huge, blue tassel hanging from a silken belt; a stray earring caught up in a ringlet – and still other impressions. 'At that precise point on the border between sleeping and full consciousness, I witnessed the brilliant dance of the close-ups.'

The 'trifling' impression had such a profound effect on Eisenstein that when, well over five years later, he first tackled the subject of collective farm life, it came back to him with full force.

The ear and wrinkles – huge as the screen itself – on the nape of one kulak's neck, the immense nose of another, a heavy paw hanging limp and somnolent over a pail of kvas ... constantly insinuated themselves into the saraband of the landscape and peasant settings in *The General Line*.

Thus, though Eisenstein was unaware of it at the time, that particular evening at Kholm formed a landmark in the gestation period of his ideas about the close-up that started with the lilac bough of his childhood and reached fruition many years later in his great films.

Meanwhile his ideas continued to be influenced by his reading, which he still pursued in the unlikeliest of situations. After Maeterlinck, he devoured Ibsen while supervising trench-digging operations, and the memoirs of Saint-Simon while on the work site at Polotsk. A journey on a troop train saw him deeply immersed in Schopenhauer, whose pessimism left a marked impression on him. He was intrigued, also, by Hoffmann's powers of imagination.

Next followed a series of incidents that proved decisive for Eisenstein's future. Towards the end of 1919, the Fifteenth Army's Military Construction Unit No. 18, to which he was attached, was posted to Veliky Luky. There the local House of Culture boasted a lively theatre company whose members used to congregate in the room of the painter Eliscycv. Into this room one day walked an earnest-looking young man, his seriousness belied only by the ever-present glint of humour in his eye; his frail form wore the faded uniform of a Petrograd civil engineering student. Introducing himself as Sergei Eisenstein, he explained that the young soldiers at his site wanted to form an amateur theatrical group and were seeking professional advice. When this was immediately forthcoming, Eisenstein asked if he himself could sit in on the professional instruction at the theatre. Again Eliseyev readily agreed, and within a short time the two became friends.

Thereafter Eisenstein was always in and out of the theatre, in the actors' dressing-rooms, watching them make up, or lingering in the paint-room. Every aspect of theatrical life fascinated him. Shortly after, on 9 February 1920, his new amateur group made its *début* with several short plays, including Gogol's *The Gamblers* and Averchenko's *The Double*, which represented Eisenstein's first serious attempt as 'amateur director'. The cast included the site's chief engineer, Peyich, and Eisenstein himself in the part of 'the first passer-by'. Eisenstein's words, however, were barely intelligible because of a peculiar quirk of his voice, which apparently made it see-saw from high to low pitch – the two voices of the mother and the father, as he jokingly put it – and which forced him to give up all further thoughts of acting himself.* But

* The peculiar hoarseness of his voice and its sudden changes of pitch were the result of chronic laryngitis. Although subsequently treated with some success, his voice evidently still gave him occasional trouble in later years, when, as film director and lecturer at the Institute of

despite this the show was a success, and it was decided to repeat the experiment with Romain Rolland's *Fourteenth of July*, again under Eisenstein's direction. The production proved to be extremely impressive – more so than many professional productions, especially as far as Eisenstein's simple and logical solutions of the problems of the *mise-en-scène* were concerned. The public gave it a tremendous reception, joining in enthusiastically with cheers for the heroes and hisses for the villains. Other productions with which Eisenstein was associated at this period include Molière's *Georges Dandin.*

During rehearsals for Rolland's play, Eisenstein gave serious thought to his future career: was it to be engineering or directing? It was not, however, until the spring of 1920, when the Unit moved westwards, that he finally resolved the dilemma. Eliseyev had meanwhile been appointed director of the two theatrical groups attached to the Fifteenth Army and was planning a production of *Madame Sans-Gêne*, for which he needed a designer. He immediately thought of Eisenstein, but had no idea of his whereabouts, except that he was stationed somewhere at the front. At this point fate intervened when Eliseyev's talent-spotting for the production took him to Polotsk. There he was surprised and delighted to receive a message from Eisenstein, who was stationed at nearby Lepel, suggesting that they meet the following day. At the meeting Eisenstein confided to Eliseyev that he would give anything to exchange the construction unit for the theatrical group and was prepared to take on any work to do so. Thus it was between the end of 1919 and the spring of 1920, somewhere at the Civil War front between Veliky Luky and Lepel, that Eisenstein finally decided in favour of a career in the theatre. Happily his decision coincided with a desperate need for new blood in the theatrical unit.

Eliseyev immediately sought out Peyich to see about Eisenstein's transfer, only to meet with pointblank refusal on the grounds that Eisenstein was indispensable for the defence constructions. Eliseyev, however, was equally stubborn and, appealing to Peyich's sympathies as a former amateur actor himself, eventually won him over. That evening, in Eisenstein's room, the two friends solemnly celebrated his initiation into theatrical life, Eisenstein ceremonially opening a treasured tin of condensed milk in recognition of the portentous moment.

Meanwhile it had been decided to incorporate Eliseyev's troupe into the Political Directorate for the Western Front (Puzap), and the troupe received instructions from Dneprov, Puzap's drama chief, to report to Smolensk. The long journey there by goods train gave the two theatre enthusiasts ample

---

Cinematography, he needed to rely on verbal communication. His doctor advised him always to talk loudly – advice which he tried to follow, though his contemporaries often remarked on the unusual softness of his voice. In a recording made in late 1940, his voice sounds natural enough.

opportunity to exchange ideas. Eisenstein talked of his interest in the Byzantine and Italian primitive artists and in medieval miniatures and showed Eliseyev his sketches of medieval scenes and processions, designs for a Renaissance play, and various other imaginative settings for plays as yet non-existent, but which he thought might one day be written; Eliseyev, for his part, expounded his attitude towards different dramatic traditions, including the *commedia dell'arte*. At this point the discussion grew heated: Eisenstein declared himself a devotee of the *commedia*, and defended it fiercely (as he was later to do over his stage productions), while Eliseyev retorted that he would never allow masks to take the place of living beings in any theatre directed by him.

At Smolensk, they found that Dneprov had amalgamated the various theatrical groups and that all projects under way were suspended for the moment. Several weeks of irritating inactivity followed, during which Eisenstein, in the cramped quarters of a goods wagon at Smolensk station, was impatient to begin work. But this apparently fruitless period in fact provided Eisenstein with an experience – evoking and amplifying that fearful childhood experience when his mother had menacingly approached him – which influenced him profoundly and was to leave its mark on all his creative work. Once, many years later, when he was asked what had been the most terrifying experience of his life, he recalled the vivid and indelible memory of the station at Smolensk. The experience was the nightmare one of being in that huge station alone after dark, fumbling his way through 'the countless goods trucks standing like so many mammoth whales in a sea of cold metal railway lines' to reach his own wagon.

In the pitch blackness the changing signals clanged out with a weird, grating sound. Was it the recollection of that sound that made me think of evoking the nocturnal shriekings of the bony-feathered birds in the nocturnal scene after the battle on the ice in *Alexander Nevsky*?

More terrifying, however, than the bizarre sounds or the experience, during an illness, of sweltering in a wagon scorched by the midday sun, was

when the leading truck of an endless line of dozens of wagons loomed up at you. No one could halt the inanimate red eye that steadily approached, staring out from the flattened face of the end wagon as the line of trucks shattered the stillness of the night. How many were the times, as I picked my way amongst the railway tracks, that these nocturnal monsters came rumbling up beside me; sometimes silent and submissive, almost stealing their way from darkness to darkness, sometimes rushing upon me suddenly, sometimes overtaking me, sometimes keeping pace with me. It is my belief that these trains – with their blind, relentless onslaught – have stalked through my films, now dressed in jackboots on the Odessa steps, now turning towards us the flattened facepiece of a knight's helmet in the battle on the ice, now in the hoods and black pilgrim's garb encroaching upon the flagstones of the cathedral yard, blotting out the flickering candle in the quaking hand of Vladimir Staritsky. In film after film this metaphor of the night trains travelled with me, until in my eyes they became a symbol of fatality.

A powerful sense of this unheeding, ruthless mechanism of Fate and the 'blind implacability' of its onslaught is, indeed, transmitted by every one of Eisenstein's films, either through such easily recognizable symbols as those mentioned above, or in more esoteric ways, as when, in *An American Tragedy*, the implacable force is equated with the brute machinery of justice. Moreover, the train metaphor crops up again, albeit in a different form, in Eisenstein's unfinished memoirs written during the last years of his life: recalling with sorrow how he had let life slip through his fingers, he asserted that his whole existence had been 'an endless succession of changing trains; just as if I always intended arriving late for a train'.

Following the period of inactivity at Smolensk, the Political Directorate was transferred to Minsk, where, in the autumn, Eisenstein and four other artists were given the temporary task of decorating an agitprop train leaving for the front. They worked from dawn to dusk, arguing endlessly about their ideas for the job in hand. Eisenstein's contributions consisted almost invariably of single-stroke drawings, often in simple straight lines. Eventually a stage production was planned – of Gorky's *The Lower Depths*. Again the troupe was fully occupied with the preparations, until brought to an abrupt halt by the announcement that armistice negotiations had been opened with the Poles. Along with other members of the troupe, Eisenstein was presented with the choice between moving on with the Political Directorate and staying at Minsk at the disposal of the new State Theatre about to be set up there. He chose to move on. By this time his one aim was to get to Moscow at any price, and when, presently, the former students who wanted to resume their studies were demobilized, he decided to enrol at the Oriental Languages Department of the General Staff Academy in order to attain his object. As a first step he started teaching himself Japanese, burning the midnight oil for nights on end while he laboured away learning well over a thousand words and several hundred characters. The language was difficult, especially the unfamiliar word order and method of phrase construction. Yet at the same time it was intriguing for Eisenstein, longing as he did to visit Japan in order to learn more about the Kabuki Theatre, in which he was passionately interested, and about oriental culture in general, which, he felt, held the secret of the origins of the 'magic' of art. It was hard going and he fell back on mnemonic tricks as a help – with occasional curious results. Painstakingly he persevered with the language, though learning it seemed to him of little practical use, except as a means of getting to Moscow. Later, however, he was to realize the value of these studies in helping him to understand the principles of montage. As he wrote years later in one of his theoretical analyses, 'the principle of montage can be identified as the basic element of Japanese representational culture'.[8]

On his arrival in Moscow it was a chance encounter one evening with his childhood friend, Maxim Strauch, that set Eisenstein on the tempestuous but fruitful career that followed. Strauch, himself a theatre addict, was loitering outside the Kamerny Theatre trying to pick up a black-market ticket for that evening's performance, when he became aware of a young soldier's eyes fixed on him. Fearing that his intended illegal transaction had been spotted, he quickly dodged into the foyer. There, to his alarm, he discovered that the young soldier had followed him. Again he dodged away, but again in vain. Only after several more unsuccessful attempts to evade the soldier did he eventually recognize him as Eisenstein. After the performance the two friends eagerly exchanged their news, wandering the streets for hours on end until, as dawn broke, Strauch discovered that Eisenstein had nowhere to sleep and offered to put him up at his home on Chysti Prudi.

Both were equally stage-struck. That very night they decided that for them it was the theatre or nothing. The existing theatres, they agreed, were out-moded, useless hangovers from the past that needed shaking up from top to bottom; it was up to them personally, they felt, to revolutionize the whole theatrical movement.

In November 1920, all thoughts of the Academy abandoned, Eisenstein set out with Strauch to try to join one of the new workers' theatres.

3. Through Theatre to Film

My thirst for that mysterious thing called art was unquenchable and insatiable. No sacrifice seemed too great.
EISENSTEIN

Eisenstein's period in the theatre had a dual significance: as his contribution to theatrical annals, and – of prime importance – as a preparation and experimental ground for his film work that it foreshadowed. It is from the latter viewpoint – as a prelude to his subsequent activity – that we shall examine this chapter of Eisenstein's life,* our main concern remaining the same: how did Eisenstein become Eisenstein?

The beginning was not easy and involved many sacrifices. The first had been the toil of learning Japanese characters in order to reach Moscow at all, and the renunciation of a secure life as a student in Petrograd for the vagrant and uncertain existence that Moscow then offered. During that bitter winter of 1920 rationing was the order of the day; but, as ration cards were issued

---

* The information relating to this period presents a problem, being not only scant, but in many cases unreliable. Even Eisenstein's own reflections on his theatrical career, which he wrote three years before his death – and from which the basic material for this chapter is drawn – are not without their inaccuracies, probably due to the normal fallibility of memory. Many of the other surviving records are contradictory or so subjective as to need treating with reserve. From this point onwards Eisenstein is, in testimonies published by some of his acquaintances and close associates after his death, credited with thoughts and qualities which must be viewed with caution. (Even the most dependable of his biographers have sometimes been led astray by unverified information.)

46

only to those in work or to students, Eisenstein was not eligible for one. Until his meeting with Strauch he was, in fact, without food or lodgings. Yet neither cold, hunger nor the prospect of endless footsore hours could deter Eisenstein as he set off eagerly with Strauch in search of work at one of the workers' theatres. At first they got nowhere. These theatres were, by definition, restricted almost exclusively to the working classes; only 10 per cent of their personnel could come from other social strata, and this allocation had long since been filled. Yet neither would give up. Undaunted, despite the doors repeatedly shut against them, they kept on trying until they were both eventually taken on at the Proletkult Theatre – Eisenstein as a scenic designer.

Contacts

The first distant thundering of revolutionary art on the move was
audible all around, convulsing the heavens.
EISENSTEIN

Despite the crippling shortage of both food and heating in Moscow that winter, the general thirst for culture and the enthusiasm pervading artistic circles gave the city a new warmth and creative fire. It was the time of Isadora Duncan's visit and the controversy raging round her ideas on plastic movement; Mayakovsky was thundering out his views; Ehrenburg was writing his novels and poetry on the backs of old bills; after a year and a half of free performances, the theatres were reinstating the ticket system, and theatre mania was so widespread that demand for tickets far outstripped supply. At the same time, the young Muscovites, taking their cue from the Italian futurists,* were demanding the overthrow of all previous art forms in favour of a new revolutionary art. Similar ideas convulsed the Moscow theatres. Everywhere as Eisenstein later recalled

there was the same frenzied assault on art: the demand that its symptomatic 'figurativeness' be supplanted by blunt reality; its content by absence of a subject; its laws by arbitrary rules; its very existence by a concrete, realistic reconstruction of life, without fiction or plot as intermediary.[1]

A widespread movement to reinvigorate the traditional theatre had, of course, long existed – in Antoine's Théâtre Libre, the naturalist theatre in Germany, and the psychological realism of Stanislavsky and Nemirovich-Danchenko in Russia itself. The experimentation for which the movement called involved revising the repertoires and modifying the whole structure of stage presentation and acting. George Fuchs, Adolphe Appia, Max Reinhardt

* Although the Russian futurists named their movement after the Italians, they differed from Marinetti's followers in many respects. As Mayakovsky, a member of the movement, recorded in *Lef*: 'The Russian futurists broke definitively with Marinetti's poetic imperialism and even greeted him with catcalls during his visit to Moscow.'

and Gordon Craig figured among its numerous and powerful reformers. The widespread stir created by Craig's ideas had reached Russia when he visited the country at Stanislavsky's invitation, before the Revolution, to stage a production of *Hamlet*. In Russia, Meyerhold and Tairov had led the protest against the 'old' theatre. Thus a revitalizing spirit had been in the air for some time; but it had met with fierce opposition. Now, in Russia, it had suddenly been given free rein, an eruption of loudly propounded, diverse views had occurred, and the theatre was being turned inside out. Meyerhold launched the slogan 'October in the theatre' and joined the 'left' wing in opposing the academic faction of the 'right', in which even Alexander Tairov's Kamerny Theatre was now included. Theatre after theatre sought to establish its own particular line: the Proletkult Theatre, the Heroic-Experimental Workshop Theatre, Foregger's Theatre of the Four Masks, as well as the improvised Semper Ante Theatre, which gave its performances in a two-room flat. At the same time vast and elaborate productions, akin to modern mystery plays, with casts of up to ten thousand, came into vogue: *The Taking of the Winter Palace, The Mystery-Play of Liberated Toil, In Favour of a World Commune*. With each day that passed – as Stanislavsky observed – new precepts were expounded and instantly taken up, only to be torn to shreds and replaced by others before the week was out. The weirdest ideas saw the light of day on the stage. Dramaturgy as such ceased to exist, and even the classics were rewritten to suit the new, changing ideas.

At this chaotic period, one outstanding theatre was Meyerhold's R.S.F.S.R. Theatre No. 1. There was also Mayakovsky. For the stage-struck Eisenstein the possibility of meeting these two great personalities was an opportunity not to be missed. One day during that bitter winter of 1920 saw him slipping into the unheated R.S.F.S.R. Theatre where the shivering actors were rehearsing Mayakovsky's *Mystery-Bouffe* under Meyerhold's eagle eye. Suddenly the rehearsal was interrupted by a giant of a man, who stalked, cape flying, over to Meyerhold and launched into a furious tirade. 'Between his coat collar and cap protruded an enormous, square chin. His lips were drawn back and a cigarette . . .' But at this point the intruder – Eisenstein – was shown the door. This was his first glimpse of the two theatrical giants at work. Though ignominiously ejected from their presence on this occasion, he was soon to become their peer and to collaborate with them on an equal footing. For the moment, however, he was still plodding round the different Moscow theatres in search of work. And presently he hit upon the Proletkult Theatre.

The Proletkult Theatre had been set up during the February Revolution, but only during the Civil War and the immediate postwar years of reconstruction had it begun developing its own distinctive line. Meanwhile it had expanded considerably into a union with almost two hundred local branches, dozens of theatres, literary and musical circles, studios and so on throughout

Russia. Its basic precept – originating from A. A. Bogdanov, one of its founders – was that 'bourgeois' culture must be forced to give way to a new one of 'purely proletarian' character. Bogdanov ran the Petrograd branch of Proletkult, and remained unchallenged as the movement's leading ideologist until 1920. Then, during the Proletkult Congress held in Moscow in the autumn of that year, Lenin insisted on incorporating the movement into the People's Commissariat of Enlightenment, ostensibly to counteract Proletkult's continued 'damaging' attempts 'to set up a culture of its own', but in reality to curb Bogdanov's increasingly powerful influence.* After the Congress, the Moscow and Petrograd Proletkults became entirely separate entities. In Moscow itself the movement was further broken up into the Central Proletkult with its headquarters in the old Hermitage Theatre and the Moscow Proletkult, which were not only at loggerheads one with the other, but also torn internally by the most conflicting views. The latter, housed in the bizarre town residence villa of the former millionaire, Morozov, became a centre for conferences, lectures and discussions attended by the young Muscovite workers. Here Stanislavsky lectured on his 'method', Meyerhold expounded his diametrically opposite views on biomechanics, Mayakovsky his artistic credo; here Foregger called for a futurist theatre, Lunacharsky spoke in defence of the Bolshoi Theatre, Arbatov rejected the cultural heritage of the past, and Mikhail Chekhov propagated the philosophy of the 'Yogi' Rāmacharaka (real name: William Walker Atkinson); here there were study sessions on Marxism, Freudian psychology and so on. And this is where Eisenstein landed. This chaotic focal point for a profusion of different ideas – where he studied Pavlov, Freud and Meyerhold, continued to read a phenomenal amount, and gained experience as scenic designer and director – provided the formative ground for Eisenstein's emergent artistic thinking.

The first link

I must kill it, destroy it!
EISENSTEIN

On joining the Proletkult Theatre, then headed by the writer and revolutionary Valeri Pletnyov, Eisenstein had no very clear ideas about the theatre. His experience till then, including his reading and contact with contemporary ideas, had influenced him in certain directions, but he had scarcely begun to find his feet in the theatre, let alone (as his biographers have tended to assume) to formulate the distinctive concepts of his own that came only later. He worked with passion, was bursting with ideas and constantly in a state of

* Some time after the Congress, Proletkult reviewed its 'political errors', Bogdanov was replaced, and the whole organization came under the control of the People's Commissariat of Enlightenment.

excitement; his activity, however, was not concerned with applying any precise ideas, but was primarily a means of broadening his knowledge. It was without conscious intent, almost by accident, that, searching for an approach towards entertainment in general, he hit upon techniques more properly associated with cinematography. And this he did with his next theatrical venture, *The Mexican*, which was also a first step towards his subsequent work in the cinema.

The Mexican was a propaganda-style adaptation by Arbatov of a well-known story by Jack London, which Valeri Smishlayev had been appointed to produce. Eisenstein, as a new employee at the theatre, was given the job of designing the décor and costumes. This he set about with the deliberate intention of breaking with accepted theatrical traditions, and his décor took on a highly stylized form. For the prologue and epilogue sets, representing the establishments of two rival boxing promoters in Mexico, he conceived a style closer to surrealism than cubism, one establishment being constructed entirely in spherical forms, the other entirely in square ones. The props and costumes followed the same pattern: one of the boxing promoters wore a full, circular costume and similarly shaped wig and had round plaster patches on his cheeks, while everything about his rival was cubic. The makeup, likewise, gave the characters pronouncedly grotesque, caricatured features. Only the hero of the play, the Mexican, who doffed his long, black costume and wide-brimmed hat on entering the stage, appeared without makeup as a sympathetic, human figure, contrasting with the grotesque caricatures of people around him. A combination of Eisenstein's childhood love of the circus and his passion for the *commedia dell'arte* suddenly erupted in this weird scenic conception.

Thinking beyond the purely decorative aspect of the production, Eisenstein made a further suggestion affecting the actual direction of the key scene in the play – as a result of which he was invited to cooperate with Smishlayev as co-director. The scene was of a boxing-match, which, according to theatrical convention, would normally have taken place – like the bull-fight in *Carmen* or the horse-race in *Anna Karenina* – off stage. Eisenstein, however, proposed constructing the boxing-ring in the centre of the auditorium, thus creating an authentic setting and having the audience participate directly in the event as spectators. Although fire regulations prevented the exact arrangement envisaged by Eisenstein, the ring was, nonetheless, set up in full view of the audience on an extended forestage. Eisenstein's aim was to stage the actual fight as realistically as possible, in contrast with the stylized acting of the rest of the play. In the event the realism was overwhelmingly convincing, with 'real fighting, bodies crashing to the ring floor, panting, the shine of sweat on torsos and, finally, the unforgettable smacking of gloves against taut skin and strained muscles'. So true to life was the action that Alexandrov (who, as the

Sketch for *The Mexican*

Mexican, had to defeat the professional boxer, played by Ivan Piriyev) still remembers with amusement how the outcome of the fight was in doubt up to the last minute of every performance.

The Mexican created an enormous stir, and its young co-director became the talk of Moscow theatrical circles for the originality of his ideas, which attacked the fundamentals of theatrical aesthetics. By unfolding the action on two planes simultaneously – thereby exposing the audience to a dual emotional shock – Eisenstein not only disregarded completely the conventional unity of action, but at the same time foreshadowed a film-making technique; for the audience was, in effect, witnessing a sort of embryonic montage. As Eisenstein later recognized, bringing the events on to the stage was 'a specifically cinematographic technique as distinct from the purely theatrical element of "reacting to events" '. Thus, though there was as yet no question of any precise or systematic conceptualizing on Eisenstein's part – his theoretical concepts were only to crystallize as he gained in experience as a stage director – *The Mexican* represented a first step on the path towards his later film creations.

Throughout this period Eisenstein more often than not went cold and hungry. One day during that bitter winter, as Alexandrov recalled to Marie Seton, Eisenstein arrived for a rehearsal of *The Mexican* with only a piece of black bread, which he left on the lighting switchboard. Famished with hunger himself, having only just obtained work at the theatre, Alexandrov leapt on the bread and began wolfing it down until Eisenstein spotted him, when a fierce fight ensued. Only when Alexandrov managed to explain that he had been without food for two days did Eisenstein, who had eaten the day before, part with the rest of the bread. This incident marked the beginning of a friendship that was to last for more than ten years.

Generally speaking, however, Eisenstein scarcely even noticed the chronic hardships of daily life; he was twenty-two, had an enormous capacity for work and was passionately devoted to his art. Throughout rehearsals for *The Mexican* he was absorbed in the work to the exclusion of all else. But one day, during a rehearsal watched by the seven-year-old son of one of the usherettes, his attention was distracted by the child's face. Eisenstein was instantly struck by the way it registered everything that was going on at the rehearsal; the child was not only mimicking the expressions of each individual actor, but at the same time catching the atmosphere of the proceedings as a whole. It was this simultaneity that amazed Eisenstein, and on the long journey home that day – the trams were still not running and he had to walk – he began musing on its implications. He had long been intrigued by William James's paradoxical assertion that people do not cry because they are sad, but are sad because they cry; and similarly by the idea that through the imitation of a certain expression or mannerism the corresponding emotion can be experienced. 'But that being so', conjectured Eisenstein,

then must not the boy, in mimicking the actors' gestures, also be experiencing their emotions, or at least the emotions they were trying to transmit? The adult spectator is far more inhibited about imitating actors. But for precisely this reason his *fantasy* identification with the whole wonderful gamut of majesty and heroism purveyed by the drama must be all the more intense. *Fantasy* in the sense that it finds no outward expression and is without physical action. Or he must, by way of fantasy, give free rein to the base promptings and criminal tendencies in his nature – but, again, not through gestures or actions, but through the play of the *real* emotions that go with his *fantasy* complicity in the horrors perpetrated on stage.[2]

Eisenstein became absorbed in the implications of such fantasy experiences which made it possible, he thought, for the spectator to share in the passions of Romeo or the intelligence of Faust, or to evade every inner conflict with the help of Brand, Rosmer or Hamlet. He grew more and more excited as he elaborated this train of thought, realizing that this *fantasy* involvement afforded the audience a pleasure that was in every way *real*. They felt themselves to be the hero, experienced the emotions of the martyr, were overcome by their own generosity. . . . When he reached Trubnaya Square his agitation brought him to a standstill:

What a horrifying discovery! What diabolical mechanism lies hidden in this art that I serve! It's not merely a cheat and a swindle. It's poison – a dreadful, terrifying poison. For, if you can get your enjoyment through fantasy, who is going to make the effort any more to find in real experiences what can be had without moving from the theatre seat?

Eisenstein continued on his way in a frenzy, the picture he had glimpsed gradually taking on the proportions of a nightmare: 'I must kill it, destroy it!' But who was he, a mere novice, green to the theatre, to attempt such a thing? Slowly the solution dawned on him. First he must master his art, then destroy it:

I must probe its secrets, draw aside its veils. I must become a maestro. Then I can tear off its mask, expose it for what it is, destroy it.

Thus began a new phase in Eisenstein's theatrical activity.

'The assassin flirts with his victim . . .'

. . . He tries to gain her confidence. He tests her, studies her.
Like a criminal he creeps up on her stealthily. . . . At length he
engages her in conversation. . . . He gets on intimate terms with
her, but, so as not to be seduced by this friendship, he surrepti-
tiously fondles the blade of his dagger whose sharpness helps
him retain his cold judgement. . . . Thus art and I took stock of
each other. . . . She – enveloping me, ensnaring me in her
meshes. I – secretly fondling my dagger. A dagger which in this
instance was the dissecting scalpel of analysis.
EISENSTEIN

So Eisenstein began studying the various art forms, applying himself to the task with the systematic thoroughness of the trained engineer he was. It was not long, however, before he became discouraged; the more deeply he probed into the essence of art, the more inaccessible its mysteries seemed to become, 'the unfathomable beauty hiding her secrets beneath seven veils – a sea of muslin'.[3] Abandoning, therefore, this frontal attack, he decided on the subtler stratagem of trying to penetrate its secrets from the inside – a thing he could set about immediately through direct creative activity.

Avid to learn more, he immersed himself in work – in preparation for the next production, Pletnyov's *Precipice*, which Smishlayev was again directing and for which he himself again designed the décor and costumes. His compulsive urge to find new ways of expressing himself led to further *trouvailles*, all of which basically represented further steps towards the cinema. In one of the scenes an inventor, staggered by his latest discovery (or perhaps chased by gangsters – Eisenstein could not remember exactly when he came to write about it later), had to rush wildly through the town. For this scene Eisenstein wanted to create a certain relationship between man and his environment so as to point to the helplessness of the individual at the mercy of the big city. He conceived the idea of suggesting the tremendous dynamism of the metropolis, and of linking the characters inextricably with it, by the use of mobile props; the actors would move around on roller skates pulling 'a piece of the town' with them. This idea of interrelating man and his environment * owed something to Picasso and the Cubists, but Eisenstein's method of putting it into effect was entirely original:

I still remember the four legs of two bankers, supporting the façade of the stock-exchange, with two top-hats crowning the whole. There was also a policeman, spliced and quartered with traffic. Costumes blazing with perspectives of twirling lights, with only great rouged lips visible above.[4]

All this was meant to convey a sense of nonstop movement in which everything intersected, disappeared and reappeared. And the formula involved was, as Eisenstein later recognized, a cinematographic one, embodying close-ups and 'double and multiple exposure – "superimposing" images of man on to images of buildings' – in short, 'a film element that tried to fit itself into the stubborn stage'. But he was destined not to make conscious use of these complex filmic means of expression until he began his film activity with *Strike*; for a clash of opinion with Smishlayev brought the production – and with it Eisenstein's ideas – to an abrupt halt.

On 29 April 1921, following the abortive *Precipice*, Eisenstein started designing the costumes and scenery for a contemporary play, Andreyev's *King Hunger*. By this time, however, he was growing dissatisfied with the Proletkult Theatre. His thirst to learn more plagued him unremittingly, so that when, in the autumn of 1921, he saw an advertisement announcing the opening of the State School for Stage Direction, to be run by Meyerhold, he promptly presented himself for the entrance examination. The School, he found, was situated in a former lycée, where Meyerhold himself had a small flat, and boasted a tiny classroom and an adjoining hall with a stage. Meyerhold, dressed in a faded sweater, trousers drawn in tightly at the ankles by gaiters, gigantic slippers, a woollen scarf and red fez, presided over the Examining Board. Its other members included the poet Ivan Aksyonov, a member of the 'Centrifugal' literary circle and author of a monograph on Picasso, the mysterious Valeri Bebyutov and the actor Valeri Inkhizhinov, who later starred in *The Heir to Genghis Khan* (known in the West as *Storm over Asia*). Eisenstein presented his huge portfolio of sketches to the Board and before leaving made the acquaintance of the candidate next to him – Sergei Yutkevich, who later became famous as a director. Examinations

---

* This theme of the relationship between man and his environment was to crop up repeatedly, becoming a key feature of Eisenstein's works.

proper were held the following day. First came questions to test general cultural knowledge, followed by a practical problem, Eisenstein's being to draw on the blackboard a stage setting for the subject: 'six men in pursuit of a seventh'. With swift strokes, he sketched an ingenious and complicated *mise-en-scène*, of which Yutkevich was to be reminded several years later on seeing Meyerhold's production of Gogol's *The Inspector-General*. For the final test, in expressiveness of movement, the candidates had to draw an imaginary bow. The next day Eisenstein heard that he had been accepted; thus began a two years' association with Meyerhold that was to prove decisively important for his subsequent development as a film director.

On the first day of lectures, Eisenstein and Yutkevich made a dash for the front seats, determined not to miss a word of the two courses to be given by Meyerhold: on stage direction and on biomechanics. The latter was a new system for developing expressiveness of movement, the basic principles of which, Meyerhold explained, he would be elaborating with the students as they went along. His lectures on stage direction were exactingly precise, incorporating formulae for the calculated planning of each separate step in stage production. It was, paradoxically, to meet the demands of this system that Meyerhold's brilliant effects of improvisation were introduced; and it was almost certainly through Meyerhold's influence that Eisenstein, in turn, developed his own chameleon-like creative mode – that mixture of spontaneous improvisation and scientifically calculated planning that later produced the phenomenon of *Battleship Potemkin*. Given his innate improvisatory powers – in the sense that one idea often unleashed a whole chain of associated ideas – combined with the logical and analytical way of thinking instilled by his mathematical and technical training, Eisenstein would, no doubt, in any case have arrived at the same method in due course; but in the event it was Meyerhold who demonstrated how these two contradictory approaches could work so effectively side by side. Thus the young Eisenstein was lucky enough to meet with just the right teacher at the most propitious moment.

From the very beginning Eisenstein felt that in Meyerhold he had struck a gold mine which he must exploit to the full. But he was impatient to learn everything at once, and after only a few lectures he itched to goad Meyerhold into revealing the secrets of his creative process. With this in mind, he engaged him in conversation after class one day. Meyerhold soon warmed to the subject and from that point on began illustrating his lectures with examples drawn from his own past and current productions. And it was these illustrations that first opened up to Eisenstein the true meaning of stagecraft.

The parallel course in biomechanics included training in acrobatics, in which Eisenstein enthusiastically joined. He took the training sessions with great seriousness – though there was one nearly disastrous occasion when he absentmindedly forgot to catch Yutkevich at the end of a *salto-mortale* – and he appreciated Meyerhold's aim in endeavouring to revive acrobatics, along with other systems on the fringe of stagecraft, which had been abandoned by the contemporary theatre. Eisenstein himself was intensely interested in discovering the maximum expressiveness attainable through movement and, well-grounded as he was in the theory as a result of his extensive reading, he now welcomed the opportunity afforded by Meyerhold's biomechanics course to put his theoretical knowledge to practical use.

Meyerhold insisted on his students gaining direct, practical experience of the stage and, when the theatre season opened, arranged for them all to take part in the ball scene in Ibsen's *The League of Youth*. At the end of the first term he also set three students the task of staging a short production, giving Eisenstein Ludwig Tieck's *Puss in Boots*. For his *mise-en-scène* Eisenstein conceived the original idea of constructing a stage within a stage, the imitation stage being viewed as if from the wings. Thus the actors were shown in two distinct roles: as actors, addressing an imaginary audience from the imitation stage; then relaxing in the wings, when, in fact, they were playing to the real audience. This *mise-en-scène*, which underlined Eisenstein's subtly ironic attitude towards romantic characters, was to reappear later in his sets for *Heartbreak House*.

All told, the years spent with Meyerhold were to have an enormous influence on Eisenstein's subsequent creative work.* It was not without justification that Meyerhold later claimed:

All Eisenstein's work has its origins in the laboratory where we once worked together as teacher and pupil. But our relationship was not so much the relationship of teacher and pupil as of two artists in revolt, up to our necks and afraid to swallow for fear of the disgusting slime in which we found the theatre wallowing in 1917 [i.e. 1921]. The theatre was sinking in a swamp of naturalism, feeble imitation and eclecticism, with even the epigones imitating epigones.[5]

Eisenstein for his part was to look back on Meyerhold as his spiritual mentor, acknowledging towards the end of his life that he had never 'loved, revered and respected' any other man as he had Meyerhold.

Throughout his period at the School, Eisenstein lived – scholarships being non-existent – a tough, hand-to-mouth existence. Fortunately he still had lodgings with Strauch, while Yutkevich, whose mother regularly baked him

---

* In Meyerhold's work he came across a developed form of several ideas – that for instance of the 'cinefication' of the theatre – which were beginning to form in his own mind, even though he was not to clarify them in theoretical analyses until over a decade later. Of interest, too, in this context is Grigori Kozintsev's claim that the cinema learned more from Meyerhold than did the theatre. (Proletkult, knowing Meyerhold's interest in cinematographic problems, tried, in 1925, to get him to make a film of John Reed's *Ten Days That Shook the World*. Two years later Eisenstein made *October*.)

potato pies, saw to it that he never starved. During this time of shared hardships, Eisenstein and Yutkevich made a pact that whoever got work first would bring the other in as his assistant. By chance it was Yutkevich who received the first offer of work, in which they duly joined forces. For some time afterwards they kept up this system of working together, but it seems fairly clear that Eisenstein was the main provider of ideas.

Their first joint venture was at Foregger's Workshop Theatre, designing the settings for a triple bill of parodies that satirized in turn Nemirovich-Danchenko's penchant for operetta, the propaganda style of certain contemporary plays (*Don't Drink Wet Water*) and Tairov's excessively stylized performances. Foregger, formerly Baron Foregger von Greiffenturn, the last surviving member of an aristocratic German family, was a slender, elegantly dressed young man, who in many respects was the exact antithesis of Meyerhold. Yet Eisenstein soon found common ground with him, particularly in their appreciation of the *commedia dell'arte* and medieval French farce. It was Foregger's use of masks (to portray in a generalized way certain contemporary figures) that first introduced Eisenstein to an embryonic version of the 'typage' idea that he was later to develop in his films and expound in his writings.* When the parodies opened at the 'Mosaic' Hall, they met with immediate success. Eisenstein's work on them necessitated his delving into the very essence of stage satire, and thus provided him with a unique opportunity of analysing the theory and application of yet another aspect of theatrical art.

The same was true of the next production he worked on, a play by the poet Vladimir Mass, an associate of Foregger, entitled, after Mayakovsky's poem, *A Human Attitude to Horses* – though the title had just about as much in common with the substance of the play as has Ionesco's title, *The Bald Prima Donna*. Yutkevich barely recalls this play, but according to Marie Seton (who bases her story on a conversation with Eisenstein) and the bio-filmography of Eisenstein by Jay Leyda and Ivor Montagu, it figured, along with a parody of Tairov's production of *Phèdre* and *The Kidnapper* by d'Ennery, in a composite triple programme.†

A Human Attitude to Horses was divided into two parts, the first having a bitingly satirical content, highlighted by the use of 'typage' masks, while the second was an effervescent music-hall parody. Eisenstein was responsible for the costumes and designed a series of strange and fantastic creations, particularly for the musical numbers: instead of skirts, the chorus wore wide, bell-shaped, wire frameworks bedecked with multi-coloured ribbons, which were

---

* Typage has been defined by Jay Leyda (*The Film Sense*, page 125) as 'type-casting (of non-actors), elevated by Eisenstein to the level of a conscious creative instrument'.

† According to Yutkevich *The Kidnapper* was not performed until some time later; the contradictions have not yet been reconciled, and a correct chronology has still to be established.

so thin and revealing, by the austere standards of that time, as to set audiences goggling;* the Poet's costume was half flowing peasant's smock, baggy trousers and boots, half stylized evening dress. When the show opened on New Year's Eve, 1921, it was an immediate resounding success.

Shortly before the première, Meyerhold, who had been following Eisenstein's activities with interest, expressed a wish to take his students to see *The Mexican*. Eisenstein sat in the front stalls of the Proletkult Theatre, his hands clammy with emotion as he watched Meyerhold's reactions. Overjoyed to find that Meyerhold liked the show, he remained in high spirits for the rest of the evening, which ended up in the futuristic coffee house known as 'Sopo' (Soyuz Poetov, i.e. Poet's Union), with Meyerhold and Lunacharsky wrangling over the merits of Isadora Duncan's art. (Many years later the situation was to be reversed when Meyerhold invited Eisenstein to his Leningrad production of Tchaikovsky's opera *The Queen of Spades* and was intensely curious about the reactions of his former pupil.)

In the spring of 1922, Eisenstein was offered the job of designing the settings for Tikhonovich's production of *Macbeth*. As Tikhonovich had no fixed ideas for the *mise-en-scène*, Eisenstein was able to give free rein to his imagination. His chief preoccupation was with creating a spatial effect, and one idea for this – influenced by Appia – was to abandon the curtain and have a single décor throughout the play, with changes only of detail. A further idea was to swathe the entire sides and back of the stage in a neutral, grey canvas devoid of any additional colour, and to produce a tonal effect matching the action through changes in the lighting and the colour of the background sky. For this he used a simple three-tone colour range of black, gold and purple – the colours that years later he envisaged employing for the colour scenes in Part II of *Ivan the Terrible*. Thus Eisenstein's ideas for *Macbeth*, when he was still only twenty-four, contained the first seeds of his conception of the dramatic function of colour which he was to elaborate in his mature years. *Macbeth* also marked the first appearance in his creative work of the theme of 'the faceless ones' that was to recur again and again in all his films. Here it took the form of the helmets of the Scottish warriors who so strikingly foreshadowed the Teutonic knights in *Alexander Nevsky*. The theme of *Macbeth* itself was also to recur.

The play failed with the public and ran for only a week. After this Eisenstein attended rehearsals for Meyerhold's production of Crommelynck's *Le Cocu Magnifique*, before accompanying Foregger's theatre company on a tour to Leningrad, where he remained for the rest of the summer. It was there that he met Kozintsev and Trauberg, both members of the FEX group. FEX

---

* Six months or so later the painter Yakulov used the idea for an operetta, much to the annoyance of Eisenstein, who at one stage even considered lodging a public protest against the plagiarism.

(Factory of the Eccentric Actor) had been launched in December 1921 when a group of young actors and directors issued a manifesto elaborating their principles. Eisenstein soon found a common platform with these young artists and was present at their first production – an unconventional rendering of Gogol's *Marriage*, which was less an enactment of the play itself than of 'the product of their own imagination'. Eisenstein's contact with the FEX group had an influence on his own theatrical thinking,* and when in the autumn the group split up Eisenstein and Yutkevich returned to Moscow, intent on propagating the ideas of FEX there.

During that same summer Eisenstein decided to write a play with Yutkevich which he himself would produce. The idea of abandoning design in favour of direction had been simmering for some time and seems to have reached a head at this point, although Eisenstein continued to design theatrical settings. The outcome was an adaptation of *Columbine's Scarf* – a pantomime by Schnitzler, with music by Dohnanyi, that had earlier been produced by both Meyerhold and Tairov. Eisenstein and Yutkevich entitled their play *Columbine's Garter* and gave it an up-to-date setting, turning Pierrot into the epitome of the contemporary bohemian, and the exploiting Harlequin into a *parvenu* banker. For the first act the setting, a garret, was to be constructed entirely on the vertical plane, with the actors clambering about the frame of a huge window looking on to a contemporary Parisian scene ablaze with dazzling, illuminated advertisements. The second act, the ball at Harlequin's house, was to be even more novel in that it unfolded against a background of jazz music, then considered decidedly *avant-garde*. Eisenstein further envisaged Harlequin entering the stage on a tightrope – an idea (later used with resounding success in his production of *Even a Wise Man Stumbles*) which was sparked off by the presence in Foregger's company of an outstanding tightrope artist, F. F. Knorre. At the end of two months, Eisenstein had elaborated the *mise-en-scène* down to the last detail. Its dedication, written on the first page, ran, 'to Vsevolod Meyerhold, the Maestro of the Scarf, from the apprentices of the Garter'. His basic aim was to bring together a whole host of different 'attractions', including the tightrope act, as a new theatrical principle. He was pondering one day on what to call this principle, when Yutkevich burst into the room straight from seeing the roller-coasters, a type of entertainment of which they were both ardent fans, known in Russia as The American Mountains, and began telling him excitedly about their 'favourite attraction', as they called it. Eisenstein suddenly cut him

---

* Kozintsev, in answer to my enquiry, remarked on the influence of the first FEX production on 'Eisenstein's similar show based on Ostrovsky's play' a year later and pointed out that their Manifesto of December 1921 which spoke about 'a chain of tricks' preceded Eisenstein's Manifesto on the 'montage of attractions' by two years. Kozintsev added that 'there was certainly no question of plagiarism; all these ideas were in the air' at the time.

short: 'I've got it! What about calling our work "stage attractions"? After all, what we're aiming at is to stir our audience just as forcibly as that attraction stirs them up!' And so 'stage attractions' became the first name for the idea that Eisenstein was soon to elaborate into his famous theory of the 'montage of attractions'.

On his return to Moscow in the autumn, Eisenstein tried unsuccessfully to talk Foregger into letting him produce this play. Piqued at the refusal, he accepted Meyerhold's invitation to become his assistant and started work on Shaw's *Heartbreak House*. His conception of the play was full of 'eccentricities': again there were to be acrobatics, including hair-raising somersaults; again there was to be no curtain and the actors were to remain in full view of the audience throughout, resting on striped couches at the back of the stage during the intervals − much as they had done in his student production of *Puss in Boots*. Although rehearsals reached an advanced stage, the play never actually opened. All the same, *Heartbreak House* marked an important half-way stage in Eisenstein's theatrical career, for it both incorporated the fruits of his previous experience and foreshadowed in certain clearly defined respects his later decisive production, *Even a Wise Man Stumbles*.

The end of *Heartbreak House* also marked the end of Eisenstein's association with Meyerhold. The rupture was apparently precipitated by Eisenstein's reply to a question posed by Meyerhold during one of his lectures, which Eisenstein was again attending. Meyerhold appeared downcast, and Eisenstein feared that he had made a fool of himself with his reply. Instead, he was surprised to receive a note from Meyerhold via the latter's assistant, the actress Zinayida Reich: 'When the pupil is not merely equal, but superior, to the teacher, then it is best for him to go!' And so Eisenstein went. At the time it was a bitter blow to both of them. But some years later, when they were reconciled, Eisenstein was capable of attempting to explain it objectively: he saw it as a re-enactment on Meyerhold's part of 'that personal trauma provoked by his own break with his first teacher', Stanislavsky. Drawing the further parallel of the tragic parent−son relationship of Rustum and Sohrab, he acknowledged that Meyerhold, in forcing the rupture, was guiltless of 'the evil intentions of "the parent" but was only giving rein to the "over-proud son's" independent will to create'. Yet, in commenting on the less amiable traits in Meyerhold's character, Eisenstein noted that he could be malicious, and recalled how upset he had once been at his teacher's indifference and biting sarcasm when he sought his advice on a personal problem. On that occasion the look he received from his 'spiritual father' had been only too reminiscent of that of his own father: 'I was, beyond all argument, unlucky with my fathers.' This remark, together with the Rustum-and-Sohrab parallel, prompts the question whether Eisenstein did not have Meyerhold in mind when, nearly twenty years later, he poignantly recalled the fable in connection with the script for *Ferghana Canal* and felt compelled to give the film a happy ending. Some time after their reconciliation Meyerhold sent a photograph to his former student, inscribed with the words:

I am proud of the student – who has become a maestro. I regard with great affection this maestro who has created a school. To this student, this maestro – Sergei Eisenstein – my admiration.

The dedication is dated 22 July 1936. The first draft scenario for *Ferghana Canal* dates from July 1939 – just three years later and very near the time of Meyerhold's disappearance as yet another victim of the Stalinist purges. In this context, the question posed above would seem to be all the more pertinent. Some idea of Eisenstein's reaction to Meyerhold's fate may be gauged from an interesting fact which I learned from a reliable source in Moscow: that Meyerhold's personal papers were found among Eisenstein's belongings after the latter's death, Eisenstein having evidently salvaged them, despite the risks implicit in such an action, before the search of Meyerhold's house and theatre and the confiscation of all his possessions at the time of his arrest.

At this stage in his career, Eisenstein seemed maturer than his years, had an unshakable confidence in his artistic talents, and an inner assurance reflected in a calm and smiling exterior, which his friends vividly recall. It was the period marking the end of his theoretical probings and the beginning of his first independent productions. As Eisenstein himself described it,

for a time, art and its potential assassin co-existed harmoniously in the unforgettable ambience unique to those years. All the same, the assassin had not forgotten to keep a tight hold on his dagger (which in this instance, as I have already said, was the dissecting scalpel of analysis).

'Let us seek a unit for measuring the force of art'

And so began for me a 'double life' – a life in which every
second was taken up with a combination of creative and artistic
activity, of analysis and the verification in practice of my
theoretical hypotheses.
EISENSTEIN

As he systematically sought to elaborate the secrets and innermost workings of art, Eisenstein bore in mind a particular axiom retained from his engineering training: 'Knowledge starts at the point where it is possible to apply a unit of measurement to the object under investigation.' And so he set about finding the 'unit for measuring the force of art'.

Eisenstein felt intuitively that art must have its own precise laws similar to those which had intrigued him during his brief engineering training; it was only a question of formulating them by means of systematic analysis. Circumstances were in his favour, as a group of fifteen members of the Central

Proletkult Theatre wanted to transfer to the Moscow Proletkult and found an independent group, the 'Pere Tru' (Peredvizhaniya Trupa, or Strolling Troupe), which they invited Eisenstein to lead. Thus, in the autumn of 1922, Eisenstein became their chief manager and artistic director. At last he had a theatre of his own, which, as he made no secret, he intended using for his primary purpose of destroying the traditional theatre. He was evidently taken seriously, for Alexandrov recalls a conversation in which Lunacharsky practically went on his knees begging Eisenstein not to force him to close down the Maly Theatre.

One of Eisenstein's first 'actions was to establish a systematic study programme that included conferences, serious study sessions on circus art, and practical training in acrobatics, his aim being to imbue his actors with an attitude of precise application to their work. The day began at nine in the morning and continued until the evening with sports, boxing, athletics, team games, fencing and special voice training. Eisenstein lectured on his theories about the laws of art, little realizing that many of his ideas were similar to those being propounded by the lecturer in Marxism–Leninism in the adjoining class. When his students drew this to his attention,

I unexpectedly discovered the relation between the things I came across in my analytical work and what was going on around me. . . . [This stimulus] was enough to put on my desk the works of materialist dialecticians instead of those of aesthetics.[6]

Eisenstein's first production was an adaptation of Ostrovsky's *Even a Wise Man Stumbles* (also known as *Enough Stupidity in Every Wise Man* and as *The Diary of a Scoundrel*), a play he had seen at the Moscow Art Theatre in the cold and hungry days, when he had cajoled an usherette into letting him in without a ticket. It was while watching this performance, according to Maxim Strauch, that Eisenstein got the idea of taking the bare bones of the plot and adapting them to a contemporary context. Simultaneously with working on the *mise-en-scène*, he also began formulating his theoretical ideas on dramatic art. These, early in 1923, he incorporated into an article expounding his theory of 'the montage of attractions', which he took along to *Lef*, the review of the Artistic Left Front – a group of artists of varied persuasions and ideas, united in the common aim of declaring war on art. Mayakovsky edited the review, and it was his office that Eisenstein entered with his article. 'Here you are then,' exclaimed the jovial giant, swamping Eisenstein's hand in his own massive one; 'all yesterday evening I was exceptionally polite with director F., mistaking him for you!' Such, then, was Eisenstein's reputation; the rehearsals for his new show were already the talk of theatrical circles, and even Mayakovsky, who had not previously met the young director, was duly impressed. He accepted the article immediately and it appeared in *Lef* (No. 3, 1923) under the title 'The Montage of Attractions'.

The evolution of Eisenstein's theory of the 'montage of attractions' was essentially bound up with his quest for a 'unit of measurement' for gauging art's effective force. 'The basic materials of the theatre,' he argued in his article, 'derive from the spectator himself – and from our guiding of the spectator in the direction we desire (or into a desired mood).' And in this guiding process all the resources of the theatre were – as he had deduced from the behaviour of the usherette's small son – potentially important:

a roll on the kettledrums as much as Romeo's soliloquy, the cricket on the hearth no less than the cannon fired over the heads of the audience. For all, in their individual ways, bring us to a single idea – from their individual laws to their common quality of *attraction*.

The attraction (in our diagnosis of the theatre) is every aggressive moment in it, i.e. every element of it that brings to light in the spectator those senses or that psychology that influence his experience – every element that can be verified and mathematically calculated to produce certain emotional shocks. . . .

Sensual and psychological, of course, in the sense of efficient action – as in the Theatre Guignole, where an eye is gouged out, an arm or leg amputated before the very eyes of the audience. . . . Rather in this sense than in that branch of the psychological theatre where the attraction rests in the theme only, and exists and operates *beneath* the action. . . .

I establish attraction as normally being an independent and primary element in the construction of a theatrical production – a molecular (i.e. compound) unity of the *efficiency* of the theatre. . . .[7]

It was a 'unit of measurement' that Eisenstein had been seeking. And, just as physics had its ions, electrons and neutrons, so art, he concluded, had its 'attractions', with varying degrees of force. As for a comprehensive label for these units of measurement, one that would incorporate them into a system, he chose the technical term 'montage', usually applied to the operation of assembling parts of a machine. It was certainly not a term fashionable in the art world at that time. If Eisenstein had been more conversant with Pavlov's theories, he would – as he later acknowledged – probably have called his system 'the theory of aesthetic excitements'. Instead it was the term 'montage of attractions' that was destined to go down in the annals of theatrical history.

Briefly then, Eisenstein's 'montage of attractions' was not concerned with the 'static reflection of an event when all the possibilities for activity are kept within the limits of the event's logical attraction', but rather with the 'free montage of arbitrarily selected, independent (within the given composition and the subject links that hold the influencing actions together) attractions – all with the aim of establishing certain final thematic effects'.

This article represented Eisenstein's first attempt to rationalize the effectiveness of dramatic art and to reduce its varied powers over the audience to a 'sort of common denominator'. It was to find its 'definitive expression' many years later in Eisenstein's celebrated theory of vertical montage.

But at that time Eisenstein's one aim was to find a way of applying his theory as a production method at the Proletkult workshop. 'Schooling for the *montageur* can be found in the cinema,' conjectured the young theoretician (who, very shortly, was himself to enter this school), 'and chiefly in the music-hall and circus, which invariably put on a good show from the spectators' viewpoint.' And it was with this thought in his mind that he started work on his production of Ostrovsky's *Even a Wise Man Stumbles*.

This production, often known simply as *The Wise Man*, provides an important key for understanding Eisenstein's later works of film art. Paradoxical as it may seem, the artistic miracles of his great emotive films, including *Battleship Potemkin*, have their roots in the eccentricities of this production which Eisenstein himself characterized as 'purely cerebral and almost abstract eccentric'.[8] In this sense – as well as in the literal sense that it included the first, short film he ever made – *The Wise Man* marked the beginning of Eisenstein's film career.

Though it preserved nothing else from the original play (even the dialogue was new), Eisenstein's show did retain the bare outline of the plot. But he placed the elaborate tissue of intrigue within a contemporary setting, the characters including the French general Joffre, the British Foreign Secretary Lord Curzon, the former Russian Foreign Minister Milyukov and a creature and servant of the New Economic Plan. As far as the décor was concerned, Eisenstein went a step further than in *The Mexican* in breaking with theatrical tradition. The stage in the huge salon of the former Morozov mansion was arranged exactly like a circus arena, down to the huge carpet and red barrier edging it. The audience surrounded three quarters of the arena, while the fourth was draped in striped canvas and had a platform with several steps in front. In the ring itself were the usual circus paraphernalia of hoops, top hats, parallel bars, a vaulting-horse, a trapeze, a tightrope and so on. Throughout the show there was a motley coming and going of actors from all parts of the auditorium. Some juggled with tin plates and others performed a variety of acrobatic stunts; one actress, her false bosom lit up by light bulbs, sang risqué ditties in true music-hall style, while another performed on the vaulting-horse. But the show's highlight came when Alexandrov crossed the auditorium on the high wire. (At this point Eisenstein always hid in terror until applause indicated that the incident was safely over.) One grotesque political satire followed another at a dizzy speed. A solemn procession of priests with placards denouncing religion as 'the opiate of the masses' was succeeded by three prelates of differing rites, who, instead of holding serious ecclesiastical discussions, quickly reached agreement, squirting water and tumbling about the stage the while. As a final rousing climax, the near-exhausted

The Wise Man: Grigori Alexandrov on the high wire

audience were subjected to the sudden explosion of fire-crackers under their seats.

Chaotic as all this seemed, the whole show in fact followed a precise inner logic. The acrobatics served the deliberate purpose of reflecting and intensifying the emotions purveyed by the actors:

a gesture expands into gymnastics, rage is expressed through a somersault, exaltation through a *salto-mortale*, lyricism on 'the mast of death'. The grotesque of this style permitted leaps from one type of expression to another, as well as unexpected intertwinings of the two expressions.[9]

Eisenstein aimed to introduce 'a *new measure* of tension'; to extend 'the *conventional* tension of acting' and to raise it to 'a new level of *real* physical tension'. From Ostrovsky's original he retained only as much as was necessary to enable the informed spectator to recognize it. He maintained that

the music-hall element was obviously needed at the time for the emergence of a 'montage' form of thought. Harlequin's parti-coloured costume grew and spread, first over the structure of the programme, and finally into the method of the whole production.

The short film included in *The Wise Man* was an entertaining idea for illustrating Glumov's diary. It depicted the masked and caped Glumov continually transforming himself into a variety of different objects beloved by one or other of his friends: with his doting aunt, for example, he becomes a suckling babe, with Joffre he turns into a machine-gun, and so on. Later it showed him wandering over the rooftops before jumping into a car which speeds off to the theatre where the show is taking place. As the film ended at this point, Alexandrov simultaneously burst through the screen on to the stage, triumphantly holding up the reel of film. This final ingenious idea had been used several years earlier by Max Linder in Moscow,* in a show which Eisenstein had probably heard about, though almost certainly not seen. It was perhaps a case of his applying Molière's maxim: 'Il m'est permis de reprendre mon bien partout où je le trouve.' But in any case the film's novelty lay less in this particular *trouvaille* than in its satire on the first news films of that time, Dziga Vertov's *Kino-Pravda* series.† From this point of view, Eisenstein's first film venture was a *negation* of a certain cinematographic form.

With this, his very first film, Eisenstein caused considerable alarm in the studios – something which he was often to do in later years as an experienced director – over the shooting of Glumov's rapid personality changes. One of

* Linder's show opened with a film showing the actor's arrival in Moscow by plane. The plane hovers over the theatre where the show is running, while Linder lets down a rope ladder out of one of the windows and begins to descend. At this point of the film the screen suddenly collapses to reveal the flesh-and-blood Linder finishing his descent on to the stage.

† *Glumov's Diary* was later included in Vertov's *Kino-Pravda* anthology.

the studio technicians considered it an impossibly dangerous task and refused to try. By way of insurance, the studio decided to appoint a specialist to supervise the shooting and chose Dziga Vertov. Not surprisingly, he too walked out of the improvised set after the first shooting session, leaving Eisenstein to his fate. But in spite of everything, including the mad rush (the film was started on a Thursday and had to be ready for the show's first night the following Saturday), the shooting was, in fact, successfully completed in a single day.

As we have noted, however, it was not the inclusion of this short comic film, but rather the entire organic structure of Eisenstein's *mise-en-scène* that gave the show a cinematographic character.

In the first place, *The Wise Man* contained unmistakable elements of 'a sharply expressed montage'[10] that foreshadowed his later film techniques. Thus, in order to emphasize the dualism of Glumov's character − a comic figure, but with some of the characteristics of Balzac's Rastignac − Eisenstein had him playing on two planes at once: in the circus arena when receiving his uncle's instructions, and on the platform when he relayed them to his aunt. These 'intersections of the two dialogues sharpen the characters and the play, quicken the tempo, and multiply the comic possibilities'.[11] Glumov leapt from one part of the stage to another, carrying over a fragment of dialogue from the first and continuing it in the next, where it took on a new significance and meaning in its totally alien context. His leaps served as *caesurae* between the fragments in this 'cross-montage of dialogues'.[12] The intercutting of dialogues as a literary technique was, of course, familiar to Eisenstein from his reading; he had been particularly impressed by the scene in *Madame Bovary* where the conversation between the future lovers, Emma and Rodolphe, is interlaced, to such dramatic effect, with the speech of the orator in the square below. The connection he saw between, on the one hand, things in literature, painting and the Japanese he had studied and, on the other hand, his own experiences was certainly what led Eisenstein to the discovery and clarification of, first, the concept of cinematographic montage, and, subsequently, its possibilities as a means of expression. *The Wise Man* opened up his path towards the film. Haphazard and motley though the eccentricities in it may have seemed, in reality they represented the clearest possible ordering of the means of expression through a montage effective in achieving his intentions.

Thus, with *The Wise Man*, Eisenstein laid the foundations of modern cinematographic montage long before he began his actual filming activity. Moreover, as has been mentioned, it was from the eccentricities in this show that the emotive quality in *Battleship Potemkin* and other Eisenstein films − or more precisely his method of achieving it − paradoxically derived. For in the eccentric theatre were to be found two major premises that became decisive in his later artistic programme and its realization. First, he had taken *'a maximum degree of passion as a point of departure'*; second, he saw *'a breaking of the customary dimension as a method of its embodiment'.*[13] In this sense the difference between his eccentric shows and 'pathetic' films lay merely in the fact that in the former he applied his theses *'directly and literally'*, and not as guiding principles, so that they found expression in buffoonery and eccentricity. As Eisenstein explained, the leap

from one type of expression to another . . . – a *dynamic* characteristic in a successive process – always proceeds from inside a *static* condition – of a forced external observance of *simultaneity* (i.e. of the same dimension). The 'new quality' was treated as if it were the old – the 'preceding' quality. This is in itself one of the means of achieving comic effects. How amusing it is, for example, when the latest stage of conveyance is forced to be dependent on the conveyance of an earlier epoch – when an automobile is harnessed to . . . oxen . . . or to mules. . . .[14]

Eisenstein's film work was logically and organically linked with his eccentric theatre.

The Wise Man was a resounding success. But Eisenstein lived through some anxious moments, particularly when he presented an excerpt from the show to a select audience of theatrical and artistic personalities at the Bolshoi Theatre. When the show ended to a burst of clapping, followed by another and yet another, culminating in a torrent of applause, his surprise was so great that he forgot to call for the curtain, and after it had finally fallen he was still so dazed as not to notice when he caught and ripped his brand new suit on a nail – and at that time a suit was worth its weight in gold.

The first to celebrate the show's success over a bottle of champagne was Mayakovsky. Though critical of Eisenstein's textual adaptation of the original, he was sorry that 'he himself had not thought of collaborating in this gay and lively show', which soon won the reputation of being the gayest of the 1923 Moscow theatre season.

But however pleasant the successes of his work at that period, the essential thing about it, Eisenstein maintained, was that it brought him to an understanding at last of 'the method of art'.[15] And his arrival at this understanding he attributed in equal measure to two factors: to his theoretical analyses and to the verification of his theories through practical application – that is, to the 'double life' that he now began to lead.

'The victim proves more cunning than the assassin'

While the assassin believed that he was cornering the victim,
she had already seduced him. She had seduced him, ensnared
him in her thralls and finally absorbed him completely.
EISENSTEIN

From this point onwards Eisenstein's productions were to be based on the principle of the 'montage of attractions', and to follow the path opened up by *The Wise Man*, which led inexorably towards the cinema.

One project – which fell through for want of a suitable auditorium – was a production of *Patatra*, 'planned with chase tempos, quick changes of action, scene intersections, and simultaneous playing of several scenes on a stage that surrounded an auditorium of revolving seats'.[16] It represented a further step towards cinematography. There followed the production of Sergei Tretyakov's propaganda play dealing with recent revolutionary events in Germany, *Listen Moscow*; Eisenstein dates this in the summer of 1923, but other reliable sources suggest that rehearsals took place in September–October, the first night being in November. Staged in Grand Guignol style, it had many similarities with *The Wise Man*; there was the same geometrical stylization and the same 'attractions', only this time Eisenstein's thinking was carried a stage further, the incipient cinematographic elements becoming more pronounced. The *mise-en-scène* singled out groups from among the mass of actors, shifting the spectators' attention from one focal point to another and accentuating details – a hand holding a letter, a raised eyebrow or a glance – in a way that was pure cinema. He was, indeed, approaching the limits of what he could achieve in the theatre by cinematographic means of expression. He had reached, as he put it, a 'threatened hypertrophy of the *mise-en-scène*', the only way out of which seemed to be a cinematographic presentation of details through montage in direct transitions from shot to shot. In other words, the film; and the concept born at this point in his thinking and experience was none other than the *mise-en-cadre*, which Eisenstein should be given due credit for having introduced, through his theoretical discovery, into the aesthetics of film art. 'As the *mise-en-scène* is an interrelation of people in action, so the *mise-en-cadre* is the pictorial composition of mutually dependent *cadres* (shots) in a montage sequence.'[17]

In Eisenstein's following production,* *Gas Masks*, the cinematographic elements were still more pronounced. His overriding aim with this play was to introduce an even greater degree of reality than hitherto and to reconcile the conflict between realism of action and artificiality of décor. With this in mind, he wanted to break out of the confines of the conventional stage and proposed creating a setting specially suited to the action – which takes place in a gasworks. Eisenstein was always telling his colleagues that 'the theatre should become real life' and, in conformity with this contention, hit on the novel idea of staging the play in a real gasworks. And so a floor – half empty of machinery – of the Moscow gasworks became his 'stage'. Benches were brought in to replace the conventional theatre seats. True to life, the actors

---

* Under this year, 1923, the catalogue of the Eisenstein archive lists, without giving details, some preparatory material for another production: *Garland's Inheritance*, by Pletnyov.

themselves wore no makeup, while the final scene was timed to coincide with the entry of actual night-shift workers, who took over from the actors and set about lighting their fires as a grand finale to the show. The pitfalls soon became only too evident, however: not only was the work of the gasworks being seriously disrupted, but the audience did not take kindly to the effects of the evil-smelling gas. After only four performances, on 4 and 6 March 1924, the actors were asked, none too politely, to leave.

But the essential reason for the show's failure was the incompatibility of real-life décor and theatrical illusion; the reality of the surroundings totally eclipsed the play-acting, making it appear trivial and absurd. Eisenstein realized that without meaning to do so he had trespassed, with a vengeance, on to film ground. But there was nothing unintentional about his subsequent plunge from theatre to cinema.

Three factors led up to this plunge. The first was his stage experiments. The second was his awareness of the limitations of the theatre as far as putting them into effect was concerned. Previously he had wanted to replace traditional theatre by realism. Now he renounced the theatre altogether: 'The theatre as an independent unit within a revolutionary framework . . . is out of the question. It is absurd to perfect a wooden plough; you must order a tractor.' He was convinced that the only reason why the theatre survived at all in its traditional form was apathy. He was fond of telling the story about a museum where Alexander the Great's skull when he was twenty-five was exhibited alongside his skull when he was forty; he dubbed the theatre and the cinema the two skulls of Alexander, considering their co-existence nonsensical. The third and decisive factor was his direct contact with filming itself – with 'the tractor'.

Film encounter

I would never have believed that my passion for cinematography
would one day exceed the limits of a platonic love.
EISENSTEIN

In making *Glumov's Diary*, Eisenstein had scarcely scratched the surface of film-making techniques, yet by the spring of the following year, a matter of days after the failure of *Gas Masks*, he was already delving deeply into their secrets.

By this time the cinema as such was no novel revelation to him. The revelation had come several years earlier when, as a penniless student, he had wormed his way free in to Mikhail Boitler's cinema and seen the repertory of American films showing there. The undreamed-of possibilities which they opened up overwhelmed and excited him, just as the new-fangled cars arriving from America were later to enthrall the young Russian mechanics. At that same period he had also seen the first German expressionist films showing at other cinemas. But most significant of all for Eisenstein had been his encounter with the films of D. W. Griffith and, through them, with the principle of montage.

All this had, however, been merely a prelude. It was the last three days of March 1924, when he first actively participated with his friend Esther Shub in putting a film together, that marked the real beginning of his cinematographic apprenticeship.* Esther Shub was herself a highly respected film-cutter at that particular period when all films imported from abroad had to be closely censored to eliminate any 'unhealthy tendencies' before their general release to the public. In this censoring process the entire sense of a film could be radically altered: there was the case, for instance, of selected excerpts from two completely separate films being edited into a single film so as to point up the contrast between the life of leisure enjoyed by the passengers aboard a trans-Atlantic luxury liner and the sweat and toil of the stokers below deck.

Eisenstein frequently visited Esther Shub in her cutting-room, watching her at work and seeing the run-throughs of films she had just edited.

It was there that he first handled a spool of news-reel film depicting the events of February 1917, which he was later to recall in making *October*. At the end of March 1924 she was busy cutting Lang's *Dr Mabuse*; she virtually remade it, in fact, with Eisenstein as a fascinated onlooker, and it was eventually released in a much shortened version under the title *Gilded Putrefaction*. Esther Shub was also deeply interested in Kuleshov's activities and used to experiment with the assorted fragments of film left over from the films she had cut. Sometimes these were films compiled to standard length from several serials, when the fragments consisted mainly of the introductory recapitulations. Together with Eisenstein at her home, where she had a small cutting-table and projector, she would study their possibilities, putting together the most unlikely pieces with the most bizarre results. The knowledge Eisenstein gained from these experiments with Esther Shub was to have a substantial influence on his later work: they not only opened up to him the 'mysteries' of montage, but also sowed the seeds of many ideas that he subsequently brought to fruition. (Even the beginning of the second part of

---

* Lev Kuleshov, who was a close friend of Eisenstein, told me that Eisenstein studied with him and learned from him at the beginning of his film career. He recalls 1923 as the year of his meeting with Eisenstein and even remembers details from those times. As he related to the American Professor Steven P. Hill in a long and valuable 'bio-interview' published in *Film Culture*: 'Eisenstein got his first lessons in film direction from me. True, he didn't study with me very long – about three months – but Eisenstein himself said that any man can be a director, only one needs to study three years and another three hundred years. . . . Together with Alexandrov, he attended our workshop in the evening (in the attic of Meyerhold's Theater), and together we did some work on developing shooting scripts mostly for crowd scenes. . . . We studied together how to work out editing scenes on paper, when there wasn't any film. That was before his début – that is, before *Strike*.'

Ivan the Terrible may have owed something to a memory from that period.) But probably the most significant lesson he learned was that a piece of celluloid is a neutral thing as long as it remains in isolation, taking on meaning and the power to communicate only when it is united with a second piece of celluloid.

Shortly after this Eisenstein decided to part company with Proletkult, following a further clash of opinions. He turned for help to Eliseyev, who by then was editing the review *Red Pepper*, and who readily accepted Eisenstein's suggestion that he should join the review as a cartoonist. The very next day, however, saw Eisenstein apologetically explaining to Eliseyev that he had changed his mind overnight, having meanwhile been offered the prospect of film work with Proletkult in connection with a projected cycle of films, *Towards the Dictatorship*, intended as a sort of historical panorama of the Party and the working-class movement; Pletnyov, who had been given the job of writing the script for one of the films, *Strike*, had invited him to join forces on it – a temptation he had been unable to resist. And so Eisenstein set to work with Pletnyov on the script for the film which was eventually to turn into a joint production of Proletkult and the cinematographic enterprise Goskino (whose director, Boris Mikhin, had, paradoxically, been most unfavourably impressed by *The Wise Man*).

In Eisenstein's view the work was in no way an extension of his theatrical activity, but rather a complete negation of it.* Cinematography represented for him virgin territory wide open for exploration:

We came like bedouins or gold-seekers to a place with unimaginably great possibilities. . . . We pitched our tents and dragged into camp our experiences in varied fields. Private activities, accidental past professions, unguessed crafts, unsuspected eruditions – all were pooled and went into the building of something that had, as yet, no written traditions, no exact stylistic requirements, nor even formulated demands.[18]

* He was later to modify this dogmatic attitude. Not only did powerful theatrical influences appear in his films, but he was actually to return to his first love, the theatre, later in his career. Furthermore, as lecturer, he was to assert categorically that 'the study of cinematography should, without fail, begin with the study of the theatre'.

4. *Strike*

The man who first stated that two and two make four was a great mathematician, even if he got this result by adding two pebbles to two other pebbles. All other men, even those who add incomparably greater things, locomotives for instance, are not.
MAYAKOVSKY

The world cinema on the eve of 'Strike'

When Eisenstein began his film-making activity, cinema history was not yet thirty years old. Yet in this time the film had long since ceased to be a mere technical novelty and had begun to be recognized among the arts. In France, Georges Méliès had already created his films, Max Linder had won a following both at home and abroad, Feuillade's films had appeared and Abel Gance had begun to make his name among the leading lights of the film universe – a universe that included such luminaries as L'Herbier, Dulac, Feyder, Delluc and Epstein. The Swedish cinema had made its presence felt, while that in Germany was flourishing: expressionism had been born and was compelling recognition; Robert Wiene, Lubitsch, Lang and Murnau had become celebrities in the cinema-loving world at large. The United States of America had produced the primitive art of a Porter, followed soon after by that of D. W. Griffith – of paramount significance – and of Thomas Ince; Erich von Stroheim had begun his film-making career, Cecil B. De Mille, Robert Flaherty and Buster Keaton had become famous. . . . A film directory of the time, though brief and incomplete, nevertheless records the existence, in the period 1920–22, of twenty-one film-making countries whose productions commanded some recognition. By 1923 Germany's annual production had risen to 347 films, that of the United States to 467. The year of Eisenstein's eruption on to the cinematographic scene – 1924 – was rich in quality films: Lang's *Niebelungen*, Murnau's *The Last Laugh*, Stroheim's *Greed*, Lubitsch's *Forbidden Paradise*, Cecil B. De Mille's *The Ten Commandments*, René Clair's *Entr'acte*, and other films by Griffith, Sjöström, Epstein, L'Herbier and Feyder. Thus Eisenstein's advent was not that of a messiah eagerly awaited by history to make the desert rejoice. On the contrary: the Gardens of Semiramis were in full bloom and the fading of one or two blossoms was followed by the flowering of many others to take their place. The cinema had claimed its place as an art form and was establishing its own language and means of expression. From the vast ocean of historical facts let us choose three that played an important part in Eisenstein's development as a creative artist.

First and foremost there was Griffith, the American director whom Eisenstein later acknowledged to have played 'a massive role in the development of montage in the Soviet film', adding that 'all that is best in the Soviet film has its origins in *Intolerance*'.

What was Griffith's contribution to cinema history? The techniques he used – the close-up, intercutting, camera movement, changing camera angles and so on – had all been discovered before him. But Griffith was the first to use them creatively. He was the first to make conscious use of abrupt cuts in action, to juxtapose with dramatic effect two different lines of action through parallel montage, to create a distinctive tempo during editing and to employ a wide variety of angled shots – all techniques now basic to the language of cinematography. The morphology already existed, but Griffith created the syntax, thereby giving the cinema an articulate language. The Soviet film school in general, and Eisenstein in particular, took over his methods and transformed them into a means of communicating ideas and emotions.

Two examples – the close-up and parallel montage – will illustrate more clearly Eisenstein's debt to Griffith and make possible a better appreciation of Eisenstein's genius. The close-up was not, as we have seen, Griffith's invention. Edwin Porter had used it as a technical device – his bandit fired, in close-up, at the audience – but without attracting more than momentary attention. But when Griffith used the close-up to show a woman anxiously awaiting her husband's return, followed immediately by a shot of the absent man, he unleashed a storm of criticism. In reply to critics of his abrupt cut from one scene to another, he claimed there were precedents in Dickens' novels: 'The difference isn't all that great; I compose novels in pictures.'

Griffith's use of the close-up, however, was merely a way of looking at an object or character, whereas Eisenstein was to use it to symbolic rather than purely illustrative effect. In other words, the purpose of his close-up was not merely to show a cheek or some other object in detail, but to express an idea through it – to endow it, as it were, with a new significance. Griffith told a story; Eisenstein composed a poem.

Similarly with parallel montage, which Griffith was the first to use deliberately (again after Porter had done so casually), in order to bring together two convergent actions – thereby discovering the expressive potentialities of montage. Again, Eisenstein was to go still further, employing the two juxtaposed images to introduce a new concept. By cutting, for instance, from the shot of strikers being slaughtered to that of oxen being butchered in a slaughterhouse, he was to convey not two disparate actions, but the single idea of the savagery of the Tsarist police. He was to enlarge the scope of parallel montage found in Griffith's films and, by extending it 'from the sphere of action to that of significance', as he put it, was to endow it with new values and new qualities.*

A second factor that influenced Eisenstein's development was his contact with German expressionist films, which were frequently shown in Moscow, and in which he encountered many methods of expression similar to those he had himself been trying out in a rudimentary way in the theatre. Though he was later to claim that the expressionist films scarcely influenced the art of the young Soviet film makers, including his own, a very different inference might be drawn from his immediately following remark that the technical equipment available in Moscow at the time was not capable of producing such 'phantasmagorias'. There is, indeed, little question – despite his unaccountable disclaimer – that the expressionist films of that time made a powerful impression on him and affected his development as a film-maker.

The final factor was, of course, the Soviet cinema itself.

The Soviet cinema at that period

Even before the First World War the Russian cinema already enjoyed an international reputation. By the end of the war there were over two thousand cinemas in Russia, and of the total footage of film that passed through the hands of the distributing houses – about twelve million metres – only 30 per cent came from abroad. Quantitatively speaking, therefore, national production was important. After the Revolution, a move was made to nationalize the film industry, a move which at first met with determined and systematic resistance, especially from the industrialists: distributing offices blocked films, refusing them to cinemas controlled by the Soviets, while production companies hid or destroyed both film and equipment. Raw film stock was impossible to import during the early years of Communist rule,† and the filmmakers used any odd pieces and left-overs they could lay hands on.

---

* Even the French term 'montage', though used as early as 1914, only became known and adopted in most countries after its acceptance by the Russian school and, in particular, by Eisenstein and Pudovkin.

† Jay Leyda notes that neither filming equipment nor film was being produced in Russia at that time.

Following nationalization, the Soviet regime began to exercise control over all film production. Films with a revolutionary content began to appear, marked by the cloying, eulogistic manner then in vogue. Two party congresses recorded the precarious state of the Soviet film and issued directives designed to improve the situation. Production started to increase. Kuleshov, who had set up his famous workshop in 1920, was continuing his experiments and training. Dziga Vertov began his *Kino-Pravda* newsreel series, setting a trend in film-making whose effects are still felt throughout the world today. The same issue of *Lef* that carried Eisenstein's first theoretical article on the montage of attractions also included Vertov's manifesto on the 'cine eye' (*Kino-glaz*), initiating ideas that were to have an international influence.

Some knowledge of the then accepted ideas on art and its application to the cinema is also important for understanding the emergence of Eisenstein's theories. His artistic thinking during that period did not exist *in vacuo*, nor did it represent a mere intellectual whim; it was a consistent and logical development of contemporary ideas. Vertov was maintaining that the exceptional flexibility of montage construction made it possible to introduce political or economic ideas of virtually any kind into the 'cine-essay'; the appearance of Eisenstein's *Strike* is thus less surprising than it might seem at first sight. It was also Vertov who, about this time, reached the conclusion that drama or *mise-en-scène* was no longer essential to the film. According to Lebedev, the official historian of the Soviet cinema, one of Proletkult's basic principles was 'collectivism', which rejected individual heroes in favour of the masses, or the collective. The idea of 'typage' had, as we have seen, been applied by Eisenstein himself in his theatrical work, reflecting in turn not only his own passion for the *commedia dell'arte*, but also the influence of Meyerhold's theatrical thinking. *Lef* was demanding the abandonment of traditional art forms. (Not until 1928 was Mayakovsky to make his public declaration: 'I grant Rembrandt a reprieve!') Finally, Kuleshov's celebrated experiments in cutting, carried out around 1920–21, were exerting a powerful influence.

Methodological parenthesis

While working on *Ivan the Terrible* Eisenstein published a series of notes[1] outlining his methodological approach to filming. Though written many years after his first film, *Strike*, these notes are well worth considering in parenthesis at this point for their considerable relevance to his earliest film work.

In these notes Eisenstein distinguished three distinct creative stages, beginning with what he called 'the first vision'.

The most important thing is to have the vision. The next [i.e. the second stage, that of elaborating the script] is to grasp and hold it. In this there is no difference whether you are writing a film-script, pondering the plan of the production as a whole, or thinking out a solution for some particular detail.

You must see and feel what you are thinking about. You must see and grasp it. You must hold and fix it in your memory and senses. And you must do it at once.

When you are in a good working mood, images swarm through your busy imagination. Keeping up with them and catching them is very much like grappling with a run of herring.

Dialogue, characters, costumes and movements — Eisenstein explained — all swarmed simultaneously into his mind. Often a new thought appeared before he had noted the preceding one; or his initial idea was modified or enriched by suggestions from his collaborators. But, even if changes occurred, 'you will strive to convey in the finished work that invaluable seed that was present in your first vision of what you hoped to see on the screen'.

When Eisenstein wrote these notes, it was by way of explaining his working sketches, his 'stenographic' method of recording his thought processes. It is not clear whether any such sketches were made for his early silent films, since it was only later that he developed this stenographic method to a fine art. But the successive stages of creation were always the same, although utterly different methods and creative processes went into the gestation of each individual film. His 'first vision' and its 'fixing' always constituted decisively important stages in the creation of Eisenstein's films, including *Strike*.

The third stage was what Eisenstein called 'facing the camera'. This was the point at which the flights of fancy were translated to the technical sphere in order for 'the dream' to become reality.

Fancy is now in harness. The earlier free play of fantasy has now become depth of focus, choice of the properly dense filters for the lens, the clicking of the footage metre.

At this stage, too, amid the turmoil of the studio set, the pursuit of the first vision still remained a prime objective.

Eisenstein's notes stopped at this point without elaborating on the final stage in his creative process. This fourth stage — the montage stage — was of singular importance. On the cutting-table the filmed material revealed many surprises and accidental intrusions which had to be eliminated or modified where they threatened to obscure the original vision. But in this final stage the 'first vision' itself underwent deliberate modifications, necessary corrections. A new vision was born, and in accordance with this new, superior vision, Eisenstein — past master of montage 'in hindsight' — virtually recreated his film.

The first vision

Goskino's director, Boris Mikhin, had been determined to draw Eisenstein

77

into filming despite his unconcealed dislike of Eisenstein's theatrical work and, in particular, of his *Even a Wise Man Stumbles*. It may have been – as he was later to claim – that he intuitively recognized Eisenstein's potentialities as an outstanding film director. Proletkult, which had its own film branch in Proletkino, was reluctant to let Eisenstein go, and Mikhin got his way only after prolonged discussion, and on condition that the film was a joint production.

Strike was intended, as we have seen, to be one of the films in the series *Towards the Dictatorship*. The series was to comprise eight films, covering themes ranging from the smuggling of forbidden political publications to deportations and subsequent escapes. The film on the strike, though planned as the fifth in the series, was the first to be made, since, as Eisenstein pointed out, it involved 'the most mass action' and would be 'the most significant'. From the very beginning the three basic features of the film were prescribed: that it should present a generalized picture of a strike and not an actual historical event; that instead of individual heroes the workers should be portrayed as collective heroes in their clash with the capitalists; that the film's method of construction should be based on the principle of the montage of attractions. Thus, when he set to work, Eisenstein had to contend both with the ideas prevailing at Proletkult and, it is clear, with those originating in his own theatrical experience. For his conception of the film was determined by the fact that

the seething lava of inventiveness in the theatre, the frantic search for the most effective means of heightening emotional intensity, the temperament that is irrepressible in its struggle against aesthetic canons that refuse to yield – everything that attracted us in the theatre spills over from it into the art of the film.

The first step towards making *Strike* was a gigantic task of documentation. For months Eisenstein studied his subject with scientific thoroughness, helped by his collaborators. There were meetings with formerly outlawed Party activists and strikers, lengthy visits to factories, and much frenzied reading. With a seriousness and application that was to mark all his film-making activities, Eisenstein assembled a prodigious mass of documentary material, which he then sifted before writing the shooting script. He worked, as he was always to do, day and night; and, since he was working in a still unfamiliar medium, he asked the experienced Esther Shub to collaborate with him. For two months they worked on the script at her house; but after its official acceptance he left her out of the filming team – an action which she never understood and which wounded her deeply. This is, indeed, the only known instance of Eisenstein's offending one of his friends.

Before shooting started, the cautious Boris Mikhin began breaking Eisenstein in to the technical aspects of the film studio, and exercised care in selecting the people to work with him. For the all-important cameraman he chose Edward Tisse, explaining his reasons to Eisenstein:

In the theatre you get carried away by your passion for acrobatics. You'll probably be just as rash when it comes to filming. Edward has an outstanding record as a news reporter and he's also still an excellent . . . athlete. You'll doubtless get on well together.

This prophecy was borne out by one of the most successful artistic partnerships in film history. Their first meeting took place in the sunlit garden of the Morozov mansion, the headquarters of the Proletkult Theatre. The discussion was brief: Eisenstein showed Tisse the plan for *Strike*, which Tisse went through carefully, before calmly correcting several errors in the text – substituting, for example, 'double exposure' for what Eisenstein had poetically described as 'profusion upon profusion'. Tisse was probably the person with whom Eisenstein talked least about filming. There was no need: 'Why tell your heart to beat in such and such a rhythm? It beats by itself.' Nor did they even address each other by the familiar form of address, bound though they were by a deep inner affinity that outweighed every difference of temperament.

And indeed the two men could not have been more different in temperament. There was Eisenstein with his massive head yet boyish face that often lit up in laughter to reveal a perfect set of teeth, his dishevelled hair often crowned by a cloth cap, and his somewhat careless dress; his was a restless, volcanic temperament, continuously on the boil. Tisse, by contrast, was quiet, calm, modest and level-headed; as a cameraman he was remarkable both for his skill and for his daring which he had demonstrated while filming at the front during the Civil War. Eisenstein was well aware of these qualities; for Tisse had been present at a performance of *Even a Wise Man Stumbles* when, as Alexandrov was making his way along the tightrope, it suddenly snapped. Alexandrov had almost been killed; and the metal support had crashed down on to the seat next to Tisse's and pulverized it. But Tisse had hardly batted an eyelid.

Despite his ignorance of the technical problems of filming, Eisenstein displayed an unnerving self-confidence from the moment Mikhin gave him the opportunity for some test filming. The first two tests were rejected by Mikhin. But thanks to post-mortem sessions every evening, at which Eisenstein learned from the criticisms of his two colleagues, the third test was approved, and Eisenstein concluded that he had passed his third 'examination' with relative ease. Not until some time later did he discover that it had, in fact, been touch and go. The leaders of Goskino and Proletkult had been following his every step with apprehension and, when the first two trial runs only confirmed their worst fears, Goskino decided to part company with the young director. Only the persistent efforts of Mikhin and Tisse, including their willingness to give a written guarantee of the film's successful completion, enabled Eisenstein to carry on with the work.

When it came to the filming proper, Eisenstein seemed to be playing with film, to be inventing for his own amusement an artistic game in which he indulged with childish abandon. In reality, *Strike* was a serious venture, however incomprehensible it may seem – given Eisenstein's insatiable curiosity about everything, coupled with his technical training – that he envisaged the film and worked out a detailed scheme for its direction before mastering the technical equipment at his disposal. The explanation can only be that he was an artist whose artistic objectives and crystal-clear 'first vision' took precedence over practical and technical means for converting his ideas into concrete terms. This in turn explains how the apparently impossible technical demands he so frequently made were successfully realized the moment the technicians understood the artistic effect he was aiming to produce.

His aim, first and foremost, was to produce a cinematographic 'montage of shocks' (he even talked about a 'science of shocks')* – in other words, to transplant his principle of the 'montage of attractions' from stage to screen with new, intensified effect. *Strike* was, indeed, an experimental film. The content of a film, he believed, should be unfolded in a series of shocks linked together in a sequence and directed at emotions of the audience.

But this material must be organized in accordance with a principle that leads to the desired effect.

Form is the realization of these intentions in a particular material, as precisely those stimulants which are able to summon this indispensable per cent are created and assembled – in the concrete expression of the factual side of the work.[2]

Eisenstein regarded this as the 'concrete and realistic' aspect of composition. Thus from his very first film he was absorbed with compositional problems. At the same time he was obsessed with precise mathematical calculations – an obsession which was to go hand in hand with all his creative work. He often gave the impression of a latter-day alchemist mixing up a variety of elements in test-tubes and retorts, weighing and measuring with infinite scientific precision, in an attempt to discover the 'philosopher's stone' of art.

This sprang into existence, however, by spontaneous combustion. For *Strike*, like all Eisenstein's work, was a spontaneous artistic creation, owing nothing to his precise, academic calculations. This is not the paradox it may seem; the time-honoured example of Leonardo da Vinci is very much to the point. Eisenstein's scientific and analytical approach served a purpose, but

* At this point, however, there was no question of Pavlovian influence, as Marie Seton erroneously states; Eisenstein's discovery of Pavlov's theories did not, as emerges from his writings, come until some time later.

only that of grasping hold of ideas in their pure form, *in vitro*, as it were, in order to lay bare their origins and innermost mechanics. It could even be argued that the alchemy practised by Eisenstein was really a form of affectation in an artist whose volcanic creative temperament could not conceivably be stimulated by carefully labelled laboratory samples; that basically he was a very timid, perhaps even inhibited, man who sought to damp his spontaneous fire by laying exaggerated emphasis on cold, scientific reasoning – as in his provocative claim that he approached the making of a film as he would the setting-up of a chicken-farm or the installation of a plumbing system. But the inner law of a work of art comes, of course, not from the logician, but from the artist. And in this respect there was a constant, if hidden, conflict between Eisenstein the creator and Eisenstein the logician. The latter strove jealously to snatch all the credit, often instantly translating the creator's artistic inspiration into complicated algebraic formulae which obscured its very spontaneity. Much later Eisenstein was to admit in his personal notes that all his creative life he had been 'engrossed in discovering *theses* – proving, explaining and teaching others'; and in view of this, even 'the first vision' might also be seen as a retrospective rationalization.

In his 'first vision' Eisenstein set himself several specific tasks. These included a frontal attack on the 'bourgeois' film and its influences, and the creation of 'a revolutionary art without compromises'. He proposed introducing Marxism-Leninism into films, finding its equivalent in cinematographic terms and 'forging a reciprocal and unbreakable link' between dialectics and film. Basically, Eisenstein set himself the task of discovering a new and original method of tackling revolutionary themes. *Strike*, along with the other films in the series, was meant to explain the 'technique' of revolutionary struggle and Eisenstein proposed doing this in cinematographic terms. There was no need for a dominant narrative thread, a transposition of the idea into the realms of fiction in order to make it intelligible. His aim was a direct and immediate communication of the theme – and this was achieved by discarding the conventional rules of drama, dropping the scenario and working straight from the montage notes. Eisenstein wanted a film that would answer the general questions: what is a strike, how is it organized, what are its antecedents, its developments, its effects? Hence the virtual absence of fiction and the replacement of individuals by personified concepts: organizer, worker, spy, foreman, etc.; hence, too, the need for metaphoric montage. Eisenstein's aims compelled him to plunge to the heart, the very essence, of the problems of montage. Hence the profoundly inventive character of his montage method, hence his discovery and definition of the essential sources and techniques of the modern film. For the 'first vision' of *Strike* laid the foundations for artistic discoveries which have been of decisive importance to film history and have made Eisenstein's name immortal – the name of a phenomenon in which there coexisted an explosive talent, breaking established laws and creating new ones in their place, and an intense, lucid intellect of rare acuity.

The filming

The first scenes were filmed at the studio in Zhitnaya Street, which for that time was relatively well equipped. The Proletkult Theatre provided the actors, who were joined by students from the Proletkult studio as well as young Moscow factory workers for the later crowd scenes. Every evening, after filming, the team used to discuss the work they had done and decide on a programme for the following day. At these discussions, which Mikhin also attended, Eisenstein almost invariably made demands considered excessive by the management, as when he insisted on using 1,000 extras for the episode in which the police and firemen drive away the workers with jets of water. Mikhin tried to prove the futility of such a huge number, for which, as he pointed out, the shooting schedule contained no provision; but Eisenstein categorically refused any concession. After a fierce quarrel, Mikhin resorted to the stratagem of pretending to agree, while secretly giving orders for only 500 extras to be called in. The shooting, so Mikhin affirms, proved his point, since even with the reduced numbers it proved extremely complicated and protracted.

Mikhin records that Eisenstein visualized every scene in precise detail and tried to reproduce his thoughts exactly during the shooting – even when they seemed misconceived. In consequence he was, from the very first filming sessions, taxed with long-windedness. Yet anyone who has seen the effectiveness of the long battle scene in *Alexander Nevsky* will understand Eisenstein's determination, while filming *Strike*, to make a major episode of the clash between the workers bent on striking and the boiler-house mechanics opposed to them. Eisenstein elaborated at length on this clash, to the increasing horror of his colleagues at the difficulties involved; for Eisenstein wanted to direct this scene as 'a series of complicated circuses', with men leaping and vaulting about, brawling, throwing each other into barrels and so on. And, when a stool had to be smashed over the head of one of the fighters, he insisted on the splinters of wood being clearly visible. Everything was rehearsed to perfection, but repeatedly failed to work out right when it came to the shooting. When, after many futile takes, everything at last went well, Tisse discovered that he had run out of film, and the whole agony had to be repeated. Although Eisenstein insisted on filming the fight in full, at the editing stage he finally agreed to shortening it, from dramatic considerations.

The management regarded all these demands as pure caprice on the part of the director, though, as the finished sequence proved, they were in fact intrinsic to the following-through of his initial intentions. But the protests and anger they provoked at the time were not unreasonable. On one occasion, during filming on location at the Simonov Monastery, Eisenstein wanted to liken the factory manager to a grinning frog – whereupon filming came to a standstill while everyone went off to the lake in a desperate search for a frog. On a freezing October day, one of the property men had to wade into the water up to his waist; but all to no avail, as Eisenstein rejected every frog produced as being too small, or unsuitable in some other way. One of the team actually went to the length of trying the zoo, but still drew a blank. At long last the right frog was found. Too late, however: it was already getting dark and the frog had to be thrown back. Everyone was short-tempered – except Eisenstein. The only thing that interested him was the realization of his ideas, irrespective of the difficulties involved.

This incident illustrates Eisenstein's meticulous attention to the tiniest detail necessary for realizing his mental picture of a particular scene. He was never to lose this characteristic as a director: in *Potemkin* he was to supervise the blacking of the soldiers' boots for the steps sequence, and in *Ivan the Terrible* was to go to incredible lengths to make the boyars' robes fall in exactly the rhythmic folds he had envisaged.

'What if we should turn our backs on all that?'

Strike was completed at the end of 1924, had its première in Leningrad on 1 February 1925, and on 24 April was released in the Moscow cinemas (Eisenstein having meanwhile resigned from the Proletkult Theatre and gone to work at the Moscow studio of Sevzapkino). It was received as a major event and had lengthy reviews in the press. Mikhail Koltsov in *Pravda* considered it 'the first revolutionary creation of our cinema', *Izvestia* 'an immense and interesting triumph in the development of our cinematographic art', while *Kino-Gazeta* characterized it as 'a gigantic event in the Soviet, Russian and world cinema'. But the press was by no means unanimous; other publications criticized the film for signs of an incipient eccentricity and lack of harmony between ideological content and form. Generally speaking, however, press reaction was favourable to the documentary-type parts of the film, while reserved about, and puzzled by, the satirical and grotesque elements. Public reaction, too, was conflicting, though mainly unfavourable. This lack of success with the general public was compensated to some extent by its prestige success in specialist film circles. Victor Shklovsky recalls that *Strike* set the film-makers asking questions about their own future work. Kozintsev told the FEX group that 'everything we've been doing up till now is mere childish nonsense' and recommended that *Strike* be seen over and over again. Of the many controversial discussions provoked by *Strike*, the most important took place at ARK (Association of Revolutionary Cinematographic Workers) on 19 March, and subsequently in polemical articles in the press.

Recollections of *Strike* by Eisenstein's contemporaries almost invariably emphasize the film's success. But these recollections were recorded at a much later date, when his reputation was established, and seem to have become coloured with the passage of time, for Marie Seton records that Eisenstein was depressed by *Strike*'s reception and gnawed by the conviction that it was a failure; and, although he wrote fiercely in its defence at the time, it may well have been that his polemical attitude was adopted for public consumption only.

Why was *Strike* considered — by some people immediately, by most rather belatedly — such an event? Without analysing the film in detail, we need to look at certain of its aesthetic properties, which were unique at the time. Before starting to make *Strike*, Eisenstein had given some thought to the aesthetic problems involved, and has described how the main ideas first came to him:

It was by the curved wall of the now demolished Strastnoi Monastery. Along it ran a path that led to 'Kino Malaya Dmitrovka 6', noted for its showings of the most triumphantly successful American films. ... How to beat these 'giants' of the American cinema — and just as we were taking our first timid steps in film-making? Where could we find stories that would be just as sharp if not sharper, than the plots of these American successes?

Where should we find native 'stars' whose radiance could compete with whole 'constellations' from America and Europe? And heroes whose originality would displace the accepted heroes of the bourgeois cinema?[3]

These questions led to the following reasoning:

What if we should turn our backs on all that and build with quite different materials?

And in 'countering' all — abolishing story, discarding stars — to push into the dramatic centre the mass as the basic *dramatis persona*, that same mass that heretofore had provided a background for the solo performance of actors.

(In 1924, Eisenstein published an article, 'Down with the Story and the Plot!') The aesthetic ideas embodied in *Strike* had their origins, therefore, in the fierce competitive spirit embodied in Eisenstein's crusade against the 'bourgeois' cinema. And no sooner was the film completed than he drew attention to its political significance from this point of view, acclaiming it as 'the October of the cinema'.

The originality of *Strike* lay as much in its theme as in its form of expression. Yet at the time of its release, and on many subsequent occasions, an arbitrary distinction was drawn between the new portrayal of the class struggle that it brought on to the screen and the film techniques it introduced. This alleged arbitrary split in the unity of form and content was, in fact, the basis of the polemic that raged round the film, then and subsequently. Eisenstein joined in, pointing out the anomalous nature of the argument and adding, to spite his critics, that the form had turned out to be 'more revolutionary than the content'. For him the originality in form lay in the methods of expression: in the practical application of new concepts and a new technique for dealing with facts. The novelty of form thus sprang from the novelty of content, since, to use Eisenstein's own analogy, the steam-engine was not created by revolutionizing the shape of the carriages, but by understanding the technical factors, in particular the action of energy contained in steam.

It was by applying the principle of the montage of attractions to filming — 'the method for making any kind of film', as he then considered it — that Eisenstein arrived at his innovations in form. Although he soon afterwards modified this opinion, it nonetheless has an important place in a biography of Eisenstein the creator, since *Strike* contained in embryo — and sometimes in much more developed form — the momentous artistic innovations that came later (and most notably those in *Battleship Potemkin*). Nearly every aspect of Eisenstein's montage method can be traced back to *Strike*. Its metaphoric and associative functions were clearly apparent in the familiar sequence of the massacre of the workers and the butchery of the oxen in the slaughter-house. Examples of this kind abound in *Strike*. Montage was becoming a language, a means of communicating thoughts, emotions and even abstract ideas. What *Strike*, in effect, represented was a first step towards discovering the functions of modern editing (and, simultaneously, the first step towards the intellectual film of later years).

Strike had its origins in Eisenstein's experiments in the theatre, traces of which it still bore.

Our first film opus, *Strike*, reflected, as in an inverted mirror image, our production of *Gas Masks*. But the film floundered about in the flotsam of a rank theatricality that had become alien to it.[4]

On the other hand his experiments with certain aspects of *mise-en-scène* while staging *Precipice*, *Listen Moscow* and *Gas Masks* had led him to the new concept of the *mise-en-cadre*, and this now became an aspect of montage. As Jay Leyda has commented, 'it is no surprise to see all of Eisenstein's future films "introduced" in *Strike*'.

Strike marked the first stage in the development of Eisenstein's montage method. It was based, at that point, on the view that two juxtaposed images give rise to a new idea and that the whole thus created is superior to the sum of its two constituent parts. Or, in Jean Mitry's description,

for him montage consists in using the relationship between two images to create a certain shock effect (in harmony, of course, with the dramatic sense of action) aimed at making the audience aware first of a single idea and then of a complex idea, by means of which the work can be brought to its emotional or dialectical climax.[5]

Strike: montage

Eisenstein, indeed, discovered a complete science for generating emotions. Through the impressive analysis of his creative works that he started with *Strike* and continued to the end of his life he discovered fundamental laws about the work of art in general. From that point onwards, his aesthetic thinking was to run parallel with his practical creative work, serving at times to elaborate on it and, quite often, to provide its motivating force.

Finally, something must be said about a question with a bearing on Eisenstein's sources of inspiration, namely, his artistic relationship with Dziga Vertov, the creator of 'cine-eye'. The question is controversial. When Eisenstein described *Strike* as the October of the cinema, he added: 'an October which also has its February, since what else are Vertov's activities but an "abolition of the tyranny" of the fictional film . . . nothing else'. Certain critics maintained that *Strike* was profoundly influenced by Vertov's activities, and Alexandrov, who was in a position to know the facts, claims that Eisenstein took Vertov's *Kino-Pravda* methods as his ideal. There is no question that Vertov stood for a presence in the Soviet cinema which Eisenstein could scarcely have overlooked and which, in fact, he greatly admired. At the start of his filming career, however, Eisenstein chose to attack Vertov in connection with *Strike*, comparing him disparagingly with the impressionists and pointillists, and provocatively asserting that the need was 'not for a cine-eye, but for a cine-fist'. Vertov, for his part, regarded *Strike* as 'an experiment in adapting some of the "cine-eye" methods of constructive editing to the fictional film'. But the real truth is unlikely to emerge from these subjective or personal views (Alexandrov's, for instance, seems clearly exaggerated), but rather from an analysis of the facts and documentary evidence – an operation which is outside the scope of this biography. Vertov's *Kino-Pravda* series certainly came before *Strike*, but his *Kino-glaz* was not made, according to Eisenstein, until the shooting and part of the editing of *Strike* had been completed. The difference between the two works are, in any case, structural ones, despite superficial similarities.* Eisenstein's denial of Vertov's influence on *Strike* appears all the more persuasive when it is known that, in the far more important instance of *Battleship Potemkin*, he openly attributed to Vertov the inspiration for the meeting of the mourners round Vakulinchuk's body.

After *Strike*, Eisenstein began work on two screen projects: *The Iron Flood*, by Serafimovich, and Isaac Babel's *Red Cavalry*. There was thus, it seems, some question of a film about the Civil War. In connection with the

* Both men were hostile towards traditional film fiction; but their ways of 'destroying' the fictional scenario differed widely.

former, a version of the scenario based on Serafimovich's novel which was found among Eisenstein's papers includes news items, impressions recorded by contemporaries, and other material — indicating, in effect, a detailed piece of documentation. Both projects were, however, soon interrupted: elaborate preparations were being planned for the anniversary of the 1905 Revolution, and the Jubilee Committee set up to coordinate them decided that several films should be made in honour of the event — one of which they assigned to Eisenstein.

5. Battleship Potemkin

. . . J'essaie de voir, à travers les oeuvres, les mouvements multiples qui les ont fait naître et ce qu'elles contiennent de vie intérieure; n'est-ce pas autrement intéressant que le jeu consiste à les démonter comme de curieuses montres?
CLAUDE DEBUSSY

In considering the significance of *Battleship Potemkin* in Eisenstein's evolution as a creative artist, we must again distinguish between two aspects of his work: the creation of the film itself, and his subsequent detailed analysis of it. It is with the former that we shall primarily concern ourselves, while bearing in mind the vital importance of Eisenstein's incredibly thorough scientific analysis – in which he used both mathematical and physical formulae to explain the film's emotional content – for understanding the intellect whose development we are tracing in this biography.

One of the first things to emerge from the facts surrounding *Potemkin* is that Eisenstein, though fully conscious of his artistic and intellectual capabilities, had no inkling of just how important a work of art he was to produce. He certainly did not set out with any world-shattering intentions. Yet the differences between Eisenstein, the creator of *Strike*, and the Eisenstein of the following year, 1925, are not contradictory. It was simply a question of a rapid maturation: his youthful, competitive spirit had given way – without, however, disappearing altogether – to an authentic, essentially creative one. The *enfant terrible* had grown up – although, as far as temperament is concerned, the 'terrible' side of his nature was never to disappear. Ontogenetically, the period between *Strike* and *Potemkin* was a decisive one: it was the period when Eisenstein became Eisenstein.

In making *Potemkin*, Eisenstein was passionately intent on discovering new artistic techniques for reinvigorating film art and on finding a cinemato-graphic equivalent of the revolutionary feeling he was striving to express. But in common with Picasso, he might justifiably have claimed: 'I do not seek, but I find.' For a study of the making of *Potemkin* attests to Eisenstein's spon-taneity, and to the fact that his clear, cold, mathematical analyses – which many of his detractors invoked in alleging that he was merely a skilled engineer who constructed his films with a slide rule and pre-calculated abstract formulae – were made after the event. In fact, he might have added: 'I seek after I have found.' Vsevolod Vishnevsky wrote in some disgust to Eisenstein in 1937 à propos his analysis of an episode in *Potemkin*:

I have read this analysis and it made me sick with its mathematical and other calculations. But the sequence itself was made with spontaneity, fire and passion; it was summer, in the south; there was passionate feeling for the sea, for the subject, and there was youthfulness, while the town pulsated, reliving the events. . . . And then . . . the analysis – the cold analysis: but you cannot palm us off with another, different key.

All the same, Eisenstein did provide a new key; for in making *Potemkin* he discovered new and universally valid laws about film art which his subsequent scientific analyses served to define.

Evoking the events

Two of the main films in the series planned to commemorate the anniversary of the 1905 Revolution, *Ninth of January* and *Year 1905*, had been approved as early as June 1924; yet, as the spring of 1925 approached, a director for the latter had still to be appointed. Then came the preview of *Strike* and, almost immediately after, the Jubilee Committee's decision, at its meeting on 19 March 1925, to assign the film to Eisenstein. The exceptional importance attached to the film was reflected in the degree of understanding with which, from the very beginning, the Committee viewed the young director's problems. They allotted him ample time for making the film, setting only two conditions: that it should not have a pessimistic ending (this affected Pudovkin's *Mother* also); and that one of the film's major episodes must be completed by 20 December of that year.

Eisenstein at once started work on the scenario, together with Nina Ferdinandovna Agadzhanova-Shutko, a scriptwriter of repute. She was also well known for her revolutionary record in the events of 1905; but it was in connection with the script for *Battleship Potemkin* that she became really famous, being often mistakenly regarded as sole author – despite Eisenstein's collaboration over the original script and the fact that her contribution to the final version of the film was virtually nil.

Helped by advisers from the Committee for Documentation, they began work on the scenario, which they had to distil from a mass of detailed research into press articles, documentary records, accounts by eyewitnesses, and other basic material relating to the vast historic panorama. Starting with the Russo-Japanese War and ending with the armed uprising, the action unfolded in Moscow, Saint Petersburg, Odessa, Sevastopol, Tiflis, Baku, Batumi, Central Asia and the Caucasus, Siberia, Tombovsk, Ivanov-Voznesensk and elsewhere. The scenario, written during the summer, often compressed major events into a mere two lines, and was thus almost impossible to regard as a practical starting-point for shooting the film. Yet it was largely successful in capturing the dynamism, tempo and prevailing atmosphere of that historic period – all of which were so thoroughly absorbed by Eisenstein himself that, when it came to the shooting, he was completely at home in the revolutionary world he was depicting, and able to invent episodes not in the scenario which were completely in harmony with the atmosphere of 1905. As Eisenstein later explained:

Relying solely on this [preparatory documentary] work, the director was able to indicate simply by numbers such scenes as 'the battleship passes through the flotilla without firing a shot' or 'a tarpaulin isolates the men who are to be executed'. Much to the surprise of film historians, the director was able in this way to transform short phrases from the scenario into totally unexpected and moving scenes during the shooting. Thus the words of the scenario became visual images; but the genuine emotion with which they were charged was contained not in these brief indications but in our own feelings. As we strove to evoke the events, these feelings gave birth to characters that became living beings.[1]

In the original scenario for *1905* the *Potemkin* mutiny took up a relatively tiny part: half a page, or just forty-four shots out of the 800 envisaged for the whole film.

Eisenstein's 'vision' of the film, predictably enough after *Strike*, was extremely complicated from the technical and organizational points of view, entailing full-scale battles, night-time fires, mass movements of peasants and so on.

On 31 March 1925 shooting started in Leningrad on the scene of the Nevsky Prospekt, lit, as it had been in 1905 during the strike at the electricity-generating plant, by the Admiralty searchlight. Filming was already well under way when bad weather made it impossible to carry on. Chasing south after the sun in order not to waste precious time, Eisenstein moved the unit *

---

* In addition to Tisse (whose original co-cameramen, Alexander Levitsky and Yevgeni Slavinsky, had dropped out), the unit included five close actor associates of Eisenstein: Maxim Strauch, Grigori Alexandrov, A. Levshin, Mikhail Gomorov and Alexander Antonov. Eisenstein later jokingly nicknamed them 'the iron five' because of the imperturbable way in which – dressed in striped sweaters to distinguish them from the mass of film extras – they resolved all difficulties: on one occasion the problem of providing the stability essential for a moving motorcycle combination from which Tisse was filming – a weight of around eighty kilograms was needed – was solved by using Eisenstein himself as ballast.

to Odessa and Sevastopol to shoot the episodes set on these locations.* And so it was that he came to the subject of the *Potemkin* mutiny – the one episode that was to sum up the entire revolution.

'The fetters of space and the claws of time'

It was at Odessa that Eisenstein took the decision to limit the film to a single episode from the original *1905* scenario. At that stage he had no clear picture of the future film, but was frantically seeking new solutions to his problems, abandoning ones that proved unsatisfactory and pursuing others in a desperate race against time. For he optimistically intended completing the film in two weeks in readiness for the October Revolution anniversary celebrations. At the Hotel London, the unit's headquarters in Odessa, Eisenstein began elaborating a new outline script, at the same time consulting a number of eyewitnesses of the 1905 events and leaving the door open for any *ad hoc* ideas that might crop up.

The first essential for the filming was a battleship to represent the *Potemkin* – the real ship having been dismantled. No such stand-in could be found among either the Black Sea or the Baltic fleets, but Eisenstein's assistant director, Liyosha Kriyukov, stumbled on a surviving sister ship, *The Twelve Apostles*, moored to the off-shore rocks in an isolated arm of the Gulf of Sevastopol. But this discovery, though it caused much jubilation, was not the end of the difficulties. For one thing, the entire superstructure of the ship was missing; this, however, could be successfully reconstructed in wood from plans preserved in the naval archives. Next, the seabed around the ship's anchorage was discovered to be strewn with mines; and, worse still, the hold of the ship itself was used as a mine-store. To remove the mines would have been inordinately time-consuming; so the decision was taken to film on a reconstructed deathtrap! Consequently all the episodes on board *The Twelve Apostles*† – episodes depicting a violent mutiny – had to be made under the most restrictive conditions, with smoking and excessive movement strictly prohibited. There was a further obstacle: the ship was so positioned that, whatever angle the deck was filmed from, the rocks would have appeared in the frame, while the mutiny had taken place out at sea. Again it was Kriyukov who came up with the solution: to rotate the ship through ninety degrees, thus eliminating the rocks – but only if the camera was kept absolutely static. The

* Eisenstein was working simultaneously on the script of *Year 1905* and, with Isaac Babel, on a scenario entitled *Benia Krik*. He hoped to shoot for both films while in Odessa; but the second project was one of many that remained unrealized. Eisenstein liked Babel's script so much, however, that he recommended it for translation into English, and in 1935 it was published.

† For the parts of the filming which necessitated a fully operational ship, the battleship *Komintern* was used.

unit was thus forced to work under constant pressures of both time and space. As Eisenstein later wrote, 'the fetters of space and the claws of time held our excessive and greedy fantasy in check'.[2] And this, he added, was 'possibly the reason for the film's close-knit and unified construction'.

Even in these nightmare conditions, the work was done at a record pace. In a single day's work on the Odessa steps sequence, for instance, seventy-five shots were filmed.* Altogether 5,200 metres of film were shot, and the whole film, from start to finish, montage and all, was completed in three months. 'It seems fantastic, but it's true!' Eisenstein exclaimed. Serious casting problems also arose; for the unit included only enough actors for the principal roles, leaving a considerable number of secondary roles still to be filled. Faithful to his ideas of typage, Eisenstein insisted on suitably expressive faces being found and gave Strauch the task of ferreting them out. Strauch, in turn, got the whole unit scouring the town, searching the streets, trains, offices and meetings for the right faces. The character that presented the greatest difficulty was the doctor, and Eisenstein was not satisfied with the eventual compromise choice. In the boat on the way to the filming, however, he noticed a stoker from the hotel who had been taken on as an electrician to the unit. Sulkily he wondered:

Why do they take on such weaklings to hold heavy mirror reflectors? This one's in just about a fit state to drop the mirror in the sea or break it – a sure sign of bad luck.[3]

But looking at his face more intently Eisenstein suddenly saw him in a totally different light; and, as he pictured him with moustache, goatee beard and pince-nez, the poor, unsuspecting man took on the features of Dr Smirnov. Similarly an aged gardener was found to play the part of the priest. But when it came to the scene of his tumble down the hatch stairs, Eisenstein himself demonstrated it for him, being 'unable to resist the temptation of "trying my own hand" at this fall'.

The film, as Eisenstein later acknowledged, turned out quite differently from the way he had originally envisaged it. And this very fact makes an examination of certain steps in its creation all the more enlightening.

Eisenstein's starting-point for the film – once he had decided on limiting it to the *Potemkin* incident – was the last two pages of the initial (*Year 1905*) scenario (the shots numbered 170–213). A serious and thorough study of his montage notes has yet to be made. When, for example, were they edited – before or during filming, or between filming and cutting? Having compared the notes with Strauch's unpublished diary in which he made daily recordings of the shots filmed, and also with Eisenstein's own subsequent

---

* Eisenstein's figure; Strauch's diary indicates a maximum of forty-two shots in a single day.

At work on *Potemkin*

analysis ('The Twelve Apostles'), I take the view that they were edited before the filming, basing this conclusion on the following facts: they contain precise shooting instructions ('shot 202 should start with a disembarkation'); they include variants of the same scenes ('the steps', 'the funeral', etc.); the film in its final form does not correspond with the montage notes (the notes lack the close-knit dramatic structure of the film, and a number of episodes – the funeral, the raising of the red flag, the approach of the boats – are different in the notes, or summarily and imperfectly planned).*

At the same time Eisenstein's ceaseless gropings while composing the notes – indicated by the numerous erasures, additions and modifications that litter the original typescript – tend to confirm that his montage ideas crystallized as he went along. While some essential features, such as Dr Smirnov's famous

* Krasovsky, the keeper of the Eisenstein archive, maintains that surviving documents do not clearly indicate the changes from the initial scenario to the finished film. The archive contains 3,066 items comprising 18,000 documents (about 100,000 pages) which include, in addition to articles published to date, Eisenstein's handwritten shooting script, montage notes, the diary of the filming kept by Maxim Strauch – kindly made available to me in microfilm by the Moscow State Central Archive for Literature and Art – as well as numerous other unpublished papers. From an analysis of these papers it has been possible to reconstruct, at least in skeleton form, Eisenstein's steps in making the film.

pince-nez,* figure in the montage notes and must therefore have been thought out beforehand, others, like the pram bumping down the steps, make their first appearance in the film. Similarly, the characters took shape in the course of the filming; with the exception of Vakulinchuk, they do not have individualized characteristics, nor are they named in the original plan, although sometimes the name of the actor intended for a particular role was noted. Thus *Battleship Potemkin* was created in a blaze of spontaneous creative fire, as an examination of several of the key scenes in the film will illustrate clearly.

The episode of the maggot-ridden meat as it appeared in the original scenario, for instance, was modified at an early stage and brought closer to the actual event as remembered by one of the eyewitnesses, Matushenko. Subsequently this documentary character was accentuated still further when the authentic words of the sailors and Dr Smirnov were introduced for the titles. Again, in the first draft the priest dies after falling down the hatch, but Eisenstein had his gardener only pretend to be dead, suddenly winking an eye and thus adding to the scene a powerfully satiric note.

Then there is the famous montage sequence of the stone lions, in which three successive shots of lions in different positions give the impression of a single wild beast rearing up as if in furious protest at the massacre. This classic piece of montage was inspired, during a chance visit by Eisenstein and Tisse to the Alupka Palace, by the marble lions in different attitudes – sleeping, waking and rampant – that adorned the flight of steps leading up to the palace. The idea of filming them in succession occurred then and there, but to bring off their stroke of genius Eisenstein and Tisse had first to outwit the overzealous attendant who did his utmost to prevent them filming the lions. In a veritable game of hide-and-seek, he tried repeatedly to get in the way of the camera, while they dashed from one statue to another to dodge him. But, although it arose out of a chance visit, this improvisation nonetheless owed something to an idea contained in the montage notes, where four shots of the panthers pulling the chariots on the decorative façade of the Bolshoi Theatre were planned. The montage sequence in the film, however, was used to totally different and original effect.

Three further important sequences in the film provide valuable help in understanding Eisenstein's creative methods: the sequences of the tarpaulin, the steps and the sea mist.

In his later lectures at the State Institute of Cinematography, Eisenstein maintained that a verbal metaphor could sometimes provide the key to a production problem of a pictorial nature.[4] And this was precisely what hap-

---

* This feature, strangely enough, does not appear in Strauch's diary, which convinces me that only a minutely detailed study of *all* the documents relating to *Potemkin* will clarify the exact mechanics of Eisenstein's creative process – a study which exceeds the intentions of the present book.

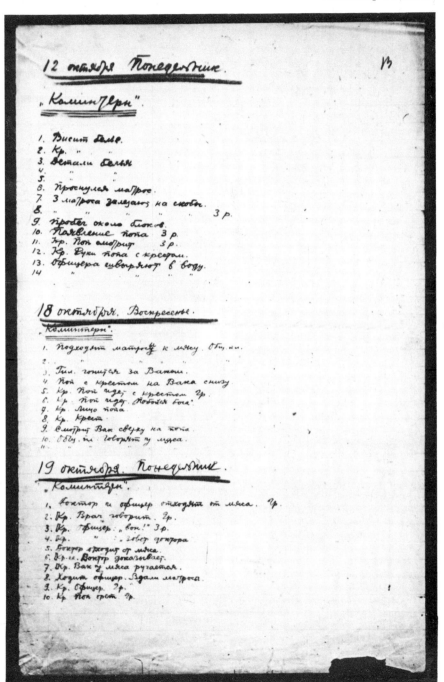

Page from the diary kept by Strauch during the making of *Potemkin*

pened in the case of the tarpaulin incident, which crystallized as an image following a chance remark by one of the mutineers that 'tranquillity hangs on the air'. That remark, coupled with Eisenstein's appreciation of Goethe's maxim – 'for the sake of truthfulness one can afford to defy the truth' – was his source of inspiration for this incident which, so far as he was aware, had no foundation in historical fact, but was purely his own invention. When he first suggested covering the condemned sailors with a tarpaulin, the naval adviser to the films was horrified: 'This was never done!' A tarpaulin was used, he explained, but the condemned men stood on it to stop the blood from staining the deck. And Eisenstein wanted to put it over the sailors! 'We'll make a laughing-stock of ourselves.' But Eisenstein, guided by his own sense of reality, curtly replied: 'If we do it will serve us right for bungling our job.' And in the event the episode proved so realistic that, after the film's première, one of the surviving mutineers brought a court case claiming part of the author's fees on the grounds that he had been under the tarpaulin on the actual occasion. The lawyers were much impressed by his apparently incontestable evidence until Eisenstein remembered that the whole incident had been a figment of his imagination, whereupon the case fell through. A similar tribute to Eisenstein's feeling for authentic atmosphere came in a sympathetic letter from another surviving mutineer, who also maintained that he had been under the tarpaulin; Eisenstein did not disillusion him, but was amused that the power of empathy could outweigh that of memory.*

The scene of the massacre on the Odessa steps – again often regarded as a true representation of the event – was based, according to Eisenstein himself, as much on other actual massacres. The sequence, which in its final shape is different from all the scripts, was conceived in several stages. First there were the powerful memories of the 'implacable force' from his childhood and youth which, as we have seen, represented the emotional basis of this scene. Then there was a contemporary picture of the Odessa steps in the French magazine *L'Illustration,*† that he came across in the Lenin Library. This illustration – depicting a smoke-wreathed scene in which a soldier on horseback is lashing out at someone with his sword – left so strong an impression on Eisenstein that, immediately on arriving in Odessa, he rushed to see the steps. He climbed up and down them again and again, exploring every one – there were 120 – and absorbing their 'feel'.

* On the basis of evidence from several survivors of the mutiny, Rostovtsev, in his treatise on *Battleship Potemkin*, maintains that the incident of the tarpaulin was, in fact, real. It is difficult to determine the truth, but there seems no reason for doubting Eisenstein's word.

† Jay Leyda has brought to my attention another illustration in the same French magazine (of 15 July 1905, pages 40–41), bearing the caption 'Omelchuk's body lying in state on 23 June on the new dike at Odessa', which is strikingly similar to the scene in the film of the meeting around Vakulinchuk's dead body. Here the influence on Eisenstein was evidently direct.

The very 'flight' of the stairs suggested the idea of the scene – this 'flight' set the director's imagination soaring on a new 'flight' of its own.

The panicky 'flight' of the crowd sweeping down the stairs is nothing more than the material embodiment of the first impressions ensuing from the encounter with the stairway itself.[5] *

Thus the next stage was one of spontaneous inspiration at the moment of direct contact with the real-life setting. And his thorough absorption, during this stage, of the atmosphere and essence of the setting was essential to the third stage – the montage stage – in recreating the intense, emotion-charged atmosphere evoked by the film. After his contact with the steps, Eisenstein wrote the scene, according to Strauch, in three days (and filmed it – the first sequence to be shot – in a further seven). But this was only its first form. The montage notes contain a version of the steps sequence different from the one that we know from the film.† The artistic rendering of the pram bumping down the steps, for instance, does not appear at this phase of the film-making, but seems to have occurred to Eisenstein only during the third stage, at the cutting-table. As he later noted: 'The filmed material at the moment of editing can sometimes be wiser than author or director.'

These, then, were the hectic and unforeseen conditions of the filming on the Odessa steps out of which finally emerged a sequence startling in its logic and closely knit construction – giving the impression that everything had been precisely calculated beforehand and carried out in optimum conditions of unhurried calm. The same impression is given by Eisenstein in his subsequent analysis of the sequence, which he regarded as the supreme example of the film's most notable features – 'the organic unity of its composition and its emotive quality'. In his analysis he explains how the emotional effect of '*the frenzied condition of the people and masses*' is heightened by the compositional structure:

186610

Let us concentrate on the line of *movement*.

There is, before all else, a chaotic *close-up* rush of figures. And then, as chaotic a rush of figures in *long-shot*.

Then the *chaos* of movement changes to a design: the *rhythmic* descending feet of the soldiers.

Tempo increases. Rhythm accelerates.

In this acceleration of *downward* rushing movement there is a suddenly upsetting opposite movement – *upward*: the *break-neck* movement of the *mass* downward leaps

* A recollection of Hans Richter strikes me as interesting: 'I remember Eisenstein relating to me how he made *Battleship Potemkin*, condensing the 1905 Revolution into six dramatic elements: the sea, the town of Odessa, the battleship, the monumental steps, the populace, the Cossacks. "Setting them in conflict" – he told me – "out of these places and objects I composed my story . . . standing on the steps of the staircase." '

† Eisenstein affirmed that the sequence of the steps did not figure in any versions of the scenario or shooting script compiled prior to the filming. Could this be simply an error, or another indication of the date when the montage notes were edited?

over into a *slowly solemn* movement upward of the mother's *lone* figure, carrying her dead son.

Mass. Break-neck speed. Downward.

And then suddenly: A lone figure. Slow solemnity. Upward.

But – this is only for an instant. Once more we experience a returning leap to the downward movement.

Rhythm accelerates. Tempo increases.

Suddenly the tempo of the *running crowd* leaps over into the next category of speed – into a *rolling baby-carriage*. It propels the idea of rushing downward into the next dimension – *from rolling, as understood 'figuratively', into the physical fact of rolling. . . .*

Close-ups leap over into long-shots.

Chaotic movement (of a mass) – into *rhythmic* movement (of the soldiers).

One aspect of moving speed (rushing people) – into the next stage of the same theme of moving speed (rolling baby-carriage).

Movement *downward* – into movement *upward*.

Many volleys of *many* rifles – into *one* shot from *one* of the battleship's guns.

Stride by stride – a leap from dimension to dimension. A leap from quality to quality. So that in the final accounting, rather than in a separate episode (the baby-carriage), *the whole method of exposing* the entire event likewise accomplishes its leap: a *narrative* type of exposition is replaced (in the montage rousing of the stone lion) and transferred to the concentrated structure of *imagery*. Visually rhythmic prose leaps over into visually poetic speech.[6]

These leaps are achieved through *caesurae* – pauses which occur throughout the film on the principle known in aesthetics as the 'golden section'. These pauses, Eisenstein explained, divide each scene of the film, and the film as a whole, in half. Or, as he more precisely pointed out, 'the proportion is closer to 2 : 3, that is, an approximation to the "golden section"'.

This exactitude of construction and precision of detail is all the more surprising in view of the spontaneous, improvised way in which the film was created.

Finally, the sequence of the sea mist. The original conception of this scene of mourning round Vakulinchuk's body was enlarged by pure chance when a mist unexpectedly descended on the harbour one day and put a stop to shooting. While other film units in Odessa at the time considered the weather conditions impossible for filming, and remained at the hotel playing dominoes, Eisenstein and Tisse hired a boat, and against all advice started filming the mist-shrouded harbour. The result was astounding, and when he came to the montage Eisenstein used it to magnificent effect – the mist representing, as it were, a symbolic funeral shroud, and heightening the emotional intensity of the whole mourning sequence.*

* Eisenstein later claimed that this sequence had previously been worked out in detail quite differently in 'over a dozen pages of directing notes'.

During the filming, Alexandrov recalls, Eisenstein returned to Moscow in response to a summons from Kalinin, the Soviet President, taking with him the parts of the film so far made. While there he sought the permission of the Red Army Commander, General Frunze, to use a flotilla of the Black Sea Fleet for filming the scene of the flotilla's meeting with the *Potemkin* and its guns firing in salute. Back at Odessa, however, the carefully laid plans for filming this sequence went awry. Everything was ready, with Tisse and his camera installed on the battleship's turret, when some officers arrived on board and asked Eisenstein how he was going to get the ships all firing simultaneously. 'Oh, quite simple; I'll take my handkerchief from my pocket and wave it three times,' he answered breezily, giving them a demonstration. Seen through binoculars from the ships, his gesture was mistaken for the real thing, and the guns opened up – far beyond the range of Tisse's camera, which in any case he had not started. After this mishap Eisenstein did not dare to ask for a repeat performance, and the episode never appeared in the film.

Generally speaking, however, Eisenstein was a brilliant organizer, even for the most complicated scenes. When filming the Odessa steps sequence, for instance, he solved the problem of getting the desired response from sluggish extras by a simple stratagem similar to one attributed to Napoleon for getting the best out of his soldiers. Shouting out the first name that came into his head – 'Put more pep into it, Comrade Prokopenko!' – he had them all galvanized into action, thinking that he knew and was watching them all individually.

When the filming at Odessa was almost completed, Eisenstein left the finishing touches to Alexandrov, Antonov and Gomorov and returned to Moscow to start on the editing and to direct the scenes that had been impossible to shoot aboard *The Twelve Apostles*. These were filmed partly in a ridiculously small studio fitted up with a very rudimentary décor and partly at the Sandunovsky Baths where a mock-up battleship was used for some of the scenes set at sea.

According to different statements made by Eisenstein, the editing of the 15,000 metres of film took him two weeks (Esther Shub says twenty-one days, including work on the final supplementary shots, and Alexandrov eighteen), working day and night with a single assistant. (Some months later this same assistant, by then pregnant, tried to have a paternity order served on Eisenstein, producing as 'circumstantial evidence' a photograph he had given her in recognition of her help, inscribed 'in memory of those nights spent together'.) He worked at a phenomenal pace in order to have the film ready for the commemorative assembly at the Bolshoi Theatre on 21 December. Yet only at this stage did Eisenstein's compositional ideas finally crystallize and, despite the rush, he was continually experimenting with different combina-

During the making of *Potemkin*

tions of shots in his striving for artistic perfection. For the finale, for example, he considered three variants – three attempts to release the action from the screen and bring it home more forcefully to the audience. In the first the screen was to split apart, revealing a huge mock-up of the battleship; in the second the model was to be replaced by a symbolic group of Budyonny's cavalrymen; and in the last by the presiding board of the commemorative assembly. Moreover, Eisenstein insisted on meticulous attention to every detail, even to the extent of getting Alexandrov and Tisse to help him paint in the flag in red on 108 frames.

A first-cut preview of the film was organized by the studio for a select audience including Lunacharsky, writers, journalists and naval leaders. As the lights went up at the end an emotion-charged silence reigned, broken only when Lunacharsky jumped on his chair and began an enthusiastic speech: 'We've been witnesses at an historic cultural event. A new art has been born. From today onwards the art of the film, an art with a truly great future . . .'[7] Only then did the applause burst. Then others spoke. A few of them disparagingly considered the film, not an artistic achievement, but merely didactic material suitable for a lecture on the 1905 Revolution. In general, however, the preview was an enormous success.

But Eisenstein was still not fully satisfied, and further montage combinations were tried out right up until 21 December. As the gala showing opened at the Bolshoi Theatre, he was still frantically putting together the last few reels of film, which Alexandrov rushed to the theatre on his motorcycle the moment they were completed. Yet, even in these last-minute panic conditions, Eisenstein continued to experiment with different montage variations, sticking the strips of film provisionally with saliva until he was satisfied with the result, when he gave them to his assistant to splice securely with acetone – except for the last reel, which, in the heat of the moment, was still held together only with saliva as they rushed off on Alexandrov's motorcycle. As they tore through Red Square the cycle broke down, and they had to run the last half-mile to the Bolshoi, arriving in the final interval – just in time to get the last reels to the projection room. Throughout the showing of this last part of the film, Eisenstein paced nervously up and down the corridor outside the auditorium, until panic seized him as he remembered with horror how precariously the final reel was stuck together. Miraculously it held, and the film ended without mishap, to a storm of applause and repeated calls for Eisenstein to take a bow. When he finally appeared with Alexandrov and Tisse, it was to a thunderous ovation from both audience and orchestra. *Battleship Potemkin*, it seemed, was a triumph.*

But *Potemkin*'s subsequent fate in its own country was far from happy, however much Soviet historians have since tried to play down this aspect of it. True, it was given a festive public première on 18 January 1926, when the First Sovkino Theatre on Arbat Square was decorated with a display representing a ship, while the ushers and even members of the film unit were dressed in naval uniforms. But immediately afterwards the storm broke with a vengeance. All the old charges from the time of *Strike* were raked up, one critic, for example, asserting that the film was 'a poor presentation of the subject'. The controversy rumbled on for years – even as late as 1933 Mikhail Kalotozov and S. Bartenev were insinuating that it was little more than a glorified documentary. And, for all the subsequent tributes to the film, nothing can erase Mayakovsky's 1927 indictment of the Sovkino executives for the fact that 'on its first showing, *Potemkin* was relegated to second-rate theatres only, and it was only after the enthusiastic reaction of the foreign press that it was shown at the best theatres'.[8] At the beginning, Lunacharsky recalls, the film played to half-empty cinemas.

One of the criticisms levelled at *Potemkin* was that it was far above the heads of the average, and in particular the peasant, audiences – an assertion disproved by its showing at the 'House of Peasants' in March 1926, following

---

* This entire version of the incidents relating to the opening performance is based on Eisenstein's own memoirs. Alexandrov, however, in his published memoirs claims responsibility for having assembled the final reel, maintaining that Eisenstein had already gone on in advance.

which it was not only hailed for its crystal clarity, but recommended for countrywide distribution in the villages.

'I awoke one morning and found myself famous.' But, as well as bringing Eisenstein fame – and, according to Victor Shklovsky, an additional two rooms in the same building where he was living in one – the film also played a part in the tragedy that overtook him in later years. For the ill-wishers who wanted to end his career and bury him alive in an Eisenstein Museum invariably attacked him by invoking *Potemkin* – the very film whose greatness is beyond dispute.

'The images . . . took shape within me'

Screeds have been written about *Potemkin*, which to the present day is acclaimed as the most perfect and concise example of film structure. They include, of course, Eisenstein's own infinitely detailed analyses. In these we find that he himself considered it to be in the Romantic tradition, but at the same time profoundly realist in structure. On the one hand, though 'outwardly a chronicle of events, *Potemkin* impresses the spectators as drama', while on the other 'the organic unity of its composition as a whole and its emotive quality' are its 'two most striking features'.[9] *Potemkin* succeeds in doing what in Eisenstein's opinion was only possible in the film, namely presenting the events on different planes *simultaneously*: the epic plane, the dramatic plane, and the lyrical plane.

What was the film's significance in Eisenstein's evolution as a creative artist? It represented not only the culmination of his experience to that date, but also the starting-point of the strictly logical sequence of his subsequent creative works.

If the clatter of hooves of the attacking cavalry in *Nevsky* grew directly out of the march of the soldiers down the Odessa steps, so, too, much of the 'visual-sound' make-up of *Ivan the Terrible* develops not so much from the achievements in *Nevsky* as from those dating from the *Battleship* and, with the use of sound, brings them to a perfection of principle.[10]

Potemkin marked a natural development from his previous work, and especially his eccentric theatre, as regards his methods for heightening emotion. As we have seen, he discovered that 'the technique of leaps which produces a comic effect in static conditions produces an emotional one in the case of a dynamic process'. Similarly, in *Potemkin* he enlarged on his montage experiments in *Strike*, bringing to perfection the new language discovered there. *Potemkin* founded a language that fundamentally affected the whole evolution of cinematography from that time to the present day.

In the process of developing montage from a technique into a language

Eisenstein discovered that a single idea contained in celluloid cannot stand in isolation from the general idea, from the overall context. There was here, he realized, a parallel with a facet of linguistic evolution: in the beginning man communicated his thoughts not in sentences, but in separate words. In fact, however, these words represented a primitive form of the sentence. And, as for the word and the sentence, so too for the image and the montage phrase, the same evolutionary process held good: the primary stage of the phrase-word (the full-length, uncut shots) gets broken down (by cutting) so that a new phrase composed of independent words (images) can take shape. Another analogy, quoted by Eisenstein from the psychologist Wilhelm Wundt to illustrate his artistic discovery, was the primitive language of the Bushman. The simple sentence,

The Bushman was at first received kindly by the white man in order that he might be brought to herd his sheep,

would in the Bushman's pidgin English be expressed in a string of asyntactic images something like:

Bushman-there-go, here-run-to-white-man, white-man-give-tobacco, Bushman-go-smoke, go-fill-tobacco-pouch, white-man-give-meat-Bushman, Bushman-go-eat-meat, stand-up-go-home, go-happily, go-sit-down, herd-sheep-white-man.

This, in essence, is a shooting-script that breaks down the idea contained in the original sentence into a series of concrete actions. Eisenstein, however, advancing far beyond this primitive stage, refined his cinematographic language to the point of expressing an abstract idea. The massacre on the Odessa steps, for instance, is followed by the canonade from the battleship, then by the three lions rearing in protest, and finally by the blowing up of the gate, marking the sailors' reply. These successive shots are concerned less with recording actions than with conveying the *idea* of revulsion against the massacre. Thus Eisenstein demonstrated that it is possible

to arrange a succession of images in such a way as to produce a forceful action [the massacre followed by the lions' protest] which, in its turn, gives birth to an idea [the sailors' outburst of fury, and their decision to intervene]. The movement thus passes from image to emotion and from emotion to thesis.

Eisenstein undertook a number of detailed analyses of this language, but we shall examine only the more important elements. He defined montage as 'an idea that arises from the collision of independent shots — shots even opposite to one another: the "dramatic" principle'.[11] This idea of collision-montage is vital for an understanding of his work. As an illustrative analogy, Eisenstein himself likened the succession of montage pieces to the series of explosions in an internal combustion engine which propel the machine forward. As well as the collision between two juxtaposed shots, there could also be a clash within the composition. This juxtaposition of two clashing shots is that montage construction of 'shocks' that has become famous throughout the world as 'Russian cutting'.

The evolution of Eisenstein's artistic thinking often owes something, as we have seen, to earlier experiences in his life. In the case of his montage theories there is a traceable link back to the course on mines which he followed at the Officers' Engineering School. An 'explosion' in art, Eisenstein concluded, and particularly an emotional explosion, is produced in the same way as the explosion of a mine. In each case there are three distinct phases: the build-up of tension, the explosion and the blast. With the film, when the explosion is an emotional one, the equivalent of the blast is the resultant outburst of feeling. And just as a mine needs a detonator to trigger off the explosion, so, too, does a film. In the film it takes the shape of a succession of 'emphases' – in which *Potemkin* abounds – which follow the build-up of tension and provoke the explosion. For example, at the start of the Odessa steps sequence, the word SUDDENLY appears on the screen, to be followed by a succession of three different close-ups of the same head. This montage is a 'release mechanism' in the sense that it shatters the calm, producing, in a silent film, the effect of a burst of gunfire. Or again, between the tension built up at the funeral meeting and the explosion of the sailors' fury on board the battleship, the dynamic emphasis is provided by the shot of a youth tearing his shirt in a paroxysm of anger. This 'detonator' is inserted between the shot of the enraged student and that of the clenched fists of the angry crowd on the quay; the crowd's fury then explodes in the revulsion of the sailors on the battleship – at which point the Red Flag is symbolically raised. Thus the Officers' Engineering School provided Eisenstein with an early concrete experience that only later crystallized into an artistic discovery (hit on spontaneously in the course of creation at the cutting-table) – the montage formula known as 'visual' or 'discovered' montage.

Potemkin also contained another new form of montage with a contrapuntal basis, which Eisenstein termed 'tonal' montage (and which foreshadowed his later audio-visual montage in *Alexander Nevsky* and *Ivan the Terrible*). He used this montage for the sea-mist sequence, which, from start to finish, is a polyphonic composition based on three elements: the mist, the water and the silhouettes. I shall not attempt to analyse the sequence, but only to uncover the emotional sources of Eisenstein's fascination with polyphonic construction, the origins of that spell-binding attraction that caused his 'whole life' to be 'plagued' by a mania for the contrapuntal and a passion for Bach.* It originated not, as might be expected, in some art form such as music or ballet, but in the construction of the pontoon bridge witnessed during his Civil War days when his first impression had been of

* For one screening at the Meyerhold Theatre the then pianist, Leo Arnstam, compiled from Bach's works a musical arrangement for *Potemkin*.

an interplay of crossing orbs, or paths joining up through continuous and varied dynamics in a complicated arabesque, to merge almost immediately into blurred, vague and sketchy outlines.

This 'rhythmic collective dance, uniting the movements of dozens of men in a single, unique symphony' and all the precise space-time calculations that went into the building of the bridge made, as we know, a deep impression on Eisenstein's artistic consciousness. And, as he later recognized in his memoirs, it probably lay behind the harmonious merging of the various component elements of his compositions,

both in the film as a whole, and in the combination of its constituent parts [of the montage sequences], and in that specific engineering of space and time that confronts the lens with extremely complicated mass episodes or gesticulations by the characters ... combining the particular action with the general action ... the action with the limited time factor, the intensity of the action with the spatial confines, the gesture with the word ... the idea with the sensorial image, the ideational conclusion with the emotional shock.[12]

Another feature of *Potemkin* is the expressive use of close-ups and detailed shots. Unlike Griffith, Eisenstein regarded the function of the close-up 'not so much to *show* or to *present*, as to *signify*, to *give meaning*, to *designate*'.[13] His 'close-up method' was based on the premise that, when the separate parts of a whole are reassembled, the whole takes on a new quality. In his montage for the massacre sequence, for example, Eisenstein first broke the scene down into fragments of detail and then reassembled them in such a way as to intensify their emotional impact and recreate the generalized idea of the savagery of the massacre. A woman struck by a bullet falls on the steps; two close-ups follow showing her hand clenching tightly before limply opening in death. Or there is the example of the old man at the funeral scene whose tears and grief are forcefully conveyed in the brief shots of his hand covering the face and his shoulders heaving almost imperceptibly.

Eisenstein further used the close-up in a way similar to the poetic use of synecdoche – to make the part stand for the whole and vice versa. The fate of Dr Smirnov, for instance, is summed up in the single detail of his pince-nez dangling from the rigging after the sailors' mutiny. As a climax this detail is incomparably more forceful than the shot of the doctor himself being thrown overboard. Similarly the figure of the doctor epitomizes in turn the whole social class for which he stands – just as, in a wider context, the *Potemkin* mutiny represents the whole 1905 Revolution.

Again, as we know, biographical influence – the lilac bough from his childhood and the evening in the village near Kholm during the Civil War – played a part in the emergence of his ideas about the close-up.

Eisenstein's metaphoric montage – of which the rearing lions constitute a

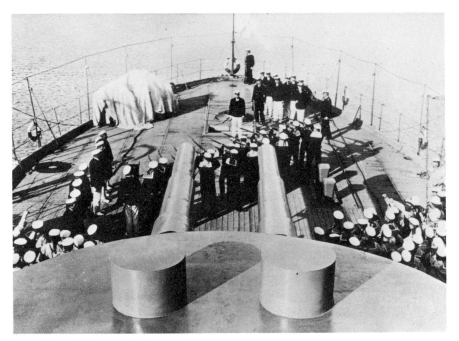

Potemkin: the execution

classic example – was also influenced by an earlier experience in his life, namely his study of Japanese. One aspect of the language that particularly fascinated him was the method of representing abstract ideas by juxtaposing two different characters: the symbols for an eye and water, for instance, to express the idea of crying. By analogy, Eisenstein based his metaphoric montage on the concept that the shot or image represents an idea, and that when two are juxtaposed they take on a completely new significance. His thinking along these lines was to be developed further in the 'intellectual montage' of his subsequent films.

Finally, among the important artistic innovations in *Potemkin*, should be mentioned Eisenstein's dramatic handling of time, on which the dynamism of several sequences depends. Sometimes the real time of an action is compressed by showing merely the start of a gesture, followed immediately by its effect. Sometimes the compression is even more stringent; when, for instance, the close-up of the bespectacled woman is followed abruptly by the shot of her shattered glasses and her eye pouring with blood, with the effect that the actual impact of the sabre is simultaneously conveyed. Conversely, his drawing out of time – by extending the massacre sequence over a much longer period than it could ever have taken in reality, or by inserting a neutral shot of the battleship between the preparations for the sailors' execution under the tarpaulin and the actual order to fire – serves to heighten the suspense and emotional strain.

Potemkin's significance lay not merely in Eisenstein's discovery of all these new techniques of expression, but in his perfecting of them. Yet he paid, paradoxically, a high price, as he acknowledged several years later, for achieving such balance and perfection – the price of exhausting the stylistic means of expression:

It was impossible to go forward after *Potemkin*, and only possible, at best, to use variations of the same methods in treating other themes.[14]

This perfection was all the more remarkable for being achieved, not through careful advance planning, but in the heat of the moment at the frantic montage stage. It was then that the film's perfect harmony of feeling was created. Hence Eisenstein's absolutely sincere claim that

I realized the emotive scenes, as the Holy Scriptures say, 'without seeing my creation'; that is, I realized them thanks to the feelings which the events inspired within me . . . and the images through which we strove to express my political attitude towards the events, these too took shape within me.*[15]

Fame

Potemkin was to be, in Eisenstein's paradoxical words, his 'first work in the sound film', for the German distributor asked Edmund Meisel to compose a score for his Berlin showing of the film. During the spring of 1926 Eisenstein went to Berlin, where he helped Meisel put the finishing touches to the score. This music was distinctly unusual for its time. Working with Meisel in much the same way as present-day collaborators on a sound track, Eisenstein dissuaded him from composing purely illustrative music for the last reel, getting him instead to accentuate certain 'effects'. This came off particularly well in the 'music of machines' – in the final sequence of the *Potemkin*'s meeting with the flotilla – which he insisted should be based on the rhythmic beat of the percussion instruments and should, in tune with the film, make a leap into a new quality of sound structure. The result was a unity of fused musical and visual images: in effect, not a silent film with illustrative musical

---

* Statements made by Eisenstein at this period are, it is true, sometimes contradictory. In a personal statement published in a Berlin newspaper in June 1926, for example, he wrote: 'According to my artistic principle, we did not depend on intuitive creativeness but on a rational construction of affective elements; each affect must be subjected previously to a thorough analysis and calculation: this is the most important thing.' But there is every reason to suppose that this statement of Eisenstein's was inspired by a juvenile artistic affectation, a form of ostentatious nonconformism, an extension of his struggle against the aesthetic canons of art. It is sincere in that it reflects Eisenstein's intentions, which were not, however, realized in practice.

accompaniment, but, as Eisenstein justly claimed, a sound film. (Eisenstein later formulated the concept of a 'pre-sound film' as opposed to a 'silent film'.) As such it helped also to blaze a trail for the sound films – in the normal sense – that were soon to come. His subsequent bitterness at being prevented for twelve years from himself making such a sound film – in the normal sense – is thus very understandable.

Since the première was postponed following the censorship's intervention, Eisenstein left Berlin without having had the opportunity of hearing this music, nor did he hear it during his second trip to Berlin, in June 1926. Although on 1 June 1926 the distributing company 'Prometheus' sent him, by mail, a complete score of Meisel's music, there is evidence that Eisenstein never heard it performed until at least November 1927, when Meisel came to Moscow, for a festive performance of *Potemkin*, to conduct his own music. Even then it is not clear whether Eisenstein was present. At all events, Ivor Montagu recalls that only later, in London at the end of 1929, was Eisenstein shown a copy of *Potemkin* 'with the Edmund Meisel musical score, which Eisenstein had never heard before'. On that occasion, Montagu further recalls, 'at the end . . . he complained that, with the Meisel music, we had turned his picture into an opera'.[16]

Potemkin's postponed Berlin première took place on 29 April 1926 at a fair-sized cinema on the Friedrichstrasse. At first only vague reports of the film's triumphant success reached Moscow. Then followed a shower of telegrams inviting Eisenstein to come at once in person. Several celebrities, including Asta Nielsen and Max Reinhardt, were ecstatic about the film; a new gala performance was to be organized and the film would move to the city centre, to the Kurfürstendamm. Finally came reports of endless queues at the box office and of the film's wider release to twenty-five Berlin cinemas and ten in other major German cities (there were fifty copies of the film for distribution). Meanwhile, after many frustrating difficulties and delays, Eisenstein was enabled to pay his second visit to Berlin. He stayed there for several days, during which time there was evidently some discussion about his making a film in Germany, to judge from an article which he published in *Berliner Tageblatt*:

I am positive that the cinema collaboration of Germany and Russia could have great results. . . . But for me personally to work in Germany is extremely doubtful. I could not forsake my native soil, which gives me the strength to create. . . .

And so, for the present I'll stay at home.[17]

Potemkin's success abroad, starting in Germany where it ran for over a year in Berlin alone, was prodigious – but chequered. The German censor, as we have seen, began by banning the film; and the final scene, in which the number and shape of the ships in the flotilla bore no resemblance to German intelligence estimates of Soviet naval strength, led to a question in the Reichstag. (In assembling this sequence, Eisenstein had, in point of fact, included shots from old newsreels of manoeuvres by another great naval power.) Official reaction to the film conflicted sharply, however, with the enthusiastic public reception and with the opinion of prominent intellectuals and cultural figures who spoke out in its support. This conflict between official and popular reaction was to be repeated throughout Europe. Cavalcanti, for example, characterized it as marking 'the beginning of a new period in film history, of a period of truth and realism'. Ernst Toller, who saw the film in Moscow during Eisenstein's absence, wrote sending his congratulations, while Egon Erwin Kisch, who also saw the film there, was equally enthusiastic; Mary Pickford and Douglas Fairbanks saw the film in Berlin at a special showing shortly after the première, the latter stating to newspaper men that *Potemkin* 'is the most intense and profoundest experience of my life'.

After Germany, *Potemkin* was launched on its wider international career in a Paris film club on 12 November 1926.

Though the French censor, too, banned it (the ban was not, in fact, lifted until twenty-seven years later) it continued to be shown at film clubs, including 'Les Amis de Spartacus', whose membership ran into tens of thousands. On 5 December 1926 *Potemkin* made its American début, following a severe censorship scrutiny that lasted three weeks. Its success was such – it was acclaimed as 'an event' and 'the best film of the year' – that even the conservative *New York Sun* recommended it as an object lesson for all American film directors. Chaplin proclaimed it 'the best film in the world'.

On his later travels abroad, Eisenstein discovered that *Potemkin* had penetrated, and made him famous, in the most unlikely corners of the world: among Mexican miners in the backwoods of Sierra Madre, factory workers in Liège and Javanese students in Paris. (The impression made by his film in Indonesia was much later brought home to him by the mutiny, in February 1933, aboard the Dutch battleship *De Zeven Provincien*, whose crew claimed at their court martial to have been inspired by seeing *Battleship Potemkin*.) And, in a totally different field, *Potemkin* had, he learned, influenced Lion Feuchtwanger's new fictional techniques.

The subsequent fate of *Potemkin* was both glorious and tragic: glorious in that even today it wins wide and regular acclaim on the world's cinema and television screens, and that as late as 1958 it was accorded the title of 'the best film of all time' by a jury of 117 film historians from twenty-six countries; tragic in that the film's original negative was mutilated in Germany and that none of the surviving copies may be identical with Eisenstein's original version. Crowning this tragedy came the sound version produced in Moscow in 1950, with its 'authorized' montage and absurdly inappropriate music

The stone lions of *Potemkin*

totally alien to Eisenstein's conception (although Meisel's score was available) – in short, a travesty of the *Battleship Potemkin* which the Polish film-historian Professor Jerzy Toeplitz described as unparalleled for its elemental force by anything in the field of art, with the single exception of the Marseillaise.

6. Searchings: from *October* to *The General Line*

Somewhere, probably, in the background of all these (the things that influenced and impressed me) also hovers the figure of Hoffmann's Lindhort, leading his bizarre life as king of the elves in, beneath the nondescript exterior of the archivist, his flame flower-bedecked gown.

EISENSTEIN

After 'Potemkin'

Moscow in 1926 was a tumultuous city teeming with life, and with odd and colourful characters – from private traders to prostitutes and down-and-out jobless loafers. In Ilya Ehrenburg's vivid description of a typically bizarre Moscow street scene of that time,

Everybody traded in everything, wrangled, prayed, swilled vodka and, dead drunk, fell like corpses in the gateways. The yards were filthy. Vagrant children huddled in the cellars.[1]

It was also a place where new and varied artistic ideas flourished. As Yevgeni Petrov summed it up: 'We thumbed our noses at everything; letter-writing was absurd, the Moscow Art Theatre was stupid. . . .' It was the period when Ehrenburg was bringing from Paris the films of Abel Gance, Léger, René Clair, Feyder and Renoir – all of which Eisenstein undoubtedly saw, being able a year later to astound Léon Moussinac by his intimate knowledge of French film developments.

Eisenstein was by this time full of self-confidence as an artist – so much so that a number of people, including his future wife, Pera Attasheva (real name Fogelman), were repelled by what they took to be his insufferable conceit. He was avidly interested in foreign comment on his work, while at the same time being, in his own peculiar way, genuinely aligned, in his ideas and feelings, with the Communist Party at home: though not a Party member himself, he had adopted the ostentatious habit of almost invariably writing letters and articles in bright red ink. A first meeting with him could arouse a reaction of antipathy; but anyone who had the perseverance to get to know him closely was won over by his charm. Generally speaking, the more enlightened were drawn by his personality, wit and intelligence, and deeply impressed by his extraordinarily fertile imagination and all-absorbing passion for artistic invention. The esteem in which they consequently held him – even hailing him as a genius – plus Eisenstein's acceptance of their admiration at its face value, was in turn a further source of irritation to his increasingly envious critics. Eisenstein, for his part, was unwilling, then or in later years, to ignore their irritation; often, indeed, he went out of his way to provoke them.

A case in point was his clash at this time with Pudovkin, who rose to fame shortly after *Potemkin* with the success of his film *Mother*. While Eisenstein gave Pudovkin his due, serious differences of opinion existed between them, not least over artistic questions. Three years later Eisenstein wrote:

In front of me lies a crumpled yellowed sheet of paper. On it is a mysterious note: 'Linkage-P' and 'Collision-E.'

This is a substantial trace of a heated bout on the subject of montage between P (Pudovkin) and E (myself).

This has become a habit. At regular intervals he visits me late at night and behind closed doors we wrangle over matters of principle. A graduate of the Kuleshov school, he loudly defends an understanding of montage as a *linkage* of pieces. Into a chain. Again, 'bricks'. Bricks, arranged in series to *expound* an idea.

I confronted him with my viewpoint on montage as a *collision*. A view that from the collision of two given factors arises a concept.

. . . Not long ago we had another talk. Today he agrees with my point of view. True, during the interval he took the opportunity to acquaint himself with the series of lectures I gave during that period at the State Cinema Institute. . . .[2]

The sarcasm suggests a deeper conflict than a mere clash of artistic principles, and there was evidently some malice on both sides. But whereas Pudovkin's attitude – his comments about Eisenstein after his death, for instance – smacks distinctly of jealousy, the same can hardly be said of Eisenstein, to judge by one of his letters to Léon Moussinac, in which he refers to Moussinac's comment that 'an Eisenstein film is like a scream, a Pudovkin one like a song':

The distinction you draw between Pudovkin and me – 'song' and 'scream' – is superb and testifies to great insight. Each of us is very pleased and his personal vanity whispers in his ear, 'You're the best.' Joy everywhere.

This is aimed at Pudovkin; Eisenstein had no need for such comparative confirmation. He continues:

On the other hand, I'm always flattered when I'm called romantic, adventurer, barbarian – unbalanced! Hexameter à la Pudovkin (I admire his work greatly, but I wouldn't want to resemble him in any way) is the thing I'm most afraid of in the world![3]

Immediately after *Potemkin*, Eisenstein projected a three-part film about China, based on a scenario by Sergei Tretyakov, to be called *Zhunguo*. The Chinese political question was then a topical one to which Eisenstein no doubt hoped to make his contribution, believing as he did that 'perhaps for the first time in history the film has become as terrible a weapon as the hand grenade'. But he was also intrigued by the theme of China *per se*, as he showed in 1934 when he contemplated making a film based on Malraux's *La Condition Humaine*. The Chinese actor Mei Lan-fang has written about a short film that he and Eisenstein made together, a recording of Mei's acting technique. At that point, it seems, Eisenstein's project had not advanced beyond the tentative stage of a memorandum on a cinematographic visit to China, some sketches and preliminary shooting notes for a three-part film.

These preparations came to a halt in the spring of 1926, when Eisenstein was asked to make a film on a more crucial, domestic political issue: the collectivization of agriculture. With characteristic enthusiasm, and after the usual massive documentary research, he set off with his team to tour the villages of the Moscow region. Even village gossip was grist to his mill; and so thorough were these 'field studies' – lasting several months – that there were jokes about the film people belonging to the Agriculture and Forestry Workers' rather than the Artists' Union. By 23 May he had outlined the scenario for the film, to be called *The General Line*, and the following day he presented it at the Centre for Agriculture and Forestry. The complete shooting script, written between 22 and 30 June, was discussed by the cinema's Artistic Council on 7 July. Filming then started, and continued for a month in a succession of villages and farms. In one village in the Ryazan district, where the team was shooting a wedding feast, all went well until the third day, when not a single woman turned up. Eisenstein eventually discovered what was wrong: the rumour was going round that the camera could see through the women's dresses and that they would be shown naked, with mermaids' tails instead of legs. Denials were of no avail, and the team was obliged to move on.

After a month, however, filming was broken off when Sovkino, which had to produce a film in honour of the tenth anniversary of the October Revolution, again called on Eisenstein's services. Pudovkin had already begun making *The End of Saint Petersburg* in Leningrad for the same occasion, his original idea for a historical epic – which he hoped would rival the grandeur of *Potemkin* – having been abandoned in favour of this contemporary theme. Eisenstein's first draft treatment for his new film, entitled *October*, was, appropriately enough, dated 7 November 1926 – or, under the old calendar, 25 October, the date on which the Revolution broke out. An item in *Kino* the previous day announced that filming would start on 1 January 1927 and was expected to last nine months.*

October

The steps in elaborating the shooting script for *October* were far more elaborate than those for *Potemkin*, involving research into newspaper reports and photographs, old newsreels, and hundreds of historical memoirs and papers – in addition to long consultations with an elderly revolutionary, N. I. Podvoysky.† A further source was John Reed's *Ten Days That Shook the World*, the title by which Eisenstein's film was later known in America and elsewhere abroad. Then there were Eisenstein's personal memories of the events he had witnessed in 1917 (the dispersal of the demonstration of the Nevsky Prospekt, for example), as well as his childhood experience at the Musée Grévin where he saw the savage scene from the time of the Paris Commune (introduced unsuccessfully in *October*).

The scenario went through a long and complicated gestation period with the result that, unlike that for *Potemkin*, it was worked out in minute detail that left little room for improvisation when it came to filming. But there was an incidental similarity in that *October* also, initially intended to cover a vast panoramic vista, was eventually limited to a much shorter time span.

Originally, the project for *October* was linked with that for *Strike*, as part of the projected cycle *Towards the Dictatorship*. Another projected film from that time that turned up again in the initial plans for *October* was *The Iron Flood*, which Eisenstein had discussed with Serafimovich.

Not all the variants of the scenario have survived, but from those which have it is possible to build up a picture of its genesis. The first outline, dated 7 November 1926, covered six main aspects of the period from the February Revolution to the years of post-Civil-War reconstruction: the events leading up to February 1917; those of June and October; the Civil War; the Red Army; and the years of peaceful reconstruction. Apart from some notes containing details of moments in the Civil War and dated 18 January 1927, there is then a gap in the extant documents. The first version of the actual scenario, worked out between 21 January and 1 February, showed no very

---

* An odd, and so far unexplained, press announcement in December mentioned that Eisenstein was planning a quite different film, based on Tretyakov's script, *Five Minutes*, about a strike aboard a foreign ship following the news of Lenin's death.

† In the film Podvoysky played the part of the revolutionary Chief of Staff, a post he is said to have held in November 1917.

great variation on the November notes: the time span of the projected film was still the same, only the fifth act dealing with the October Revolution. By the end of February, however, the panoramic vista had been drastically narrowed: five acts were devoted to the October Revolution, while a sixth touched on events from the Civil War by way of conclusion.

But still the adaptations went on, with new ideas cropping up, many of them being abandoned almost immediately. One of these abandoned ideas was to show through the eyes of an officer the contrast between life at the Winter Palace before and during its storming; another was for somebody quite unconnected with the Revolution to be swept with the in-rushing crowd into the Palace, which he would then have explored. These two eliminated characters were, it seems to me, Eisenstein's spontaneous reaction to the demands of conventional drama for a subjective viewpoint. He evidently felt, however, that they ran counter to his theoretical aims, and he quickly rejected them in the interests of preserving the objective and documentary nature of the scenario.

The final version, on which the film was based, was dated 5 March 1927. After its approval filming started on 13 April with the sequence of fraternization between the Russian and German soldiers.

Throughout shooting Eisenstein enjoyed the full cooperation of the authorities. In fact the Special Cinematographic Committee – a body set up by the Central Commission specifically to advise on the many Anniversary films – evidently viewed Eisenstein's proposed film with particular interest from its very first session on 16 December 1926.*

While everyone expectantly awaited another *Potemkin*, Eisenstein's intentions were quite different. Although *October*, like *Potemkin*, was meant to be a chronicle of historical events, Eisenstein proposed projecting the events through the filter of his own particular artistic interpretation. Overawed neither by the magnitude of the subject, nor by the importance of the occasion it was intended to mark, he experimented freely in making the film, with the aim of overthrowing his own 'system' and discovering, as he put it, 'the key to pure cinema'. In this respect *October* was the 'dialectical opposite' of *Potemkin*; whereas Eisenstein looked on the latter as being in 'the style of the Greek

---

* Eisenstein states later in a letter to Upton Sinclair: 'I made an outlay of expenses before starting. They accorded me exactly the half of the money – *without* reducing the story to a half! I accepted, making in advance the statement that this amount is enough for *half* a picture – and when I will be through with this half they will *have* to give us much more, or be without a picture. And in three months it *exactly* happened. And the whole picture costed exactly as much as I foresaw: 600,000 roubles.'[4] Was this true or was it said only to impress Sinclair, with whom Eisenstein was just then haggling about financial support for his Mexican film? Doubts arise because in another letter to Sinclair, in 1931, Eisenstein wrote about the footage of *October* as being 225,000 feet, whereas in an article published just after completing his film he quoted a figure of 49,000 metres.

temples', *October* would have a somewhat more 'baroque' flavour. He was, indeed, at this stage, trying to develop what was later to be known as the 'intellectual film'.

Once again Eisenstein insisted on the film's entire cast conforming with his 'typage' theory, and the familiar frantic search for suitable 'types' began. The task again fell mainly on Maxim Strauch, who scoured the streets, offices, pubs and doss-houses, going unshaven and down-at-heel among the jobless and suitably smartened up among the white-collar workers. The outcome was a detailed dossier, complete with photographs, of a huge selection of 'possibles', from which Eisenstein selected for closer personal inspection those approaching his ideal. Sometimes he was enthusiastic about a face, but not the beard that went with it; the luckless man was asked to shave, only to encounter his wife's stubborn opposition to the request. . . . As usual, it proved impossible to type-cast all the characters, and Eisenstein had to fall back on his colleagues for some of the parts, Tisse, for example, becoming a German officer. Hardest of all to find was Lenin's prototype, for whom Eisenstein insisted on someone resembling him so closely that make-up could be dispensed with. A protracted and widespread search finally unearthed a certain Nikandrov whose facial features were almost the exact replica of Lenin's. But there the resemblance ended abruptly: nothing in the world could hide the poor man's inner emptiness and primitive intellect. Despite this, he was drilled into walking and behaving like Lenin, down to his last characteristic gesture.

During the filming in Leningrad the Tsar's palace, the streets, virtually the whole city and its populace, were put at Eisenstein's disposal. For the crowd scenes, such as the massacre on the Nevsky Prospekt or the assault on the Winter Palace, a total of nearly 11,000 workers and soldiers took part, many of whom had actually witnessed the events of 1917. (The figure is Alexandrov's; Eisenstein once mentioned 4–5,000 workers.) For the latter sequence, the Army provided uniforms for all the extras as well as making tanks and artillery available. Much of the shooting had to be done at night and, as there was a power shortage in Leningrad at that period, most of the city went in darkness while the electricity resources were concentrated on the scene of the filming. Eisenstein was refused nothing, not even the use of the cruiser *Aurora*.

Such, indeed, was the power he enjoyed that Pudovkin was spurred to modify the scenario of *The End of Saint Petersburg*, which he was simultaneously filming in Leningrad. As Pudovkin summed up the situation:

I bombarded the Winter Palace from the *Aurora*, while Eisenstein bombarded it from the Fortress of Saint Peter and Paul. One night I knocked away part of the balustrading of the roof, and was scared I might get into trouble, but, luckily enough, that same night Sergei Mikhailovich broke 200 windows in private bedrooms.[5]

119

On the Tsar's throne during the making of *October*

After this exploit, Eisenstein was told by an elderly porter who had just been sweeping up the broken glass: 'Your people were much more careful the first time they took the palace.'

The filming was accomplished at a phenomenal pace, thanks to the two film units that Eisenstein had shooting simultaneously, to the exceptional facilities made available to him – and to the pep pills that he and his fellow workers took to keep themselves awake at night.

For the July demonstration on the Nevsky Prospekt, Eisenstein wanted to reproduce everything exactly as he himself remembered it, even down to the hats and walking-sticks forlornly littering the streets after the demonstrators' forced dispersal. When filming this episode, Eisenstein carefully arranged for the objects to be dropped unobtrusively by members of the film unit strategically positioned in the crowd – only to be thwarted when they were just as conscientiously gathered up by some elderly extras with an over-developed sense of responsibility towards state property.

Inside the Winter Palace, Eisenstein tried to absorb the atmosphere through every pore of his body, just as he had done when faced with the reality of the Odessa steps (and was again to do many times later, be it in Mexico or Uzbekistan). This entailed an exhaustive exploration of the interior. But, for all the seriousness of his researches, Eisenstein's characteristic playfulness still bubbled to the surface, as photographs of him in mock-serious poses on the Tsar's throne amusingly illustrate. One of his finds while exploring the Palace was a clock showing the local time on a central dial and the corresponding time in various world capitals on a series of smaller dials surrounding it. He later used shots of this clock for an interesting piece of montage showing the dials first as separate entities and then rotating together at an increasing speed until they seem to merge into one – to produce a plastic effect of time everywhere fusing into 'one single historic hour'.[6]

Similarly accidental and spontaneous was Eisenstein's inspiration for other plastic effects, including those in the startlingly beautiful sequence of the rising bridge and the blonde girl and suspended horse. One dawn after filming all night on the storming of the Winter Palace, Eisenstein happened to glance from the window of Tsar Nicholas's library and saw the two arms of the Dvortsovy bridge rising towards the heavens. 'Instantaneously, as in a vision, the arms of the bridge suggested the shattered carriage and dead horse, while the golden rays of the sun shining above became the dead girl's blonde hair.' Against seemingly impossible odds – filming in short spurts of barely twenty minutes each morning before the bridge had to be lowered for the day's traffic – Eisenstein filmed this sequence which has become a classic of its time. The scene of the Nevsky Prospekt massacre had likewise to be shot in brief, twenty-minute sessions daily. On another occasion, however, shooting went on without interruption for forty hours.

At times while making *October*, Eisenstein's deliberately audacious experimentation caused him considerable anxiety. He had doubts about the film's unity and foresaw its being a flop ('the public won't understand'), but consoled himself with the thought that a failure with the undiscerning public at large was no great price to pay for accomplishing an artistic experiment. Léon Moussinac recalls that another of Eisenstein's premonitions at that time was that he would be unable to realize the film exactly as he envisaged doing – a premonition that came true shortly after, the first of a long and tragic chain of artistic disappointments that dogged his career.

In the midst of the filming, on 12 October 1927, Eisenstein thought of splitting the film into two parts, starting the second with the events of the morning of 7 November (old-style 25 October) 1917. But the idea fell through for want of time, which had again begun exerting the worrying pressures familiar from *Potemkin*. (The shooting-script for the unrealized reels has been preserved and published.[7]) A further disquieting factor was a series of malicious rumours alleging Eisenstein's adherence to Trotsky – rumours which he felt compelled to repudiate publicly in a press article, explaining at the same time his reasons for the film being delayed. Normally he paid little attention to blatantly scandalous speculation; and the situation must have struck him as pretty serious for him to have broken off in the thick of work in order to write an article for the express purpose of clearing his name. The film's deadline was subsequently extended; but because of the expected delay Sovkino organized a showing of the material thus far filmed. This was attended by Voroshilov and Yaroslavsky in addition to the official advisers, and resulted in measures being taken to speed up completion of the film.

Again Eisenstein edited the seemingly endless footage of film largely single-handed, only occasionally calling on Esther Shub's opinion about certain montage effects. He afterwards said that during the editing stage his head was 'so full of celluloid' that the mere mention of the 'utterly detested' word 'film' was enough to send it spinning dizzily. 'And perhaps something of this dizziness, this chaotic confusion of kilometres of film transferred itself to the film's composition.' It was a story of haste and yet more frantic haste – a haste that allowed Eisenstein no breathing-space in which to perfect the film's structure.

In the midst of the editing Edmund Meisel arrived in Moscow to compose the music for *October* as a sequel to his successful *Potemkin* score. The film's complicated structure made for considerable difficulties, which were accentuated by the far from ideal working conditions in the projection-room, where the central-heating system was being repaired amid an infernal clatter. Eisenstein later laughingly accused Meisel of writing this cacophony into certain parts of the score that he disliked. Sometimes the music imitated certain of the film's visual effects, such as the smashing of a statue of Alexander III to symbolize the overthrow of Tsardom, and the later reversal of the procedure, which satirized the monarchists' dreams of returning to power at the time of Kornilov's offensive: for the latter scene Meisel reversed his previous music correspondingly, though Eisenstein was sceptical about whether anyone would appreciate this musical trick.

Meanwhile, throughout the period of work on the editing, events had been boiling up on the political front; Stalin's offensive against the 'Trotskyites' had reached fever pitch and 'Trotskyism' had become the dirtiest word in the political vocabulary. Eisenstein's film was naturally – though probably to his surprise: he seems to have been out of touch with events, and not to have seen that his film had political implications – expected to take account of the 'new historical facts', and this entailed far-reaching modifications. To judge from a remark about the film's length made by Eisenstein while he was editing it, and the actual length of the film as we know it, about one-third seems to have been cut. Although the full story will probably never be made public knowledge, an incident related by Alexandrov throws an interesting light on the prevailing atmosphere. Late one night, according to Alexandrov, when Eisenstein was working on the film, Stalin unexpectedly dropped in at his studios and was shown several sequences, including a certain speech by Lenin.

This he ordered to be cut, adding curtly: 'Lenin's liberalism is no longer valid today.' The cut in question amounted to some 900 metres, Alexandrov maintains.

Only a few selected reels of *October* were shown for the Anniversary celebrations. The rest had to be edited anew. In a letter to Sovkino on 15 November 1927, Eisenstein reported that he was then about to begin the editing for the second part (even at that stage, it seems, he was still thinking in terms of a two-part film). This re-editing, which seems to have involved cuts of over 4,000 feet, took several months – a letter of Meisel's indicates that Eisenstein was ill during the second half of November – and it was March 1928 before the film finally reached the screens of Moscow.

Just what this hectic period of editing meant for Eisenstein appears from a bitter statement he made shortly afterwards when he described the year of *October*'s production as 'a year . . . that took us beyond the limits of our strength . . . most of our energy being wasted in the struggle with the Sovkino Leningrad workshop's crude, recalcitrant, treacherous machinery. This year has finally broken us.' It is clear today that Eisenstein had in mind other governmental bodies as well as Sovkino. In the same statement he complains of having been refused a ten days' respite in order to cut, for the final version, such redundant padding as still remained. 'They never gave us time to bathe our new-born child properly.'[8]

Different as *October* was from *Potemkin*, the new cinematographic elements it introduced – and notably the concept of the 'intellectual film' – were logical developments from the earlier film, and more specifically from the potentialities inherent in the famous montage sequence of the stone lions. *October* contains a whole series of formulae for expressing abstract ideas. Without examining the film in detail, we shall look at several examples which Eisenstein himself analysed in detail. The sequence of Kornilov's march on Petrograd is one such elucidating example.

Among the ideas which Eisenstein wanted to convey here was Kornilov's basic militarism. This he proposed to do by exploding the myth of the General's 'crusade' against Bolshevism 'in the name of God'. In a montage sequence of religious images,

shots of a Baroque Christ (apparently exploding in the radiant beams of his halo) were intercut with shots of an egg-shaped mask of Uzume, [Japanese] Goddess of Mirth. . . . The temporal conflict between the closed egg-form and the graphic star-form produced the effect of an instantaneous *burst* – of a bomb, or shrapnel.[9]

Eisenstein also wished to discredit the concept of God by pointing out visually the essential similarity between all deities, be they Christian or pagan. This he achieved through a montage sequence of several symbolic images of deities: the Baroque Christ mentioned above (the most magnificent he could find in Leningrad); then, as if materializing out of the rays of its halo, a many-armed Indian deity, whose terrifying face gives way to another Indian head with an outline reminiscent of the silhouette of a mosque; this, in turn, has points in common with the subsequent mask of the Japanese sun goddess Amaterasu, after which – following the same associative pattern, and in increasing order of primitiveness – come another Japanese goddess, an African one, and finally a primitive idol. This step-by-step debasement of the wonderful Baroque Christ invariably raises a laugh from the audience; that is, it transports them into the sphere of the emotions. An idea, an argument, was capable of presentation on the screen. From this to the vindication of the 'intellectual film', which Eisenstein was soon to undertake, was a short step.

An unconscious inspiration for this sequence was – as Eisenstein realized some time after completing the film – a Daumier caricature of Louis Philippe which he had seen as a child. In a series of sketches gradually transforming essential features of the king's portrait, Daumier had finally reduced it to a caricature of a pear. Eisenstein's method of expressing an abstract theme in plastic terms was essentially the same as Daumier's.

Thus from the 'montage of attractions', purely emotional in its effect, Eisenstein had arrived at the concept of an 'intellectual attraction'. This he explained in an article entitled 'Perspectives', in which he outlined his basic ideas of 'intellectual cinema':

The duality in the spheres of 'feeling' and 'reasoning' must have new limits by the new art:
To restore sensuality to science.
To restore to the intellectual process its fire and passion.
To plunge the abstract reflective process into the fervour of practical action.
To give back to emasculated theoretical *formulas* the rich exuberance of life-felt *forms*.
To give to formal *arbitrariness* the clarity of ideological *formulation*.
Those are the challenges. Those are the demands that we make on the period of art that we are now entering.
To which art will this not be too much to demand?
Wholly and only to the cinema.
Wholly and only to the *intellectual cinema.* A synthesis of the emotional, the documentary, and the absolute film.[10]

October contains a whole variety of examples of 'intellectual montage', a whole range of metaphoric formulae. Kerensky's rise to power, for example, is satirized in successive shots of Kerensky climbing the Winter Palace steps at exactly the same pace in each, while, inserted between the shots, subtitles indicate the increasingly powerful rank he has meanwhile assumed. The incongruity between the high-flown flummery of the ranks and the down-to-earth monotony of Kerensky's unchanged step highlights his essential nonentity and total incapacity for his duties. The idea for this sequence was apparently suggested by a newsreel shot of Kerensky looking fixedly ahead while climbing the steps of the Alexandrinsky Theatre, followed by two adjutants obsequiously aping his bearing and tread.

Elsewhere Eisenstein attempted a 'dynamization' of documentary events with the aim of producing an emotional effect. Thus, 'the dramatic moment of the union of the Motorcycle Battalion with the Congress of Soviets was dynamized by shots of abstractly spinning bicycle wheels, in association with the entrance of the new delegates'.[11] Or he tried to extend parallel montage from the sphere of action to that of significance by intercutting shots of the tearful pleadings of the defeated Mensheviks with shots of hands plucking at harps and balalaikas. But this, as Eisenstein later described it, was 'purely literary parallelism', and hence basically ineffectual as cinema.

So much for the examples. As always, they led Eisenstein to the next step – of seeking in the particular method concerned the essence of cinematography. In this case it was the 'intellectual film', for which he had been agitating for several years and at the basis of which stood the idea that 'the first and foremost essential of cinematography is montage' – whose task was 'to restore to the intellectual process its fire and passion'.

Thus, once again, Eisenstein's theories were founded on practice – not *vice versa* as was claimed by his detractors, intent on proving his ineptitude. His natural thought process was always the same: from emotional, through intellectual experience, to practical experiment in the film itself, and thence to theory. As he himself stated quite categorically: 'To build cinematography starting from "the idea of cinematography", and from abstract principles, is barbarous and stupid.'[12]

Another feature of *October* was the originality of Eisenstein's attempt at conveying sound effects visually. The gunfire from the *Aurora* was filmed with a rhythmic opening and closing of the diaphragm so that its roar was 'visible'. Similarly the machine-gun bursts are 'seen' in the quivering of the crystal chandeliers in the Winter Palace.

October remains, indisputably, an experimental film of immense proportions. But because Eisenstein always thought in larger-than-life terms his mistakes, too, are inevitably glaring ones. They sometimes take your breath away. As daring as Achilles in his iconoclastic struggle against traditionalism, yet at the same time a strange Don Quixote pursuing his hallucinations, Eisenstein sometimes became the slave of his own revolutionary ideas.

October's release in the Soviet Union provoked a storm of criticism in which even Meyerhold and Mayakovsky joined. Mayakovsky's chief criticism was of the use of 'typage' for Lenin's role:

For all the outward similarity, there is no hiding the inner emptiness. How right the comrade was who said that Nikandrov doesn't resemble Lenin, but a statue of Lenin.[13]

Lenin's widow, Krupskaya, expressed the same opinion in an article on *October*. Eisenstein was profoundly affected by these criticisms, not even finding comfort in Krupskaya's following comment that *October* represented a 'landmark on the road towards a new art, towards the art of the future'. His sensitiveness to these attacks seems to have determined the entirely different approach to his next film.

Though *October* enjoyed considerable success abroad (in Germany it was acclaimed as the best film of 1928), nowhere did it achieve the resounding success of *Potemkin*. Nonetheless, through both the film itself and Eisenstein's subsequent theoretical analysis based on it, the concept of the 'intellectual film' was launched throughout the world.

1928

Even while immersed in the montage for *October*, Eisenstein's thoughts were running ahead to the potentialities it opened up. Since the 'intellectual film' was possible, why not a screen presentation of Marx's *Das Kapital*? At intervals between October 1927 and March 1928 he considered the possibility. He envisaged it as a film about the dialectical method that would raise the cinematographic language embryonically present in *October* into 'the realms of philosophy'. In this direction, he believed, lay the theme for the film of the future. Before branching into this virgin territory, however, Eisenstein considered a year or more's preparatory study essential. His subsequent decision to defer the project in favour of something of greater immediacy was the result, partly of Stalin's 'suggestion', imparted to him during a conversation in the spring of 1929, partly his conviction that the theme could be successfully approached only when sound-film techniques were mastered.

Meanwhile Eisenstein's position in the Soviet cinema had become distinctly precarious. He was in conflict with *Lef*. Though the 'leftists' meetings had ceased, the chief mentors of *Novy Lef* summoned him to a meeting at Tretyakov's home in March 1928. There Mayakovsky insistently tried to persuade him against breaking with *Lef*, while Eisenstein put his equally adamant view that it held no future. It was a period of bitter experiences, which he confided in a letter to Moussinac:

I am certain that cinema 'shall be'. That it will come from Russia. . . . But so what!

And I do not want to disillusion you in any way; we must always have something towards which we can turn our eyes in order to revitalize our faith, but beware of rose-coloured glasses!

We're not living a continuous holiday either! . . . It's just that I'm afraid, very much afraid. . . . We aren't rebels any more. We're becoming lazy priests.

I have the impression that the enormous breath of 1917 which gave birth to our cinema is blowing itself out. . . . We're getting classical – 'artistic!'

The bleeding wounds have healed – no more chances to scream loud and rip old film traditions apart. . . . Cream puffs instead of naked hate. . . . We're losing our teeth. We aren't fighters any more. . . . We're losing our teeth because we don't need them now: no need to chew what's going to come back up whole. And it would be very hard not to vomit when the current is carrying you straight to the island of the golden mean.

This golden mean . . . makes your stomach and guts boil! . . . If you're lording it with Jesus on the cinematographic Golgotha, I feel myself hanging at your side.

Whether as the good or bad thief, I couldn't say. (We'll see – if I give in, I will have been the bad one.)

But no matter what, there's a wound in my side!

You must never generalize about our cinema *en bloc*. . . . I am horrified to see gradually creeping into our 'avant-garde' a stultified, manneristic academy, dressed in magistrate's cap, which, while still red, is whimsically crumpled above the traditional aesthetic robes of perfect and impeccable cut. . . . It's stifling!

And it's not only the Leningrad wing which is tending towards 'classicism' – the most disgusting kind of classicism! We see this tendency in most things being done now.

And what is worse, this is the tendency of the people for whom we are working! . . . We are 'evolving' – effortlessly evolving to a point where it will again be necessary to revolutionize to the roots what has become sterile stylization instead of palpitating life and true passion. . . . Enough Jeremiads. . . . Don't let's abandon optimism!

To arms, citizens! Butt the stomach of anyone opposed to what we *must* do![14]

This letter gives some idea of Eisenstein's problems and state of mind at that time, as well as of his reasons for choosing the path he did in his following film, *The General Line*. But it also reaffirms his fighting spirit in the face of such difficulties – difficulties which were to increase and multiply as time went by.

This energetic fighting spirit characterized Eisenstein's attitude not only to his own creative work, but also towards the difficulties experienced by other artists at that time. Dovzhenko is a case in point. A year after becoming famous through *Potemkin*, Eisenstein received an urgent telephone request from the Ukrainian Cinematographic Office to attend the preview of Dovzhenko's film *Zvenigora*, which was causing much official bewilderment. As the film started, Eisenstein too was taken aback – 'God Almighty! What can't you see here!' – and dreaded the moment he would have to comment on it, only to become more and more absorbed as it unfolded. When the lights went up, he was lavish in his congratulations to Dovzhenko and full of enthusiastic praise for the film in talking with Pudovkin and other film people present. Thus Eisenstein played a large part in launching Dovzhenko on his film career. And later, though immersed in the editing of *The General Line*, he broke off work to attend the première of Dovzhenko's next film, *Arsenal*. With Pudovkin as the third, they held a splendid party over some sandwiches and bottles of mineral water, launching into high-spirited impersonations of da Vinci (Eisenstein), Michelangelo (Dovzhenko) and Raphael (Pudovkin). It was a riotous game, in and out of upturned tables and chairs, that went on till dawn. Subsequently Eisenstein's relations with Dovzhenko became more sporadic, but even then Eisenstein remained as generous as ever. A characteristic gesture, made when he was desperately short of money before leaving Hollywood, is recalled by Ivor Montagu:

Our financial situation was near the border line. Of the last resources that remained to the unit, Eisenstein . . . insisted on telegraphing one hundred dollars to Dovzhenko, who had just arrived in Germany on holiday. He remembered the shifts the three had been driven to when they had started their trip outside the border a year earlier, and Dovzhenko was one of the few Soviet film-makers he admired and recognized as a peer.[15]

Several years later, at a particularly difficult period in Eisenstein's career, Dovzhenko showed no hesitation in making a crude public attack on his former generous benefactor; and in his autobiographical notes all Eisenstein's initial help was glossed over in the single remark: 'The film was well received by the specialists.' This was just one of the ways that Eisenstein was to suffer at the hands of his fellows. He was never forgiven for his sarcasm by those who felt slighted by it, nor for his generosity by those to whom he had been generous.

With Eisenstein everything was ignited by an inner fire, at the centre of which burned his passion for art. He had absolute faith in its power, and when André Malraux later visited Russia and confided his dispirited misgivings to Eisenstein – 'If I worked here I'd be ashamed to be merely writing books' – Eisenstein was full of encouragement. Passionately he tried to convince Malraux of the epoch-making value of his novels.

Similarly, when faced with daunting opposition to his own creative work, Eisenstein decided not to give up the struggle but to continue on his innovating course.

The General Line

In June 1928 Eisenstein resumed work on *The General Line*; this is the working title by which it is still known in the West, though it was in fact renamed *Old and New* before release.

Again he intended the film to be an experiment – but this time a clear and simple experiment intelligible to a mass audience. In its first form the film had been a lament about the conditions in the villages. But in the intervening period the agricultural situation – not to mention the Party line on it – had changed radically, and, according to Eisenstein's colleagues, he had to make many substantial alterations. Eisenstein himself stated that the film paid for the stoppage 'with its shattered vertebrae and broken spine'. Of the original conception there remained only the first three reels, and the agitation scene in the second part.

For the first time Eisenstein included a heroine, Marfa Lapkina, as the focus of the film's events. These tell the propaganda tale of a peasant community's development from a state of chronic backwardness and poverty into a flourishing collective farm, thanks to Marfa Lapkina and the district agronomist. Together they combat the peasants' ignorance and fire them with a new collective and progressive spirit through the material agencies of a cream-separator (throughout this period he had a poster for an American make pinned on the wall of his room), a tractor and a bull. These three symbols – two representing mechanized modern life and one natural fertility – loomed large in Eisenstein's first vision of the film as the foci of the drama.

The scene of the bull's mating with the cow – an unprecedented and fantastic one, superb in its primitive barbarism – was to become a key scene in the film. Clasping in her hand the money saved up to buy the bull, Marfa falls asleep and dreams. The sun rises, grows larger and then, suddenly, turns into a bull. This, too, grows ever larger until it fills the whole heavens. A deluge of milk begins inundating the village, the land and seemingly the universe. And out of the fertilized ground appear superb livestock breeders, pigs, hens. . . . Suddenly the village is preparing for a wedding. Young maidens await the bride with bouquets of flowers. After a long wait the bride appears, festively decked: she is a cow. Then the groom: the bull, enormous and virile. During their mating, the earth begins to tremble, fireworks inundate the screen and then dissolve to take the form of numberless cattle.

The cream-separator, too, becomes a symbol of fertility, notably in the memorable scene where the peasants crowd round it awaiting the first drop of cream to materialize. And here, too, the drop is dramatically magnified to huge proportions, while the white liquid begins to gush, not only from the machine but from the fountain that takes its place as a symbol.

The three central symbols of the film are thrown into relief by opposing symbols of ignorance and poverty. The cream-separator sequence, for instance, is contrasted with the religious procession – a feature retained from the original film – in which the peasants despairingly invoke rain to end the drought. Eisenstein's repeated reference to liquids (the milk and the rain) is interesting: the element of earth and the element of water, continuously intermingling, themselves constitute an essential theme of the film. Another symbolic element, pointing up the misery of peasant life in the past, comes in the early scene where the brothers divide between them all the property they are left, including the house itself.*

Another influence on the film's conception was Eisenstein's interest in forms of ecstasy. This, in turn, was an extension of his interest in the emotional that had absorbed him since *Potemkin*. Eisenstein's theory was that intense feeling could only be generated by a sudden upsurge of the emotions, all of them directed towards a single purpose. Whereas in *Potemkin* this had been a grandiose one – no less than a mutiny – in *The General Line* it was the cream-separator, an everyday object of little importance *per se*, but of enormous importance for everything it signifies: namely, the hopes and fears of the peasants as the instrument in transforming their lives. Eisenstein's aim, as Jean Mitry recalls it, was

to endow with emotive qualities something which in itself does not, or appears not to, possess them . . . to attain a state of ecstasy, a sort of beatific state through which the spectator – his consciousness as it were suspended – enters into a condition of immediate receptiveness and takes part emotionally (and hence mentally) in the action represented. He had visions of a sort of hypnosis through film.[16]

It was in this sense (and not in any religious sense, since in all his films he bitingly satirizes religious mysticism) that Eisenstein was preoccupied with forms of ecstasy.† His interest in religion extended only to its outward ceremony and trappings as sources of ecstatic manifestations: 'My atheism resembles that of Anatole France – it is indivisibly bound up with the visible forms of the cult.'[17]

Few details about the shooting of *The General Line* are available, but from its start, in the summer of 1928, it seems to have been dogged by bad weather conditions. To escape the ice and snow of Rostov-on-Don, the unit moved first to Baku, then to the Kura Lowland and on towards the Persian frontier. There torrential rain and thick mud again stopped work, and again the unit had to move on, this time to the province of Ryazan, then east again to Penza. . . .

---

* On the origins of this scene, Jay Leyda notes: 'This scene was suggested, indirectly, by Shub, via Shklovsky: "I told Alexandrov that E. Shub wanted to film Byelorussian life without staging anything, and in order to show a genuine isba, she did not want to build one in the studio, but to take a real one and simply saw it in half. Alexandrov replied, 'It would be good if the sawing itself were to be shown.' " (*The Realities*, 1927.) Apparently this exchange lingered in Alexandrov's memory, for that is how the wasteful divisions between the sons of a peasant's family are shown in *Old and New*: the family house is literally sawn in half.'

† Eisenstein became an atheist only after 'a period of hysterical, puerile religiosity and juvenile sentiments of mysticism'. Father Nikolai Pereshvalsky, the religious mentor of his childhood, impressed him deeply during that time by the overwhelmingly dramatic way he officiated at religious rituals. This, Eisenstein thought, probably lay at the root of his attraction to church spectacle and ornate religious vestments. 'After that, I became an atheist.'

Eisenstein has summed up his approach to the film as 'an attempt to depict in an interesting way the daily round of peasant husbandry'.[18]

Finding the principal actors was a nightmare. As Pera Attasheva recorded it:

The filming went on but the heroine had not been found. For two months the directors of *The General Line* combed railway stations, night-lodgings, factories. They rode through the country. They summoned women for inspection by ringing church-bells. They looked at thousands of faces and tested some of them.

No heroine.

In this extremity Eisenstein even decided on a step directly contrary to all his principles originally formulated on beginning this film – he decided to test actresses for the role. Interviews of actresses began. Nothing came of this. Actresses looked insulted when they were asked whether they could milk a cow, or plough, or drive a tractor. They would proudly answer, 'No!' – and that would end the interview.[19]

At last, quite by chance, the right person was found: Marfa Lapkina, an illiterate peasant from Konstantinovka, who needed much persuasion to leave her farm work for the filming.

In the course of shooting, Eisenstein's youthful experience near Kholm after the supper with the Pudov family came back to him with force – those strange close-ups: the enormous ear and neck of the fat kulak, the gigantic nose, the hand hanging limply over the mug of *kvas*. All these, as we have seen, 'constantly insinuated themselves into the saraband of the landscape and peasant settings' in the film.

On occasions Eisenstein directed the filming with a view to parodying well-known films. One variation of the final scene, distinctly lyrical in character, was based on Chaplin's *A Woman of Paris*. Jay Leyda has also pointed out how the famous grotesque satirical scene of the bureaucrats' allocation of the tractors parodied the similar, but serious, office incident in Pudovkin's *The End of Saint Petersburg*. A parody of a western, and even of Buster Keaton's *The Three Ages*, also figured in the original version of Eisenstein's film.

Once again there was the familiar hectic rush. Shooting went on twelve hours a day, sometimes with as many as five cameras working simultaneously. The location scenes were completed in August 1928, when the unit returned to Moscow for the studio shooting. Filming was completed in November, but Eisenstein has stated that when allowances have been made for preliminary work, travel and rain, the actual shooting was done in a mere 120 days. (Parallel with the intensive work of this period, Eisenstein began his mammoth theoretical writings, analysing his works and the general aesthetic conclusions to be drawn from them.* The purpose of these writings,

---

* Towards the end of his life, Eisenstein wrote: 'I accumulated piles of conclusions and detailed observations on artistic methods, since I knew without a doubt that, as long as I had not elaborated my own system, there was very little probability of my consenting to rest peacefully in my grave.'

according to Jay Leyda, was 'to find and define the reasons behind the thoughts and acts of excited creativity, to prepare himself for *next* steps'.[20])

During work on the montage – again a long and exhausting process – Eisenstein came up against a multiplicity of problems. When hopelessly stumped over complicated sequences – probably including that of the cream-separator – he often turned back to his earlier films, trying to discover the 'secrets' of his previous artistic solutions. He ran through the Odessa steps sequence, for instance, a number of times. It may have been seeing the Red Flag incident in *Potemkin* again that inspired him to revert to the use of colour in a black and white film – this time by inserting short lengths of film painted with abstract splashes of colour in the bull's wedding sequence in an attempt 'to impregnate the narrative with feeling'.

Another powerful influence on Eisenstein's montage ideas was the Japanese Kabuki Theatre, which visited Moscow in 1928 while he was working on the film. Eisenstein was fascinated by the Japanese actors, and wrote an enthusiastic article on their methods, which directly inspired some of his original montage techniques in *The General Line*. But there was also a link with Eisenstein's own previous ideas. As early as 1923, it will be remembered, in his article on what he then termed 'attractions', he had theorized on 'the unity of the theatre', equating for their dramatic effect a roll on the drums with Romeo's soliloquy. In the Kabuki actors' methods Eisenstein saw a practical demonstration of his previously expounded principles through what he now termed 'the monistic ensemble':

Sound – movement – space – voice here *do not accompany* (nor even parallel) each other, but function *as elements of equal significance.* . . . We actually 'hear movement' and 'see sound'.[21]

And so, still deeply impressed by the Kabuki Theatre, Eisenstein worked on the montage in a 'creative ecstasy', as he described it, allowing the pieces of film themselves to transmit to him their inner meaning, 'hearing and feeling' them. Once again the discovery of the mechanics of his method of creation came after the 'creative ecstasy', at the far from poetic point when he had to review the finished film at the cutting-table in order to shorten it. This was no moment of inspiration, but a simple technical matter. As he ran the film through, he was astounded: the montage for the religious procession struck him as weird, there being no rational explanation, it seemed, for his un-orthodox arrangement of the shots. Only at this stage did he begin to discover the deeper implications of the techniques he had used. One discovery was of a 'filmic fourth dimension', through what he termed 'the visual overtone'. And this fourth dimension, or 'four-dimensional space-time continuum'[22] – Eisenstein had read Einstein – would, he predicted, soon become a familiar feature of cinematography.

What was the 'visual overtone' and, by extension, 'overtonal montage'? Eisenstein explained it as 'the furthest development along the line of tonal montage' − the montage method in which the arrangement of shots is based 'on the dominant'; that is, they are arranged according to their dominant feature, be it one of length or tempo. The emotive effect with 'tonal' montage derived − it will be remembered from *Potemkin* − from the juxtaposition of two shots with conflicting dominants (conflicting from the viewpoint of their graphic value, the length of the shot, and so on). For the mist sequence in *Potemkin* Eisenstein had used 'tonal', or 'melodic emotive', montage. 'Overtonal montage', however, was based not merely on the basic 'dominant', but on a whole series of similar vibrations − or, in other words, the various overtones and undertones:

In combinations which exploit *these collateral vibrations* − which is nothing less than *the filmed material itself* − we can achieve, completely analogous with music, *the visual overtonal complex of the shot.*

This was the method that Eisenstein discovered he had used in *The General Line*; the montage had taken

as its guide the total stimulation through all stimuli. That is the original montage complex within the shot, arising from the collision and combination of the individual stimuli inherent in it.

Using an analogy from music − from which he derived the term 'overtonal montage' − Eisenstein explained that all these stimulative factors coming together form a unity which determines the 'feeling' of the shot; there is thus a 'physiological quality' which acts directly on the spectators' senses, in the same way as music constructed 'on a twofold use of overtones − not the *classicism* of Beethoven, but the *physiological* quality of Debussy and Scriabin'.

Thus Eisenstein had arrived at a superior form of the polyphony which has been discussed earlier. An example of 'overtonal montage' from *The General Line*, the sequence of the religious procession, will help clarify his somewhat complicated thesis. Eisenstein described this sequence as being linked

not merely through one indication − movement, or light values, or stage in the exposition of the plot, or the like − but through a *simultaneous advance* of a multiple series of lines, each maintaining an independent compositional course and each contributing to the total compositional course of the sequence.[23]

He distinguished seven separate lines:

1. The line of heat, increasing from shot to shot.
2. The line of changing close-ups, mounting in plastic intensity.
3. The line of mounting ecstasy, shown through the dramatic content of the close-ups.

4. The line of women's 'voices' (faces of the singers).

5. The line of men's 'voices' (faces of the singers).

6. The line of those who kneel under the passing ikons (increasing in tempo). This counter-current gave movement to a larger counter-stream which was threaded through the primary theme – of the bearers of ikons, crosses and banners.

7. The line of grovelling, uniting both streams in the general movement of the sequence, 'from heaven to the dust'. From the radiant pinnacles of the crosses and banners against the sky to the prostrate figures beating their heads in the dust. . . .

The montage achieves its total effect through 'an uninterrupted interweaving of these diverse themes into one unified movement'. For this Eisenstein intensified the content of every 'overtonal resonator'. The sequence was, in fact, itself a resonance from a childhood experience during the torrid summer of 1914, when he had been present at the dedication procession of the Staraya Russa Church. 'This vivid procession provided the basis for my procession in the film *Old and New*.'

A simpler example is that of the mowing contest: in this the different shots make up 'a single mowing movement from one side of the frame to the other'. Eisenstein was amused during this sequence to see 'the more impressionable members of the audience quietly rocking from side to side at an increasing pace as the pieces were accelerated by shortening. The effect was the same as that of a percussion and brass band playing a simple march tune.'[24]

Though perhaps the least well known of Eisenstein's films today, *The General Line* was particularly important in his development as a film-maker. First, it marked the beginning of his preoccupation with the potentialities of colour (the colour tone as an 'overtonal resonator' was an integral element in 'overtonal montage').* Second, for all the failures inherent in any experiment, *The General Line* represented the culmination of a succession of works of art and theoretic deductions. With it, in short, Eisenstein had reached the ultimate point to which the silent film could be developed and had arrived at the brink of sound cinematography – the next step being his celebrated vertical and audio-tonal montage, which had been foreshadowed as far back as *Potemkin*. Indeed, it was while making *The General Line*, in the summer of 1928, that Eisenstein wrote his famous manifesto (signed also by Pudovkin and Alexandrov) expounding the idea of 'an orchestral counterpoint of visual and aural images', which still stands today as the basis of sound-film aesthetics. He even projected turning *The General Line* into a sound film, in collaboration with Meisel. In fact he saw the future of the cinema only in terms of sound.[25]

Eisenstein's innovations in *The General Line* did not stop here. Though no attempt is made to list them all in this biography, mention should be made of one other accomplishment of the film: Eisenstein's perfecting of the montage

* In the Eisenstein archive there is a manuscript oddly listed as a 'description of a method of colour filming and of light phonograph [sic] invented by Eisenstein', and dated 1928–29.

During the making of *Bezhin Meadow*

within a shot, or, as he himself had termed it, the *mise-en-cadre*. With this film, composition in depth – that is a shot in which background as well as foreground action is clearly in focus and both play a simultaneous and coordinated role in the drama – was perfected. The necessity for such interplay within the shot arose out of the very essence of 'overtonal montage'. But the emotional sources were those childhood impressions left by Poe's story, his love of Degas, and his reading of Pushkin, Gogol and Dostoyevsky. ('From the storehouse of creation nothing is completely lost,' Eisenstein once wrote.) Everything pointed towards the necessity, and possibility, of focusing on the different aspects of the event *simultaneously*. And this, in *The General Line*, was developed into a clearly defined film technique, which Eisenstein was to exploit further and to magnificent effect in his Mexican film and, more particularly, in *Ivan the Terrible*. The acclaim-winning device used by Gregg Toland in his work for Wyler is thus to be found more than fifteen years earlier in *The General Line* and Eisenstein's theoretical analyses.

Much later, in tracing retrospectively his creative path, Eisenstein examined the evolution of his absorption with *mise-en-scène*:

From the vast variety of elements that go to make up the production, the director will always have a special preference for one in particular. . . . In my case, in the theatre it was the *mise-en-scène*. *Mise-en-scène* in the narrowest sense of the term – the combination of temporal and spatial elements in the interaction of the performers on stage. I was always fascinated by the interweaving into one harmonious whole of the independent lines of the action, by the naturally separated tones of their rhythmic designs, and by their spatial mutations. The *mise-en-scène* was not only the favourite part of my work, but also invariably the point of departure for presenting the scene; with me the scene arose out of the *mise-en-scène*, its component parts developing later. In passing from theatre to film, the *mise-en-scène* was transmuted to conform with the legitimate demands of the *mise-en-cadre* (by which should be understood not only *the arrangement within a shot, but also the arrangement of the shots amongst themselves*) and became the object of a new passion – montage.[26]

Referring to the further growth of this absorption, at the stage immediately following the one we have reached – that is, the sound film – Eisenstein went on:

Complicating itself in a sense, the problem developed in the direction of audio-visual counterpoint in sound cinematography. Changing its character, *mise-en-scène* developed in the realm of dramaturgy, where the same interweaving and cross-cuttings are found, this time between individual persons or individual features, and between the motifs of a particular personage. Orthodox, illustrative *mise-en-scène* of the old school, with its extremely simple spatial schemes, restricted in a precise system of rhythmically calculated time, always remains, through the extremely complicated means of counterpoint, the starting-point for a prototype of movement; the reason for its extreme complexity in cinematography is the necessity of welding into a whole elements which have no common term of comparison – beginning with the contradictory pair, the image and the sound.

After the film had been completed in April 1929, and even as late as the stage when copies were already being made from the cut negative, as Alexandrov relates, Eisenstein was forced to remake the ending on orders from Stalin. Consequently two months of the spring of 1929 found him chasing from village to village in the Northern Caucasus filming the substitute ending, which he caustically termed 'a kind of emotional semi-epilogue'.* (In April, nonetheless, he found time to write several theoretical studies, including 'A Dialectical Approach to Film Form'.) Yet even the new ending did not wholly satisfy the official pundits; hence the change of title from *The General Line* to *Old and New* – implicitly dissociating the film from official policy on agriculture.

Meanwhile Eisenstein had for some time been preparing for a journey abroad. Following their visit to Moscow in 1926, Douglas Fairbanks and Mary Pickford had been trying to arrange a contract for him in America with United Artists, and since 1928 Sovkino had joined in the negotiations. Eisen-

---

* Both versions of the ending happily survive. Jay Leyda mentions another variant which, it seems, is no longer extant.

stein himself hankered after visiting the United States, attracted not by the glamour of Hollywood but by the opportunity of getting to know the country and, first and foremost, the new developments there in sound-film techniques. He had been trying to press the arrangements both through personal correspondence and through contacts with visitors to Moscow – among them the painter, Diego Rivera, who aroused Eisenstein's interest in Mexico, and the American novelist Theodore Dreiser, whose *An American Tragedy* was to become linked with one episode in Eisenstein's personal tragedy as an artist. Negotiations dragged on for what seemed an eternity. At the end of 1928 Joseph Schenck of Metro-Goldwyn-Mayer let Eisenstein know of his wish to invite him to America the following year; but at the beginning of 1929 Eisenstein commented wryly: 'I won't really be sure whether I'm going until I'm on my way back home from there!'[27]

Eventually the much-hoped-for journey materialized. On 19 August 1929, without even waiting to see the reception given to *The General Line*, which was to have a preliminary showing in September and its première on 7 October, Eisenstein set off with Tisse and Alexandrov on travels that were to take them through Europe and America.

7. Abroad

Amer savoir, celui qu'on tire du voyage!
Le monde, monotone et petit, aujourd'hui,
Hier, demain, toujours, nous fait voir notre image:
Une oasis d'horreur dans un désert d'ennui!
BAUDELAIRE

As he set off from the Soviet Union, Eisenstein's most precious possessions were a copy of *The General Line* for showing in Berlin and twenty-five dollars in cash. This was the princely sum that he, like his two companions, had been allotted for a journey that was planned to take in Germany, a cinematographic congress in Switzerland and an engagement in Hollywood.

Berlin – La Sarraz – Berlin

First on the itinerary was Berlin, where Eisenstein planned to adapt his film for German audiences and collaborate with Meisel once again on a sound synchronization. A book on theoretical problems of cinematography, with the unfinished manuscript of which Eisenstein was armed, had also been mooted.

Berlin gave him a magnificent reception, marred only by the news awaiting Eisenstein there that Joseph Schenck's offer of a Hollywood contract had meanwhile fallen through.

With his customary all-embracing interest, Eisenstein renewed his acquaintance with the life of Berlin, where on all sides he noted 'the chaos and confusion of post-war Germany'. He also renewed contacts made during his visit three years before. One of these was Jannings, who, on the occasion of their first meeting on the set for Murnau's *Faust* at Tempelhof in 1926, had received Eisenstein somewhat high-handedly (despite the warm letter of recommendation he brought from Egon Erwin Kisch), imperiously motioning Eisenstein from the heights where he was being filmed. Now, in 1929, the boot was on the other foot, Jannings practically begging Eisenstein to make a film about Potemkin – the real Prince Potemkin, of course, Catherine the Great's one-eyed favourite: 'I'd give one of my eyes if you'd make this film.'

From Berlin, Eisenstein, Tisse and Alexandrov left for Switzerland for the First International Congress of Independent Cinematography. At the frontier, however, Eisenstein's party was refused permission to enter the country by the Swiss authorities; only after twenty-four hours, and an intervention on Eisenstein's behalf, was the refusal rescinded. The congress was held from 3 to 7 September at the Château of La Sarraz near Lausanne, the estate of the cinema enthusiast, Mme Hélène de Mandrot, who was sponsoring it financially. 'La belle châtelaine', as the congress delegates always addressed her, had a secret weakness for the Russians – it was she who had vouched for them with the Swiss authorities and secured their entry into the country; and on their departure she was to sigh, 'Oh! Those Bolsheviks! . . . The only true gentlemen!'

The congress, organized on the initiative of Robert Aron and Janine Bouissounouse, was intended to bring together from all over the world filmmakers eager to establish an independent film industry unfettered by commercial interests, and to lay the foundations for an International Film-making Cooperative with its headquarters in Paris. It was attended by the most varied selection of international cinema personalities, but 'the biggest star', in the words of *Le Cinéma Suisse*, 'was the celebrated Eisenstein'.

The high spot of the congress turned out to be the Thursday, officially designated a rest day, when the delegates let down their hair to make a light-hearted film, directed by Eisenstein and Hans Richter, symbolizing the aims of the congress. From six in the morning, under the alarmed but benevolent gaze of its owner, the château was turned upside down: priceless medieval objects were commandeered as props, and the splendid lawns and flower-beds trampled mercilessly underfoot. Janine Bouissounouse, dressed in white and her bosom stuffed with two film reels to personify 'Independent Cinematography', was fastened with rusty chains unearthed from the cellars to the château's monumental chimney stack, whence, captive of the commercial industry, she had to be rescued by the army of 'independents'. The comedy developed with much horseplay on all sides. Isaacs, playing a big-business tycoon in Balázs's 'commercial' army, sweated horribly under a heavy suit of medieval armour decked with ostrich feathers, while he parried the blows of Alfred de Marset's sword. Meanwhile Mme de Mandrot plied the thirsty 'knights' with cold drinks, and even came up with sheets from her wedding trousseau for a ghost sequence. One of these she swathed round Eisenstein, while he was dressing Moussinac as d'Artagnan. In this role,

Moussinac braved the lances of Balázs's army to storm the château roof and rescue the 'independent cinema' – a feat that nearly ended in disaster when the tiles started to slip and Moussinac only just avoided falling headlong, with the filming Tisse in tow. Eisenstein later took over d'Artagnan's costume to pose, lance in hand, as Don Quixote astride his projection-horse. Jean-Georges Auriol, brandishing a copy of the *Revue du Cinéma* as a banner, joined in the fray with his typewriter-turned-machine-gun. In the culminating sequence a Japanese member of the congress, personifying 'the commercial film', went through the full ritual of a hara-kiri. Unfortunately this short film was lost, apparently by Richter.

The resolution adopted by the congress (published only relatively recently) records that, despite conflicting views among the delegates, 'the congress raised . . . as an absolute principle the difference in practice and spirit between the independent cinema and the commercial cinema in any shape or form'.

After the congress, Eisenstein left with his colleagues for Zurich where he had been invited to make a film in support of the campaign for legalized abortion – a theme on which Tisse had already made a film in Switzerland. In the event, Eisenstein turned down the offer: 'Let me abort all Zurich, then I'm interested; but abortion for only one woman, definitely no!' Instead he gave several of a planned series of lectures before the Swiss authorities again raised objections and requested him to leave the country.

Back in Berlin, Eisenstein became one of the city's most fêted celebrities: he broadcast on the radio, formed the centre of conversation at the Romanisches Café, and was sought out by intellectuals and cultural figures. He, in turn, was interested in everything, wanting to explore everywhere – even a haunt of lesbians – and to meet everyone: film-makers, painters, actors, musicians, dancers. . . . He talked with the writer Ernst Toller, with the film-directors Pabst, Fritz Lang, Murnau and Josef von Sternberg, the theatrical producer Erwin Piscator, with Dr Hanns Sachs, a disciple of Freud – whom Eisenstein had avidly studied – with Magnus Hirschfeld, director of the Institut für Geschlechts Wissenschaft, with Brecht, Georg Grosz and Pirandello. At his meeting with Pirandello in an Italian restaurant in Charlottenburg, the Italian writer expounded enthusiastically on the dramatic role of the narrator, firing Eisenstein with the possibilities his ideas opened up for the cinema.

With Meisel he again took up the question of setting his last film to music, but again without definite result. Hans Feld, who saw Eisenstein frequently at this time and got to know him well, detected, as did many of his close friends, a deep inner sadness beneath his humour and sarcastic wit. The nature and cause of this despondency that sometimes overwhelmed him, and often spilled over into the tragic episodes in his films, are uncertain. But the truth will probably emerge with the publication of Eisenstein's personal papers, which are believed to include brutally searching analyses of his innermost feelings and motivations.

During the Berlin period there was talk of Eisenstein's making a film of Albert Londres's book, *Le Chemin de Buenos Aires* (the English edition of which had an introduction by Theodore Dreiser). But although in Paris he returned to this idea, and even did some work on it with Ivor Montagu, it was to prove just another of his many unrealized projects, as was a dramatized life of Basil Zaharoff, mooted shortly after, and broached again in France, England and the United States. This latter project was still in Eisenstein's mind when he returned from the United States in 1932, and in an interview published in *Berliner Tageblatt* he spoke of it as a matter of burning interest for him: 'I would like to create one day, on film, a kind of modern *Götterdämmerung*, a visual history of the deaths of the Titans, of Basil Zaharoff, Löwenstein, Krüger, Deterding – a kind of dynamic Pergamon frieze, possibly with Richard Wagner's music post-synchronized.'

At the invitation of the workers' cinema club, Volksfilmverband, Eisenstein left Berlin for a three day visit to Hamburg. Ten cinemas had been hired for a Sunday morning showing of *October*, but so great was the demand for tickets that thousands had to be turned away. At one of the cinemas Eisenstein gave a short talk before the performance and met his audience afterwards. The rest of his time in Hamburg he spent exploring the city and meeting cinema enthusiasts, whom he fired with the idea of bringing out a film magazine. This later appeared under the title *Sozialistische Filmkritik*.

On his return to Berlin Eisenstein was unwell and forced to delay his departure for a while. He mentioned, apparently for the first time, a cardiac weakness – according to Victor Shklovsky, the phragma behind the left and right ventricles had never grown properly – which had troubled him earlier, but which he tried to exclude from his thoughts. It is the only mention at this period of the heart condition – and the fear of death it implied – that clearly linked up with the infarct which was to kill him less than twenty years later.

Paris and England

Early in November, Eisenstein arrived in Paris and immediately set about exploring everything, and inhaling the atmosphere of places already familiar from his reading. From dawn to dusk, driven on by a passionate and insatiable curiosity, he systematically toured the streets, scouring the Seine bookstalls, the cellars of the Rue Bonaparte in search of pictures, and the Saint-Germain district. Next he visited Fontainebleau, Compiègne and Versailles, before returning to the city and making further foraging expeditions in the Foire aux Puces, the antique shops of Saint-Sulpice, and the back-streets of Montmartre. On one occasion he visited 'a special resort' on the Rue Blondel, where, as Ivor Montagu recalls, 'the hostesses, all middle-aged and plain but with a special talent, sat beside us on the red plush sofas but without clothes, chatting calmly of their husbands and children and kitchens and how much they earned in the working day, until the time came to display this talent, which was an ability to pick up coins from the edge of the table with an organ not usually so employed'.[2] Nightclubs, café haunts of young painters and writers, even the salons of the social élite – all were grist to Eisenstein's mill. He ended by being paraded as a celebrity, one aristocrat congratulating him on his 'brilliant interpretation of the role of Potemkin'.

And, of course, there were the museums – the Hôtel de Cluny, the Musée Carnavalet, the Louvre – which often provided him with the opportunity of verifying his ideas about art. Jean Mitry, who accompanied him to the Louvre one day, recalls Eisenstein's words on gazing raptly at Leonardo da Vinci's *Virgin of the Rocks*:

Look at it. I *know* that the sense of balance, harmony and perfection that this work conveys to me comes partly from the geometric arrangement of line and form, from the positioning of the figures and setting. . . . Yet this knowledge in no way diminishes the intense emotion, the feeling of ecstasy that overwhelms me. The logic behind it makes everything clearer, but only *after* the emotional response. It does not detract from the feeling, it illuminates it. . . . Add to these mathematics all the associations evoked, with greater or lesser clarity, by the work's symbolism: the transfigured, idealized figures are no longer people, but incarnate ideas. And everything is symbol: the glance is a symbol, the gesture is a symbol, and the attitudes . . . and the setting. . . . And as all this (the overall impression, the emotion) is instinctively carried over into the content, you can see with what emotional richness it is instantly amplified.

This is how a film image should be interpreted, this is my reason for constructing them plastically, with this aim: to amplify the meaning of the content through all the 'harmonic resonators', through all the symbols contained in the particular form through which our eyes perceive the 'given image'.[3]

Thus Eisenstein's outings, in Paris, as elsewhere, were no mere sight-seeing trips, but occasions for comparing and enriching his artistic ideas. His comments on Leonardo's canvas should be recalled when we come to analyse *Alexander Nevsky* and *Ivan the Terrible*, made over ten years later.

Paris gave Eisenstein the opportunity of getting to know a number of personalities: Henri Barbusse, F. T. Marinetti, Abel Gance, Gordon Craig, Jean Cocteau, Fernand Léger and Blaise Cendrars, whose novel, *L'Or*, he discussed adapting to the screen. He was visited by Chaliapin – on the unlikely recommendation of a jeweller in the Rue de la Paix – with a proposal to collaborate on a film about Don Quixote (later made by Pabst) in which he wanted to play the Don. A further proposal for him to make a film came from the celebrated star Yvette Guilbert. His most important meeting, however, was with James Joyce, whom he had long admired as a 'colossus' of literature for breaking down traditional literary barriers and creating his own technique for expressing internal mental and emotional processes. Eisenstein's first impression of Joyce, whom he found eaten up by the dreadful disease that had brought him to the brink of blindness, was of a modest and jocular man totally dedicated to his work. They spent hours together at subsequent meetings, when Joyce sometimes read from his works or discussed examples of interior monologue from *Ulysses*, firing Eisenstein with enthusiasm for his technique of 'unfolding the display of events simultaneously with the particular manner in which these events pass through the consciousness and feelings, the associations and emotions'[4] of Leopold Bloom. Joyce, for his part, was fascinated by ideas Eisenstein had evolved over the previous five years for conveying the interior monologue on the screen, where, he was convinced, it would find even fuller expression. For only the sound film, Eisenstein believed, was capable of reconstructing 'all phases and all specifics of the thought process'. His montage visions were dizzying:

Like thought, they would sometimes proceed with visual images. With sound. Synchronized or non-synchronized. Then as sounds. Formless. Or with sound-images: with objectively representational sounds. . . .
Then in passionate disconnected speech. Nothing but nouns. Or nothing but verbs. Then interjections. With zigzags of aimless shapes, whirling along with these in synchronization.
Then racing visual images over complete silence.
Then linked with polyphonic sounds. Then polyphonic images. Then both at once.
Then interpolated into the outer course of action, then interpolating elements of the outer action into the inner monologue.[5]

Joyce understood. Though almost totally blind, he wanted to see parts of *Potemkin* and *October*. So impressed was he by his talks with Eisenstein that he commented to a friend that if *Ulysses* were ever to be filmed, only two people were capable of directing it – Walter Ruttmann or Eisenstein.*

During his stay in Paris, Eisenstein discussed the possibilities of making a film for one of the most influential film companies, at whose invitation he had come to France. But he was unable to agree with the producers. He was up against the commercial cinema – and this time not in fun, as in the La Sarraz parody. The proposition was that he should make a 'mass-appeal' film, using a young actress in an alluring role. Eisenstein was dumbfounded and able only to blurt out: 'But I don't use actors. . . . Actors are too artificial!' Then, accustomed to plain speaking, he countered the producers' objections furiously:

How could you suppose for one moment that I would give up my ideas? Doesn't my success in France rest entirely on their realization? Why do you think the showings of *Potemkin* are packed out?

* In 1967 it was filmed by Joseph Strick.

Meanwhile the more enterprising Alexandrov had succeeded in getting a commission from the singer Mira Giry to make a short sound film in which she would star. Thanks to this film, the three were able to finance their stay in Paris. Eisenstein was tempted to apply his own theoretical principles to the sound-track, but la Giry would have none of it. She was interested only in furthering her own image by the usual conventional means – 'singing a sentimental song while gazing tearfully at the rain', as Eisenstein sardonically told his friends, taking off her actions as he did so. Soon bored by the restrictions, he left Alexandrov to complete the film, *Romance Sentimentale*, alone. 'You'll see,' he told Mitry, 'Tisse and I filmed some fine autumn scenes that go well enough with the romantic tone and sentimentality of the music, which was what I was after; but the rest!' Despite Eisenstein's cynical prediction, the film seems to have had a success of sorts – a success that he compared somewhat bitterly with the cool reception given to *The General Line*.

At the end of November, Eisenstein took up an invitation dating from La Sarraz to lecture to the London Film Society. In England, he discovered, *Potemkin* had created less of a stir than elsewhere abroad, largely because of the ban by the British Board of Film Censors and its consequent restriction to film clubs. Later, after his experiences of the more intransigent French censorship, Eisenstein looked back almost nostalgically on the British censors, jokingly telling his friends: 'One of them is blind and probably deals with the silent films; another is deaf and so gets the sound films; the third one chose to die during the very period that I was in London.'[6]

Eisenstein's erudition and the avant-garde nature of his theories made a powerful impact on his audiences. It was the same story wherever he went in England, the impression he made stimulating new developments in cinematographic techniques.

Once again he got to know many influential people, including Bernard Shaw, with whom he discussed the sound film, and Hans Richter, whom he had met at La Sarraz and whom he visited during his film-directing classes in his studio over Foyle's bookshop. Richter was making a film in which Eisenstein took part – as a London policeman; he evidently threw himself into the role, even improvising an amusing sort of ballet for it. Stills from this survive, and the film itself has finally been found – a gift from Richter to Eisenstein.

In London he visited the historic sights, wandered the streets, dropped into auctions and bookshops as the fancy took him, and scoured the museums. In the British Museum, exhibits relating to tragic historical figures inspired an impromptu mental montage sequence, which is interesting for the light it sheds on Eisenstein's innermost thoughts and fears at the time. The sequence comprised: a letter from Mary Stuart to Elizabeth I, complaining of the

Eisenstein as a London policeman, and (below) a souvenir for his friends on the *Revue du Cinéma*

discomforts of prison life; a draft sketch of the setting for Mary's execution; an autograph letter of Queen Victoria as a child; and another of Napoleon, written during his Egyptian campaign: 'I've been through everything. Bitterness and joy, success and defeat. A single thing now remains: to become an egotist locked up within myself.'[7] It also provides an interesting example of Eisenstein's involuntary assimilation, at both the intellectual and emotional levels simultaneously, of everything he saw.

His excursions from London took in Windsor, where he paid homage to Leonardo's notebooks and Holbein's paintings; Eton, which impressed him by the sense of history it conveyed – not least through the carved names of successive generations of schoolboys including that of Shelley; and Cambridge, where he lectured at the University. Of the Cambridge visit Professor Maurice Dobb has kindly sent me the following account:

I arranged a small party of university friends in a small house where I then lived in order to meet him; and I can remember that while Eisenstein himself was anxious to talk about Cambridge, I rather ruthlessly sat him down opposite me (surrounded by a circle of guests) and fired a series of questions at him about his own country and the Russian cinema etc. When he saw that there was no escape from this inquisition, he talked magnificently and, so far as I can remember, the audience listened to him spellbound. He did not stay very long, however, since later that evening there was a performance of a Masque of Comus in one of the colleges . . . which he was anxious to see. . . . My main impression of him was of a highly intelligent and sensitive man, with a great fund of cultural experience; physically the most impressive thing was a large head on a comparatively small body. When he started to talk (and at that time he knew English reasonably well) he talked with great animation and force, using words with great deliberation and a sense of their import and meaning. He stayed on in Cambridge for a little while after that, and would have liked to stay longer.[8]

When Eisenstein left England towards the end of December, the general impression he took away was one of changelessness and immobility:*

Hidebound, petrified, traditional and conservative. It is difficult to say what exactly gives rise to this physical sensation that you feel again when your foot touches its soil. . . . The why and wherefore of this image is not important, but only half an hour from the moment you've begun to get to know London, Cambridge, Oxford or Windsor, this image is inevitably implanted in you, causing you an almost physical pain.[9]

This impression of immobility was poles apart from the 'excessive mobility' which, for Eisenstein, characterized France. For the time being, though, it was to France, with its 'ephemeral, transient, unstable changeability', that he was returning.

* Ivor Montagu had left for America in advance to smooth the way for the team. He had left with two promises: 'G.B.S. had promised me *The Devil's Disciple* for Eisenstein if an option on it would help to get him signed up, and H.G. had done the like with *The War of the Worlds*.'

Belgium, Holland, France

Eisenstein had hoped to spend Christmas in Switzerland, but once again he was refused entry and so stayed on in Paris, revising the manuscript of some theoretical studies, until the middle of January, when he set off on yet another lecture tour.

The first stop was Antwerp, followed by a suburb of Liège, where workers who had seen a clandestine showing of *Potemkin* welcomed him warmly. He intended visiting Ostend and the ageing painter James Ensor, whose grotesque sketches he much admired; but repeated pestering by the police enforced his hurried departure for Holland. His arrival in Rotterdam was greeted by a battery of journalists and photographers who thought they were meeting Albert Einstein. Their amazement was, therefore, all the greater when Eisenstein – who from childhood had associated Holland with Van Houten chocolate, pointed bonnets, and clogs – immediately asked: 'Where are the wooden clogs?' – a naïve question that received headline coverage in the next day's papers. Following a lecture in Rotterdam, Eisenstein left for the Hague. There he was impatient to visit the Van Gogh museum where, 'as if besotted', he drank in the wealth of colour. The travelling and lectures continued: Amsterdam in January; Berlin and a meeting with Einstein; Brussels and finally back to Paris. During these travels Eisenstein wrote several articles on the peregrinations 'of Eisenstein's team', which were published in the Moscow *Kino* under the pseudonym of R. Orik.

This time his stay in the French capital was characterized by more insistent harassment from the police, culminating in a stormy incident at the Sorbonne on 17 February. Eisenstein had been invited to present selected excerpts from *The General Line* in one of the University's large lecture theatres. The Censor's permission had not been obtained for the showing as the meeting was a closed one and, as the University in any case enjoyed extra-territorial rights, no serious trouble was expected. Shortly before the appointed start, however, the organizers were informed that the showing had been banned on the orders of Chiappe (the Paris Prefect of Police who had already created difficulties for Eisenstein over his French residence permit). Eisenstein arrived to find them livid at this intervention, especially as the already over-flowing theatre was now being packed by various right-wing *agents provocateurs*, including members of the 'Camelots du Roi' organization. An estimated 3,000 people eventually crammed into a theatre with a seating capacity of a thousand. The dilemma of providing a substitute programme was solved when, at Moussinac's insistence, Eisenstein agreed to give an impromptu – and in the event highly successful – lecture on the 'intellectual film' and his own aesthetic theories and filming activities. But the highlight of the meeting was the subsequent question-and-answer session, when Eisenstein not only parried the provocative queries of his attackers with wit and skill, but had the whole audience in fits of laughter in the process. An hour and a half passed; but the audience showed no sign of tiring. Suddenly someone asked: 'Is it true that laughing's forbidden in the U.S.S.R.?' A deathly hush fell, to be broken by Eisenstein's spontaneous outburst of laughter – a laughter so contagious that it had everyone joining in. That was his answer. When Eisenstein left, his passage through the cordons of police was a triumphal one.

In the right-wing newspapers the following day the event was largely glossed over, but the comment of one of them no doubt represented the general annoyance at Eisenstein's success: 'The Bolsheviks are more dangerous with a smile on their face than with a dagger between their teeth.' Chiappe's vengeful reaction, too, was soon reflected in the difficulties experienced by Eisenstein in extending his permit to stay in France. Next came an expulsion order, which was rescinded only after concerted protests by a large number of prominent personalities.

Eisenstein's activities over the next weeks were interspersed with sightseeing visits with friends, no opportunity for which was missed. One such visit was to Verdun and the battlefields of the First World War, during which he made frequent stops, summoning up a mental picture of the frightful battles that had taken place at those particular spots. He spoke little, and fell into a deep reverie whenever still-fresh traces of the events – ruins, or a shoulder-blade that he accidentally unearthed with his foot – evoked the carnage for him. But he reverted to the epicurean pleasures of everyday life when a rest was called at an inn, devouring and praising a tasty Camembert. Next came the châteaux of the Loire, the South of France and the Riviera. Everywhere he went he amazed his travelling companions by his vast and detailed knowledge of French history, literature, architecture and culture in general.

The experiences and impressions from these travels were assimilated into that vast internal storehouse of ideas and emotions, often to reappear in some form or other in his subsequent work. In a lecture to his students some years later, for example, he recalled an incident from his trip to Marseilles:

I ran into a group in the street: an ecclesiastical dignitary of high rank from the colonies wearing a crimson cassock and, behind him, two Senegalese. Imagine the bright southern sun and, sailing towards you, a crimson-red blotch with, pacing evenly beside it, two perfectly black Senegalese. For a colour complex this was a remarkably effective composition.[10]

After Marseilles, Eisenstein spent a few restful days writing at Moussinac's cottage at Toulon – one evening was spent in a bar for sailors at Saint-Tropez, where he joined in the dancing with gusto – before having to return hurriedly to Paris to face further harassments from the police.

Another cause for anxiety at this time was the failure of the Hollywood contract to materialize, coupled with the news that Douglas Fairbanks had been in London without attempting to contact Eisenstein. There is also an obscure note in the memoirs which reads: 'And finally – finally! Here lies before my eyes the ardently expected telegram: an invitation from the United States to go to Argentine and give two lectures in Buenos Aires. Finally!' At this point, however, Jesse Lasky turned up in Paris with an exciting proposal from Paramount: for Eisenstein to spend six months in America making a film for Paramount, after which it would be open to him to return to Moscow to direct a Sovkino production. The subsequent plan was for alternate work on American and Russian films until Eisenstein had completed three or four films for Paramount. The contract would be terminated only if Eisenstein failed to settle on a subject for a film and conditions of work by the end of three months in the United States. Lasky mentioned several possible subjects, including the Dreyfus Affair, a film on Zola, Vicki Baum's *Grand Hotel* and Wells's *War of the Worlds*.

While Eisenstein awaited Sovkino's confirmation and the official extension of his leave of absence from the Soviet Union, the financial side of the contract was discussed. Lasky offered Eisenstein a weekly sum of $500 until a subject was decided, and $3,000 weekly once filming began. But Eisenstein categorically refused to consider any contract that did not include Tisse and Alexandrov – in whose services Lasky was uninterested. Because of this condition negotiations were almost broken off; but eventually Paramount came up with an offer of $900 a week from the beginning, out of which Eisenstein himself could pay his colleagues.

Finally Soviet agreement came through, and Eisenstein signed the contract and set off for the United States. While on board he received a cable from Bernard Shaw authorizing a film of *Arms and the Man*. On 1 May a press announcement of the American contract provoked a host of newspaper comment. Ironically, whereas he had previously been denounced for his Communist sympathies, Eisenstein now found himself accused by *Comoedia* and *Paris-Midi* of abandoning his political ideals.

Journey through America

No sooner had Eisenstein arrived in New York than he was swept up in Paramount's publicity machinery. Under the terms of his contract he was expected to fall in with all the image-boosting arrangements: impeccable dress, the best hotels, meetings with the 'right' people, publicity photographs and so on. A meeting with film-distributors on only his second day was an unnerving experience, but he evidently impressed his audience, receiving an immediate offer for the distribution of his films in America. Eisenstein had little patience with this irksome, engineered publicity – as he demonstrated in typically outrageous fashion only three days later at a prestige luncheon at the elegant Astor Hotel, where he was to make his début before the New York press. Arriving for the occasion with three days' growth of stubble on his chin and a worker's cloth cap on his head, he proceeded to astound his conformist audience with the sarcastic explanation: 'I think you picture all Russians with beards. I did not wish to disappoint you. . . .'[11] He went on to shock them further by announcing that he had come to make 'a truly American film'. It was an ill-chosen time to risk alienating his American hosts when the militantly propagandist character of his latest film, *Old and New* (*The General Line*), then running in New York, was already causing misgivings.

Eisenstein's remark was no idle boast, however, and he now set about exploring the America that he wanted to portray in 'a truly American film'.

His first step was to move to a hotel in one of the busiest streets off Broadway; and from here he began absorbing the city's atmosphere. As usual, not only the mind but all the senses were brought into play in the process. All the antennae of perception were spread wide, and only afterwards did Eisenstein examine the sensations thus recorded. First the movement on the streets. The immediate impression was of everyone apparently bent on his own particular business, on his multiple and urgent problems. He looked at the legs of the passers-by; their movement seemed one of agitated bustle. Transferring his gaze to their faces, Eisenstein was surprised to see a deep anxiety, a marked perturbation written there. Concentrating on their eyes, what he detected was a sense of insecurity.

The exploration continued. One day he observed the city's tempo from a car. The first impression of dizzying hustle and bustle reminiscent of the Stock Exchange now disappeared. The mad rush had paradoxically given way to a snail's-pace crawl: the profusion of cars forced traffic to a virtual standstill. By another paradox, the towering skyscrapers failed to convey a sensation of height. This, he discovered, was because each of the innumerable storeys was compact in itself, so that the skyscrapers appeared as a series of intimate, homely provincial buildings piled one upon the other. Indeed, provincialism existed in the very heart of the city: in what looked like a farm-house, tucked away behind a giant block; in the washing hanging out across the streets in the Italian quarter and even at the corner of Wall Street; in the tiny church on the edge of Radio City; in people's homes, side by side with the household gadgets of modern technology; and even in the narrow outlook of many of the people themselves, in their provincial, patriarchal conventionality. But what impressed him about these things was precisely the existence of that 'dynamic of accomplishment: stability'. America was a country that 'throbbed and boomed through its technical-material stability'.

As he probed deeper into the character of the country and its society, he was to find this dualism cropping up in a variety of unexpected ways. He discovered what he later termed 'the principle of formalism' in American social life. At first he noted it in relative trivialities that shocked him nonetheless: in the theoretical part of the driving test, where the yes/no system of answering deprived the candidate of all possibility of independent thought and reduced the whole thing to a mechanical assessment of his memory. It was an intellectual conveyor-belt holding the individual in its throes. It carried over, for example, into judicial practice, where the authentification of a crime seemed of less consequence than *formal* judicial guilt. And later, when he worked on the film script for *An American Tragedy*, he felt it imperative to

sharpen the *actual* and *formal* innocence of Clyde within the very act of perpetrating the crime. Only thus could we make sufficiently precise the 'monstrous challenge' to a society whose mechanism brings a rather characterless youth to such a predicament and then, invoking morality and justice, seats him in the electric chair.[12]

He was to modify Dreiser's story – winning the latter's approval for the way he did so – in order to lay bare what he saw as the essence of American society. It was a truly American film he wanted to make. And it was this that from the beginning had prompted his successive probings into the innermost secrets of the American way of life.

He visited Sing-Sing, where he actually sat on the electric chair for himself – after first making sure that the current was switched off. His subsequent description of the feelings and associations it evoked is particularly revealing for the light it casts on his creative approach:

A monstrous experience! . . . But the most depressing sensation was evoked by various details near the chair. Beside it, for example, stood a spittoon. Gleaming, brightly polished, the sort you usually find beside you at the dentist's. From the chair, you could see, through an open door, a table, a new wooden table, where the post-mortems are carried out. Then I saw another door, through which I wasn't allowed to go. That was where the condemned prisoners sit. There was nothing fantastic about the place, no freakish lights or shadows such as people love to show in films. The condemned wear no unusual headgear; they are just bound with leather straps and a thick wire is attached to a shaved patch on their heads. In keeping with all these details, such as the chair itself, the spittoon, the scrubbed table, the benches for the witnesses, everything was very primitive and practical. It's just this primitive practicality that's so sinister. But I was even more struck at Sing-Sing by another sensation – the feeling of time turned off. Outside, back in the city – on Broadway, say – at five o'clock there's so much movement you can't get through. In the skyscrapers the lifts work without pause; half of them are empty, yet they keep on working. But when you enter Sing-Sing you sense at once that the time it takes to do anything is of no importance here; the only important time is the time you have to pass. Whether you do anything quickly or slowly – it doesn't matter. You have this feeling from the moment you come into the prison. A tiny waiting-room. One door leads to one wing, a second leads to the other. The guard who is conducting you knocks at one of the doors. . . . A long pause. Then, from somewhere far away, you hear slow, regular steps. . . . The door slowly opens. A second guard comes out and patiently hands a key to the first one. Nobody hurries anywhere. After his measured knocking on the door the guard had patiently waited, he was in no hurry – he knew the other guard was certain to come – this is a most terrifying feeling. And it is also the diagnostic, the characteristic, of prison.[13]

In his plans for *An American Tragedy*, all this turns up again: the electric chair and all the paraphernalia surrounding it, representing 'one particular embodiment of that tragedy which continues to be enacted every hour and every minute in the United States, far outside the covers of novels'.[14]

Eisenstein's process of assimilating reality included another mechanism for elevating sensations on to a rational plane. Certain commonplace experiences, as we have seen, sometimes set him off on trains of thought that culminated in some of his most profound theorizing. One such experience was his difficulty in memorizing the New York streets because of their unfamiliar designation by numbers, which, in contrast with names, conjured up for him no pictorial associations. 'To produce these images, I had to fix in my memory a set of objects characteristic of one or another street, a set of objects aroused in my consciousness in answer to the signal "Forty-second" and quite distinct from those aroused by the signal "Forty-fifth".'[15] There were, he discovered, two definite stages in this memorizing process: in the first, at the mention of the street's number, his memory responded by evoking the street's separate characteristic elements; only at the second stage did all these elements fuse into a single perceptual image. He saw a connection between this process and that of creating a work of art: in each case a 'single, recognizable whole image is gradually composed out of its elements', the same law governing 'the procedure of entering the consciousness and feelings through the whole, the whole *through the image*'. But whereas in normal, everyday practice the important thing in the remembering process was to pass as quickly as possible over the first stage so as to arrive at the second, with art the emphasis was different. For the work of art was concerned with precisely the process of instilling the images in the spectators' consciousness. The method for doing so should, therefore, reproduce the real-life process that helps the images to take shape. In short, Eisenstein concluded, the artist should reproduce the very steps that he had gone through in remembering the New York streets.

The more Eisenstein probed beneath the surface of American life, the more ridiculously inappropriate seemed the subjects suggested by Paramount. *The Martyrdom of the Jesuit Missionaries in North America*, for instance, and O'Neill's *The Hairy Ape*, he laughingly dismissed as 'one hundred per cent propagandist', reverting instead to his idea of adapting Blaise Cendrars's *L'Or*. Paramount showed an interest, but no definite decision was reached.

By far the most important of Eisenstein's American film contacts at this stage was D. W. Griffith. Their first meeting took place at an unconventional hour – between five and six in the morning – in the Broadway Hotel that Griffith had made his home for thirty years. The sky was still grey, the road-sweepers were at work, and overflowing dustbins littered the pavement as Eisenstein, absorbed in this strange atmosphere, itself so reminiscent of a Griffith film, approached the gloom of the hotel entrance. Their conversation, too, was highly unconventional, Griffith confessing that half his films were trash made only for the box-office to provide the capital to finance the ones that were really dear to him. At that moment he was looking for a sponsor for a film about the corruption resulting from prohibition; his last hope was the rich widow he had been assiduously cultivating for two weeks. Eisenstein was saddened by the sight of this veteran director having to resort to the machinations of a tiro in order to make his films. Little did he realize that he himself was destined to a still worse fate.

Soon after this Eisenstein set out to see something of the rest of the United States before his planned visit to Hollywood. A meeting at Columbia University, presided over by the philosopher John Dewey, was followed by one at Harvard, where he spoke on the new possibilities of presenting abstract ideas through the film. Next, Boston and a meeting with the city's intellectuals at the Vendôme Hotel. There the star of the day was the famous film dog, Rin-Tin-Tin – the first star he had had the chance of meeting, as Eisenstein sardonically commented. While Eisenstein was made to pose for photographers with the dog, which had been brought along for its publicity value, representatives of the local press fired a barrage of questions at him about his American plans, his work in Russia, and so on.

At Harvard, Eisenstein was the guest of Professor H. W. L. Dana, whose house had previously belonged to his famous grandfather, Henry Wadsworth Longfellow, and had witnessed the formation of the poet's literary circle; earlier still it had been a residence of George Washington during the American War of Independence. These historical associations fired Eisenstein with the idea of making a film about America's history centred on this house. Meanwhile he continued his travels, exploring the Negro quarters of the deep South, lecturing to Negro audiences in Charleston and New Orleans, and generally making contact with Negro intellectuals.

From New York, Eisenstein finally left with Tisse and Alexandrov for Hollywood, having meantime enjoyed a spending spree, buying clothes and the best filming equipment available. The long journey westward by train was broken at Chicago, where Eisenstein spent a happy week scouring the city's precincts. Shunning his hosts' futile efforts to interest him in the usual tourist attractions, he explored the notoriously unsavoury districts: the Mexican slum quarters, the Black Ghetto, and the hide-outs of Al Capone's gangsters. Friends who accompanied him on these excursions recall how he kept them alert with his insatiable curiosity, which often landed them in totally unexpected places and situations, and his unfailing exuberant good humour. In a cafeteria one day, he suddenly assumed the role of a waiter, serving an imaginary customer at an empty table with appropriate flourishes and gestures – even down to leaving himself a ten cent tip. He once said that he had remained the same, small, well-behaved, obedient boy all his life. But for a long time he also preserved the attributes of a childlike cheerfulness, of an inner freedom specific to childhood: a capacity for delight and for uninhibited childish fun, a youthful freshness of vision. All these childlike characteristics that enchanted everyone closely acquainted with His Majesty Eisenstein were, however, soon to be curbed.

Hollywood

Arrived at last in Hollywood, Eisenstein and his colleagues – who now included Ivor Montagu – installed themselves in a Spanish-style villa complete with swimming-pool at No. 9481 Readcrest Drive in Cold Water Canyon, Beverly Hills. Served by an old run-about car and the cook who went with the house, Eisenstein tasted to the full a completely new sort of life in the 'incomparably picturesque' Californian surroundings. So rich were his impressions from this period that for once he was unable even to begin recording them.

Hollywood had its less pleasant aspects, however, not least those connected with Paramount's publicity campaign, which demanded Eisenstein's attendance at innumerable meetings, banquets and other social occasions. For Eisenstein, a born gaffeur, they were a perpetual and irksome strain, and many are the stories of his social blunders – many of them, no doubt, apocryphal or deliberate. At a banquet given by a multi-millionaire he reportedly asked to change places with the butler on the grounds that he disliked being waited on; on another occasion he refused all alcohol, facetiously invoking his oath to observe the prohibition laws. Most tedious of all were the meetings with film celebrities, most of whom Eisenstein found 'stupid and mediocre'; Jean Harlow, for instance, he characterized as 'the platinum beauty queen, full of airs, gracing the marble surround of the Ambassador Hotel's sky-blue bathing-pool'.[16]

There were other, fascinating meetings, however: with Walt Disney, who corresponded with Eisenstein for some time afterwards; with Mack Sennett, Ernst Lubitsch and King Vidor, who became a close friend; with Erich von Stroheim (whose work Eisenstein greatly admired); with Marlene Dietrich and Greta Garbo. This last meeting led to the rare, almost unique, opportunity of seeing Garbo actually filming. After the experience Eisenstein quite understood her insistent exclusion of onlookers:

She possessed none of the techniques learned at professional school, acting purely by instinct – but with what force! Instinct can, of course, sometimes fail the actor. On such occasions there were hysterical outbursts and floods of tears on the set. Acting was a hard way of earning her living for Garbo.[17]

Among the few people whom Eisenstein admired and always met with pleasure were Josef von Sternberg, Robert Flaherty and, above all, Chaplin, who became Eisenstein's close friend and constant refuge from the Hollywood bores. They frequently visited each other, played tennis, went sailing in Chaplin's yacht, or gave vent to their childish high spirits in amusement parks, trying their hand at everything from the Aunt Sally shies to the moving-target rifle ranges. It was probably this shared childish streak that played a large part in their enjoyment of each other's company, helping them, as it did, to forget the sombre side of their natures, which in both was strongly developed. On a more serious level, they took, and continued to take, a similar pleasure in each other's artistic successes.

During their friendship, Eisenstein discovered some interesting, lesser-known sidelights of Chaplin's character. In a party game at Eisenstein's house one night, for instance, the King of Humour was awarded only four marks out of five for wit – evidently a fair assessment in view of his subsequent failure to see the humour of the situation.

Meanwhile Eisenstein had been installed in a two-roomed office in the Paramount buildings where he reportedly felt as ill at ease as a caged lion. A further cause for discomfort was an antisemitic and anti-communist campaign, apparently instigated by a certain Major Frank Pease, of which Eisenstein found himself the principal target. At first limited to disparaging comments, in letters and pamphlets, about Eisenstein's character and intentions, the campaign later included threats, and even protests to the Senate against Eisenstein's presence in America. As a result Eisenstein was once again faced with unwelcome visits from the police.

Nothing, however, could distract Eisenstein from his work. Under the general eye of Bachman, one of Paramount's associate producers (and later of Horace Liveright, a former publisher whose list had included *An American Tragedy*), he started work with Ivor Montagu and Alexandrov on *Glass House* – a project which, in Montagu's account, seems to have been an obsession with Eisenstein:

Paramount seemed ready to accept *Sutter's Gold*. But Eisenstein preferred *The Glass House*, which was only an idea.

The idea was this, as Sergei Mikhailovich explained it. People live, work and have their being in a glass house. In this great building it is possible to see all around you: above, below, sideways, slanting, in any direction unless, of course, a carpet, a desk, a picture or something like that should interrupt your line of sight.

Possible, I have said – but in fact people do not so see, because it never occurs to them to look. . . . Then, suddenly, something occurs to make them look, to make them conscious of their exposure. They become furtive, suspicious, inquisitive, terrified.

Fantastic, you would say? Even silly? But it was not at all in this manner that Eisenstein saw it. He did not see it as fantasy. He wanted to embody his idea on the most mundane possible plane. A serious, down-to-earth, ordinary story.[18]

The scenario soon became bogged down, however, and despite help from Paramount scriptwriters had eventually to be scrapped.

Sutter's Gold, to which Ivor Montagu alludes, was the proposed title of a project to which Eisenstein had once more reverted: a film version of Blaise Cendrars's novel, *Gold*, about the mid-nineteenth-century gold rush and General Sutter, on whose land the first gold deposit was discovered. Eisenstein envisaged the film as illustrating 'the paradise of primitive, patriarchal California, destroyed by the lust for gold in the ethical system of General Sutter himself, who was opposed to the gold'. He began work on a scenario intended to capture this basic theme.

Following his usual practice, Eisenstein embarked on a thorough course of research into the period. He read a vast selection of books on the subject; travelled throughout California, visiting the scenes of the events such as Sutter's fortress at Sacramento; talked with anyone who knew anything of the Sutter legend, including an old woman who had played as a child on the General's knee; and sought out any objects, like buttons and spurs, that evoked the period. At a San Francisco factory he was shown a blade from Sutter's two-handed cross-saw; at Sacramento he witnessed customs, such as the beard-growing contest, that had survived unchanged over the passing decades. In the course of his travels he also came across some early daguerreotypes so evocative of the authentic period atmosphere that he embarked on a frantic search for more – in shops, private houses, museums, everywhere. In short, Eisenstein was once more carried away by an insatiable desire to absorb through all his senses the atmosphere to be conveyed – the atmosphere of America before the Civil War.

Back in Hollywood, Eisenstein produced, after three days' non-stop work,* a preliminary scenario and detailed shooting-notes – only to have them rejected just as quickly by Paramount's producers, who could not give their

---

* About the method of work on the scenario, Montagu gives the following details:

'*Sutter's Gold* and *An American Tragedy* were both written straight off in a single operation lasting many hours, without sleep or rest.

(a) Eisenstein outlined the action to Alexandrov who wrote it down in Russian.

(b) Paramount translators, standing by, immediately made a literal translation.

(c) I took this translation to Eisenstein. We discussed it, changed it, I made notes on it.

(d) I wrote out in longhand an exact copy of the corrected and noted translation which then became the final script. . . . All phases of this work proceeded simultaneously. . . . After the scripts had been got down in this way, Eisenstein made his production sketches and costings of *Sutter's Gold* and sketches, notes and caricatures of *An American Tragedy*.'[19]

On the trail of General Sutter

backing to his critical view of the gold rush and the implicit criticism of American society in general. The scenario was admitted to be excellent, and the pretext for its rejection was the presumed high cost of the film. It was left to James Cruze and Luis Trenker to make films on the theme.

An American Tragedy

After the disappointment of *Sutter's Gold*, Eisenstein turned his energies, on Lasky's suggestion, to an adaptation of Dreiser's *An American Tragedy*, and September 1930 found him already deeply involved in work on this project. Meanwhile he had been developing his theoretical ideas on the 'wide screen'; and in a paper entitled 'The Dynamic Square', which he presented at a discussion organized by the Academy of Motion Picture Arts and Sciences, he launched the idea of a variably shaped screen that could be made higher or wider.

Eisenstein's interest in Dreiser's novel dated from several years earlier. He had met Dreiser in Moscow in 1927 and again in New York, where 'the old grey lion'[20] – as Eisenstein nicknamed him – had shown him the lesser-known parts of the city. Later they became more closely acquainted when Eisenstein stayed at Dreiser's villa on the banks of the Hudson.

Paramount had secured the film rights of the novel five years earlier, and several directors, among them Griffith and Lubitsch, had approached the subject, but without success. An apparently insurmountable problem, as Eisenstein observed, was that the novel contained 'ninety-nine per cent statement of facts and one per cent attitude towards them',[21] so that an interpretation was essential before it could be screened. Even to extract the essence of the novel's vast epic scope presented a mammoth task. It was probably best done by Eisenstein himself:

We shall touch upon only the outer central point of the outer story side of the tragedy – the murder itself, though the tragedy, of course, is not in this, but in that tragic course pursued by Clyde, whom the social structure drives to murder. . . .

Clyde Griffiths, having seduced a young factory girl . . . sees himself forced to marry her. Yet this would ruin all his visions of a career, as it would upset his marriage with the wealthy girl who is in love with him.

Clyde's dilemma: he must either relinquish forever a career and social success, or – get rid of the girl.

Clyde's adventures in his collisions with American realities have by this time already moulded his psychology, so that after a long internal struggle (not with moral principles, but with his own neurasthenic lack of character), he decides on the latter course.

He elaborately prepares her murder – a boat is to be upset, apparently accidentally. All the details are thought out with the over-elaboration of the inexperienced criminal, which subsequently entangles the dilettante in a fatal mesh of incontrovertible evidence.

He sets out with the girl in a boat. In the boat the conflict between pity and aversion for the girl, between his characterless vacillation and his greedy snatching at a brilliant material future, reaches a climax. Half-consciously, half-unconsciously, in a wild inner panic, the boat is overturned. The girl drowns.

Abandoning her, Clyde saves himself as he had planned beforehand, and falls into the very net that he had woven for his extrication.

The boat episode . . . is neither fully defined nor completely perceived – it is an undifferentiated tangle. Dreiser presents the matter so impartially that the further development of events is left formally, not to the logical course of the story, but to the processes of law. . . .

Almost the whole of the second volume is filled with the trial of Clyde for the murder of Roberta and with the hunting down of Clyde to a conviction, to the electric chair.

As part of the background of the trial it is indicated that the true aim of the trial and prosecution of Clyde, however, has no relation to him whatsoever. This aim is solely to create the necessary popularity among the farming population of the state (Roberta was a farmer's daughter) for the prosecuting District Attorney Mason, so that he may win the necessary support for his nomination as judge.

The defence take on a case which they know to be hopeless ('at best ten years in the penitentiary') on the same plane of political struggle. Belonging to the opposite political camp, their primary aim is to exert their utmost strength in defeating the ambitious prosecutor. For one side, as for the other, Clyde is merely a means to an end.

Already a toy in the hands of 'blind' Moira, fate, 'causality' *à la grecque*, Clyde also becomes a toy in the hands of the far from blind machinery of bourgeois justice, machinery employed as an instrument of political intrigue.[22]

Faced by the immensity of the novel, Eisenstein had three fundamental problems: to reduce the contents to the proportions of a normal-length film; to treat the action as a whole from a precise philosophical viewpoint; and thereby to resolve the dilemma unanswered by Dreiser – is Clyde Griffiths guilty or not?

This was, in fact, the first question put by the head of Paramount, B. P. Schulberg, in relation to Eisenstein's proposed treatment of the crime. And his reply to Eisenstein's 'Not guilty' was a prompt 'But then your script is a monstrous challenge to American society'.[23]

The dilemma seemed insoluble: if Clyde was guilty, then he became a totally unsympathetic character and the film was doomed to box-office failure; if he was not guilty, then, as in Eisenstein's interpretation, his crime must inevitably be portrayed as resulting from the social pressures to which he was subjected. For Eisenstein the problem was 'to make an Emile Zola from a Theodore Dreiser',[24] since his primary interest lay in the role played by destiny – that blind force of destiny that preoccupied him so obsessively and turned up in all his films. In this case, the implacable force was represented by the pitilessly grinding legal machine which inexorably caught Clyde up in its toils until it finally crushed him.

Such depth of thought was, however, beyond the producers: ' "We would prefer a simple, tight whodunit about a murder . . ." . . . . "and about the love of a boy and girl," someone added with a sigh.' Finally, they agreed that Eisenstein should continue with the script ' "as you feel it", and then, "we'll see" '.

And so, with Ivor Montagu's help, Eisenstein set to work on the mammoth task: cutting out all the superfluous padding; reinterpreting certain facts; inventing others; analysing and laying bare Clyde's psychological state of mind in the boat scene; shifting the emphasis on to the electoral question during the trial; changing some of the characters and completely eliminating others. And, for the first time, Eisenstein applied his theories about 'interior monologue', which features as an important method in the scenario, the camera probing into Clyde's very mind and soul.

On 5 October Eisenstein sent the finished scenario to Paramount with an accompanying letter:

Gentlemen:

So here we see the miracle accomplished – An American Tragedy presented in only 14 reels!

Still, we think the final treatment must not be over 12.

But we withdraw from the final 'shrinking', leaving it for the present 'in extenso', so as to have the possibility of making this unpleasant operation after receiving the benefit of notes and advice from:

1. The West Coast Magnates.
2. The East Coast Magnates.
3. Theodore Dreiser.
4. The Hays Organization.

Accordingly, gentlemen, we have the honour to submit to your 'discriminating kindness'

The Enclosed Manuscript

and . . . Honi soit qui mal y pense. The AUTHORS[25]

Almost everyone who read the scenario was impressed, and Eisenstein, confident that it would be accepted, set off to New York to meet Dreiser and the leaders of Paramount with whom the final decision rested.

Dreiser was full of praise for the adaptation. So was everyone who had read a copy: Lasky, Selznick, Schulberg, who said it was the best scenario Paramount had ever had. Nonetheless, the inevitable happened. In Ivor Montagu's account:

Lasky said:

'We must proceed without delay . . . I am going to New York. Are you ready to leave with me at once this very day?'

We hurried to pack our handbags. . . .

A day or two after we arrived in New York we were shown into Jesse Lasky's office. On his desk was a pile of papers. He said:

'Gentlemen, it is over. Our agreement is at an end.' . . .

We were shocked, but not surprised.[26]

Most of the team, indeed, had long regarded the outcome as a foregone conclusion.

The contract between Eisenstein and Paramount was wound up on 23 October 1930.* Yet despite their dissatisfaction with him, Paramount went to considerable lengths to make sure that no rival film company secured his services, buying him a ticket to return to the Soviet Union via Japan (where, on the basis of a contract which he had been offered and which only awaited his signature, he was to make a film), and actually announcing his departure to the press. Eisenstein, meanwhile, sickened by everything that had happened (including a preposterous and humiliating request from Sam Goldwyn 'to do something of the same kind' as *Potemkin*, 'but rather cheaper, for Ronald

* The novel was later made into a film by Sternberg, much to the fury of Dreiser, who brought an action against Paramount. For many years he continued to hope that Eisenstein would one day realize the film in the Soviet Union. In 1951 there was another film version of the novel, by George Stevens.

Colman'), had returned to Hollywood to pack up his things. And it was at this point that he met Flaherty.

Eisenstein was immediately taken by this white-haired man who talked interminably to anyone ready to listen, passionately relating a fund of wonderful stories, which, he maintained, cried out to be made into films. Invariably he ended with: 'There, I'll make you a present of that one.' This was the nearest that, for want of a backer, Flaherty, author of *Nanook of the North*, got to making the films himself. It was he, among others, who stimulated Eisenstein's interest in Mexico. Eisenstein, for his part, aroused Flaherty's interest in the Soviet Union. 'The old man was fired . . . with determination to work in Russia on a series of films devoted to the national minorities.'[27]

Eisenstein was not to be beaten by his disheartening experiences. The creative fire burnt as fiercely as ever within him, driving him on to new ventures with a compulsion that he was to compare with the mania of the millionaire William King Gillette – whom he met shortly after – for building bigger and better villas and palaces in the desert. It was an endless chase, 'like the donkey, mule or horse lured on by the carrot hanging in front of his nose, reaching out for it, running with all his might in a hopeless, never-ending pursuit'.[28]

For Eisenstein the carrot was now Mexico – a country that had attracted him long before his meeting with Flaherty. He had read numerous books on the subject, including the reportage of John Reed and the stories of the American writer Albert Rhys Williams, whom he had met in Moscow in 1928. Then there were the tales and fresco reproductions of Diego Rivera, who now urged Eisenstein to make a documentary film, *Life in Mexico*. Tempted by the project, Eisenstein sought advice about a sponsor from Chaplin, who referred him to Upton Sinclair.

Sinclair, in turn, recommended the project to his wife and persuaded her to back it, and also obtained the financial support of Gillette, who insisted, however – according to Alexandrov – on remaining in the background.* Delighted at the prospect of making the film, Eisenstein paid little attention to the clauses of the contract, signed on 24 November – clauses that the Sinclairs were repeatedly to invoke in justifying their actions in the tragedy that ensued. At the beginning of December he said goodbye to Hollywood. On the day of his departure, Chaplin showed him the first edited version, without sound, of his new film *City Lights*. While Eisenstein watched the film from Chaplin's armchair, Chaplin himself sat at the piano, explaining his plans for the sound and humming the melodies. Then friends took Eisenstein to the station, where he left looking, as one of them recalled, 'like a little boy

---

* This does not emerge from the Sinclair archive. There were, it appears, other financiers, who also wanted to remain anonymous.

taking his first long trip. . . . Eisenstein, the king and master of flaming images of turmoil and the world's war for freedom — seemed so completely, so pathetically and tragically, innocent. This was what stared from the Pullman window.'[29]

On 5 December 1930, together with Alexandrov and Tisse, Eisenstein crossed the frontier into Mexico. Thus began a new chapter in his life and one of the most controversial tragedies in the history of the cinema.

8. *Que Viva Mexico!*

Death – the twin sister of love.
HEMINGWAY

Eisenstein got off on the wrong foot in Mexico. *En route* for Mexico City, he found his reserved sleeping-berth in the *wagon-lit* already occupied. A vain attempt to sort out the situation ended up with Eisenstein and his companions forcibly ejecting the intruder. At some point after their arrival in Mexico City they were summoned before the Chief of Police, to be confronted, not only by this powerful personality himself, but by their adversary from the *wagon-lit* – who turned out to be none other than his brother, and on whose evidence they were arrested. The prime reason for the arrest, however, soon proved to be not personal vindictiveness but the now familiar political pressures which had followed Eisenstein to Mexico and which again culminated in demands for his deportation. And again it was Major Pease who was responsible, having written to the Mexican authorities to warn them of the Communist 'danger' that Eisenstein represented.

There are conflicting versions of the arrest incident. In Eisenstein's own account they were arrested immediately, before they had even unpacked their belongings at the hotel, and eventually released only after numerous interventions by twelve United States senators and other personalities including Einstein, Shaw and Chaplin. According to the Sinclair archive,* however, the

* From the published Sinclair correspondence it seems that there was no question of as many as twelve senators protesting.

In Mexico, with local inhabitant

arrest occurred at 10 a.m. on 21 December 1930 — that is, about two weeks after the film unit's arrival. Sinclair's brother-in-law and personal representative with the unit, Hunter Kimbrough, was apparently released the same evening, Eisenstein and his colleagues the following day after spending the night at the hotel under police surveillance. Immediately the news reached Sinclair he contacted Chaplin, Fairbanks and some senators, seeking their help. Senators Borah and LaFollette subsequently intervened with the Mexican authorities.*

Whatever the differences in detail, both stories agree on the outcome: the Mexican authorities apologized and declared the Soviet visitors honoured guests — the President himself later shaking them by the hand at an anniversary celebration in Mexico City.

We have already seen some of the reasons for Eisenstein's attraction to Mexico. But there was another important one — the impression left by a photograph he had once seen of a window display in a Mexican hat shop during the traditional Death Day celebrations on 2 November, in which hats were ranged on skulls dressed up with collar and tie. The impression had aroused in him the same excitement as he had felt in his youth when he dreamed of travelling to the land of Fenimore Cooper's Red Indians or

---

* In 1961 Professors Harry M. Geduld and Ronald Gottesman of Indiana University began work on a detailed study of Upton Sinclair's personal papers and records. Their researches — which shed new light on the whole tumultuous affair of Eisenstein's dealings with Sinclair and clear up several of its hitherto obscure aspects — have now been published in book form.[1] Thanks to the kind cooperation of Professor Gottesman, I was able, in writing this chapter, to consult some of the unpublished material in the Sinclair archive and take account of the incontrovertible facts revealed there.

At my request, Professor Gottesman was also kind enough to prepare the following brief comment on the affair. As he was still engaged on his work, these conclusions (dated 16 August 1966) were of necessity rather generalized ones, reflecting his opinion at a particular stage of his researches:

'While the relationships between Upton Sinclair and Sergei M. Eisenstein during and just after the filming of *Que Viva Mexico!* have been the subject of commentary, the relationships, typically, have been over-simplified. This has been true whether Sinclair or Eisenstein was the one being vilified or defended, accused or exonerated. Indeed, the whole story of the relationships between these two famous men has suffered from too much partisanship, and too few facts. When the facts are fully presented and interpreted I think the effect will be to dispel the atmosphere of half-truth and ignorance which has obscured the fascinating complexity of that relationship and the making of *Que Viva Mexico!* For the story is not a melodrama — neither Sinclair nor Eisenstein was merely the virginal victim of villainy. Nor was either of them guilty of acting with Iago-like "motiveless malignity" towards the other. Rather, when the documentary evidence is presented, the dramatic movement will be seen to develop against the rough-textured backdrop of history and to involve a considerable cast of real people and the gritty, sometimes grimy, stuff of human nature. What will reveal itself then, I think, is an extraordinarily complex drama of two generous-spirited men doomed to be tested, and, in part, defeated by the times, by other men and by themselves.'

Dumas's Château d'If, and had obsessed him 'like a festering splinter', filling him with an 'irresistible urge' to witness the Death Day carnival and get to know 'the whole of a country which could celebrate in such a way'.[2] With this obsession now reawakened by contact with Mexico itself, his idea was to make a travelogue film of the country. His contract with the Sinclairs specified a period of three to four months for filming – a period which Eisenstein had no intention of exceeding, as he told Esther Shub in a letter written soon after his arrival in Mexico: 'My leave of absence expires in February and I expect not to delay overmuch. I may perhaps stop off in Japan on the way.'[3]

And so Eisenstein set about exploring Mexico, simultaneously taking advantage of any opportunities for filming, such as the festival of Our Lady of Guadalupe. These travels were of paramount importance to his evolution as an artist; for the great 'Mexican adventure' represented a major crossroads, a catalyst for all his experience to date – and a springboard to the new, superior heights of his subsequent work. Though accounts of this period usually concentrate on its tragic aspects, it is rather the burning intensity of Eisenstein's inner experiences, and the simultaneous upheaval in his thinking and feelings, that constitute the more fascinating aspect.

From the beginning of his travels Eisenstein came into contact with many leading Mexican painters and creative artists: Fernando Gamboa, Best Maugard, José Clemente Orozco, David Alfaro Siqueiros and others, whose impressions on him added to that already made by Diego Rivera. Marie Seton has, moreover, pointed out a number of interesting similarities between certain scenes in *Que Viva Mexico!* and the paintings of Olga Costa, Miguel Covarrubias and Frida Kahle, while the influence of Mayan and pre-Columbian art is also clearly discernible. Every episode of the film was intended to incorporate something of – and to be implicitly dedicated to – one or another Mexican painter, and echoes of Siqueiros, Charlot, Rivera, Orozco and Posada can be recognized in what has survived of *Que Viva Mexico!*

Mexican adventure
Eisenstein travelled the length and breadth of Mexico, uncovering the secrets of its life and history, despite the difficulties – often aggravated by language problems – of probing into some of the more obscure and esoteric customs. He was assailed by a fantastic variety of intensely powerful impressions: the corridas; cock fights; pagan Indian dances, anachronistically devoted to Catholic saints; the asceticism of self-flagellating monks; ancient pyramids; constellations turned on their heads; the rose-coloured, blindingly sharp silhouettes of mountains suspended in a void between the ultramarine of the sky and the purple haze of their foothills; luxuriant vegetation swallowing everything in its irresistible growth, so that it seemed as if a few days' neglect on the part of the rail inspectors would be sufficient for the lianas to engulf the

In Mexico

railway lines, the viaducts or even some stray train; sun-scorched scrub springing out of endless miles of bizarrely sculptured stones; the remains of ancient Toltec settlements, upturned and laid waste as if by the hand of some angry giant; the fruit of the palm cactus, offspring of the infernal desert, whose purple flesh, seething under an inhuman sun, had absorbed every last drop of sap from the wilderness to remain ice-cold.

The eye no longer sees at all, but perceives and feels things just as a blind man would perceive and feel them with his hands. It is not, however, as though these things penetrate my consciousness and feelings; on the contrary, here the whole complex of my emotions and reactions, welling up inside me and amplifying endlessly, becomes a complete gigantic world of mountains, bridges, cathedrals, men and fruit, with wild beasts and tidal fluxes, with droves of cattle and armies, with painted saints and with the majolica of azure spires. . . .[4]

In the strange cosmic silence of the vast landscape, he felt at one with nature and experienced 'a most sublime sensation of the happiness of ecstasy'. That ecstasy, whose laws he had for so long tried to probe, became a living reality; caught up in it and experiencing for once an unprecedented peace and perfect internal harmony, he felt cinematography, by comparison, to be unimportant, except to the extent that it could become a microcosm of human experience. Technical problems of film-making, montage and even sound, faded into

In Mexico

insignificance. And so all his initial ideas for a travelogue film were over-thrown. As far as filming was concerned, he felt the need for a 'period of purification' and metamorphosis, at the end of which 'not a stone of our precious dead work would be left standing'.

Another aspect of Mexico that fascinated him was the intermingling of past and present. In Tehuantepec, there were survivals of a time-honoured matriarchal system. Elsewhere the Catholic festivals, self-punishing penitents and popular pantomimes preserved in living form the tragedy of instilling by fire and sword the Spanish brand of Christianity. On the other hand, former Catholic monasteries, expropriated during the Liberation period, had been turned into the haciendas of wealthy landowners, and still exuded from their thick walls the barbaric atmosphere of feudal times. Superimposed on all this were the massive, capitalist, industrial constructions of Mexico City; while, at the same time, among a community of farm workers living in the shadow of millenium-old pyramids, effective control over production was in the hands of the workers, 'almost as if Communism had been put into practice'.

As he looked over the vast Mexican landscape, the thought that 'Eden did not exist between the Tigris and Euphrates, but rather here, somewhere between the Gulf of Mexico and Tehuantepec' kept stubbornly recurring to him.

You suspect that when the land was still in its infancy the same all-pervading indolence reigned supreme, and, along with it, the same creative potency as prevails on these plateaux and lagoons, deserts, thickets and pyramids which, when you are face to face with them, you expect to start erupting like volcanoes at any moment; palm trees piercing the blue cupola of the sky in their upwards thrust, tortoises that emerge, not from the slime of the gulf but from the very depths of the ocean where it meets the centre of the earth.[5]

In this Mexico, which lived thousands of years behind the times and projected the future of centuries to come, the most revered word was the relaxed *mañana*. Even nature herself seemed to pander to man's indolence.

Not just for imitation's sake, quite certainly, had she coloured the feathers of the tiny parrots in tones of greenish-yellow. But so that the gaze that wanders idly over the verdant tapestry of the foliage is not distracted from the spell woven by the colour green. The tangled green knots of the lianas stretch for miles on end. You can scarcely breathe. Yet the lungs are not parched by the desert's scorching aridity. The embrace of the tropics is a humid one.[6]

Everything in the landscape, palm forest, rivers, wild beasts and even man himself, seemed scarcely to have emerged from nature's workshop – or rather to be still in the process of taking shape.

This impression was heightened by the plastic forms and graphic severity of the landscape, which led Eisenstein to resume the practice of sketching.

In his youth, as we have seen, Eisenstein sketched profusely. He had begun doing so after watching spellbound while an engineer friend of his father doodled animals in chalk, and a 'white arabesque of line' sprang into existence before his eyes, miraculously giving shape to dogs, stags and cats. The dynamism of 'shape-taking', whether movement of line or of phenomena was involved, was to fascinate him all his life – a fascination with the genesis of things; and as a student at the Polytechnic the arid stuff of analytical geometry soon came to exercise a compelling attraction for him through its power to translate into mysterious formulae precisely this movement of line. His youthful sketches suffered from being overloaded with detail, under the influence of a certain Russian school of painting, and contrary to his natural instinct, which was towards linear design. Then, with his first films, after he had dropped sketching, there followed an absorption with 'the mathematical purity of montage in its movement'. His taste for sequence came later, Eisenstein himself invoking a dictum of Engels to explain the oddity of the delay: first of all movement attracts the attention, and only after do you think about what is moving. It was, indeed, in Mexico – and again in connection with drawing – that this taste for sequence developed; only then, when his drawing had 'passed through the stage of inner purification, aspiring to mathematical abstraction, to linear purity'.[7]

In Mexico he was intoxicated by the extraordinary linear structure of the landscape, by its purity and by the graphic severity in everything around him: the square cut of the peons' white shirts and the curve of their hats came to stand almost for graphic symbols. Everything had a graphic exactitude: the perfect line of the pyramids; the white peaks of the Popocatepetl range cleaving the azure sky; the clear-cut lines of the shadows thrown on the ground by maguey leaves; the black silhouettes – of a vulture tearing at its prey, of a Franciscan monk, or of the black crosses on the tombstones. Everywhere and at all times there was this clash between black and white.

It all made him dizzy, as did 'the tormenting cruelty of the line wrenched with blood from the many-coloured body of nature'.

For me the delineation seems to stem from the image of the ropes constraining the bodies of the martyrs, from the lashes of the whip on the body's white expanse, from the swish of the sword before it makes contact with the condemned neck. Thus the naked line shatters the illusion of space, thus the line makes its way through the colour, thus the law of harmony splits open the varied chaos of form.

Then

the whips swish no more. The searing pain has given way to a state of warm numbness. The marks of the blows have lacerated the surface of the body, the wounds have opened up like so many poppies and the ruby blood has begun to flow. Thus the line has given birth to colour.[8]

Everywhere he came across this phenomenon: in, for example, the crimson flower growing on the trunk of a leafless tree amid the arid rocks around Tasco. It was called the *sangre de toros*, its name evoking the stain spread by the gush of blood from the black body of the bull as the matador's sword thrusts home.

As Eisenstein traversed the country, so the lines and colours changed. The harsh lines and strident colour tones of the north – matched by the cruelty of nature and many customs of the human inhabitants themselves – softened towards the south, the spiteful, razor-sharp maguey leaves giving way to the peaceful green lianas, and the brutality to a happy-go-lucky atmosphere. In this 'paradise of graphic art' Eisenstein again began sketching – on a phenomenal scale. First came drawings recording his visual impressions of the country; these were soon superseded by abstract, intellectualized line drawings featuring an extremely sensual relationship between human figures in various eccentric postures. There was a cycle of exotic sketches of Salome, one of which shows her sucking through a straw protruding from the lips of the decapitated John the Baptist. In another cycle devoted to bull-fighting the corrida theme is intercut with that of Saint Sebastian to symbolize two martyrdoms: that of the Saint and that of the bull. One drawing shows the crucified bull pierced by lances like the Saint. Then there is a whole series of bizarre sketches on the Macbeth theme, or original variations on that of *The*

Two sketches: the corrida theme, and Lady Macbeth

Death of Werther, in which the limbs take on weird forms (an arm, for instance, tapering off into the sword which decapitates him, leaving his head suspended in an attitude of tortured reverie). According to Moura Budberg, there are some 120 versions of Duncan's death alone, which Eisenstein sketched during an illness in Mexico. These drawings, coupled with our knowledge of the circumstances that inspired them, provide a revealing insight into Eisenstein's artistic thinking. As the painter Jean Charlot recorded, they were done 'very quickly so as not to disturb the subconscious elements' and were thus 'highly interesting documents to his mental workings'.[9]

This pictorial preoccupation with death was symptomatic of a profound interest in the whole life–death cycle probably aroused in Eisenstein by the sensation of a primeval, nascent world that he experienced all the time in Mexico and by the sensation of everything being reduced to its basic, primary elements. First, the bull-fight; that barbarous play of blood, gilt and sand whose savagery fascinated him. Bull and matador, each bent on dealing the mortal wound, represented for him a fusing of man with nature, of life with death, of instinct with art. Trying to analyse the 'miracle' of this bloody spectacle, Eisenstein noted that everything led up to that split second of release, vocalized in the shrieks of thousands of spectators in a state of ecstasy – to that moment of bloody sacrifice when the matador achieved his freedom.

The idea of death, indeed, was ever-present in Mexico. At first only Death Day itself had attracted him. But everywhere he found life emerging triumphant over death – death purging everything decrepit and obsolete and generating a new birth. Death and birth were closely interwoven at every step: a sarcophagus made you think of a cradle; from the peak of an ancient crumbling pyramid sprang a clump of roses; on a carved skull you could still make out the words, 'I was like you – you will be like me'; on Death Day, the children played with miniature skulls and bolted down chocolate coffins and sugar skulls. Death Day, however, remained supremely impressive: a day beginning with a ritual feast at the cemetery for the souls of dead relatives and ending in riotous, sensual parties.

This, then, was the emotional context, this the sensory ambience, and this the landscape, 'carrying a complex of plastic possibilities for interpreting the emotions', in which Eisenstein conceived his epic film – the film that was to remain tragically unrealized.

In Eisenstein's conception *Que Viva Mexico!* was to represent the history of successive civilizations, not in 'vertical', chronological sequences, but on a horizontal plane – that is, by unfolding the various stages of Mexican culture coexisting in their geographical context. It was to encompass Mexican history from prehistoric days, through the Spanish conquest, feudalism and civil war, to the present day, and finally project forward into the country's future. The central episode, epitomizing the idea of national unity from the historical viewpoint, was to be the simultaneous entry into the capital of the armies of Villa and Zapata.

Underlying all this was the basic theme of life, death and immortality. It was a theme on which Eisenstein had pondered, long before his Mexico days, in connection with the Revolution. Biologically speaking, he had then reasoned, man is mortal and achieves immortality only through his contribution to society, the ultimate goal of which is man's freedom. Now, in Mexico, he saw this general idea symbolized in the bull-fight. At this stage there emerged the linking thread for marshalling into a coherent presentation of the theme the multitude of whirling impressions and sensations absorbed by Eisenstein during his months of travel.

In Eisenstein's general conception, the film was to open amid the petrified symbols of the death-cult practised by the ancient Aztecs and Mayas, and end with the sardonic gaiety of the Death Day carnival, when the Mexican sense of irony confronts death with laughter, pokes fun at it and celebrates the irrepressible triumph of life. The spectre of death, before which their Christian ancestors knelt in fear and trembling, becomes the object of fun to the latter-day Mexicans of the finale. Everyone takes part in the carnival wearing a death-mask. And, when these are stripped off one by one in the final scene, the film's sympathetic characters – recognizable throughout by their clothing – appear with happy smiling faces, while the characters representing brutality and savagery reveal, not human faces, but lifeless skulls. The skull thus takes on a new significance, becoming the symbol not merely of the lifeless corpse, but of 'the corpse who is living man . . . a terrifying *memento mori* of the power of the corpse over the living'. But death is left behind. The Mexican peon lives, laughs, makes fun of death, leading life onwards to the attainment of his freedom. And the last mask to be lifted reveals a healthy, sun-tanned boy whose smiling face fills the screen.

Mexican Calvary
The scenario for *Que Viva Mexico!* was thus totally different in structure and character from anything previously created by Eisenstein: full of poetry, romanticism and a sensuous love of life. A number of versions are known to exist – those written in Mexico, others edited after Eisenstein's return to the Soviet Union, and a commentary in the form of an *Afterword* written in 1947. In none of the scripts written in Mexico did Eisenstein commit to paper the full extent of his ideas. Moreover, he intended changing quite drastically, when he came to the editing, certain episodes as indicated in the scenario. Only later, in Moscow, when Eisenstein knew he would never be able to realize the film, did he rewrite the scenario and send it to France for publication.

The brief outline scenario which Eisenstein sent to Upton Sinclair from Mexico gives – despite the omissions – a clear general idea of his first vision:

Do you know what a serape is? A serape is the striped blanket that the Mexican indio, the Mexican charro – every Mexican wears. And the serape could be the symbol of Mexico. So striped and violently contrasting are the cultures in Mexico running next to each other and at the same time being centuries away. No plot, no whole story could run through this serape without being false or artificial. And we took the contrasting independent adjacence of its violent colours as the motif for constructing our film: six episodes following each other – different in character, different in people, different in animals, trees and flowers. And still held together by the unity of the weave – a rhythmic and musical construction and an unrolling of the Mexican spirit and character.

Death, skulls of people. And skulls of stone. The horrible Aztec gods and the terrifying Yucatan deities. Huge ruins. Pyramids. And faces. Faces of stone. And faces of flesh. The man of Yucatan today. The same man who lived thousands of years ago. Unmovable. Unchanging. Eternal. And the great wisdom of Mexico about death. The unity of death and life. The passing of one and the birth of the next one. The eternal circle. And the still greater wisdom of Mexico: the *enjoying* of this eternal circle. . . .[10]

In a scenario later published in the United States and England some years later Eisenstein explains:

The story of this film is unusual.

Four novels framed by prologue and epilogue, unified in conception and spirit, creating its entity.

Different in content.

Different in location.

Different in landscape, people, customs.

Opposite in rhythm and form, they create a vast and multi-coloured Film-Symphony about Mexico.

Six Mexican folk-songs accompany these novels, which themselves are but songs, legends, tales from different parts of Mexico, brought together in one unified cinematic work.[11]

The time setting for the prologue is eternity. In the realm of the dead, where past dominates present, a funeral procession is winding its way – like some ritual farewell to the ancestral Mayan civilization – among pagan temples and majestic pyramids. Taking part in it alongside the stone idols and masks of ancient gods are the people of today, who accompany the cortège with stony faces exactly like those on the temple façades. To the bizarre rhythm of drums and the unfamiliar strains of Mayan hymns, these living faces participate, together with their replicas sculpted in stone, at the burial ceremony.

The four stories are entitled *Sandunga, Maguey, Fiesta* and *Soldadera*. Set in different historical periods, and containing different characters, the four stories continuously interrelate. Beside bull-fights, *Fiesta* also depicts a Catholic procession, a symbolic Calvary which foreshadows the real one of the peons in *Maguey* who are buried up to their necks and then trampled to death by horses' hooves. Structurally, in terms of both content and, particularly, composition, the themes reappear and interconnect. Again the epilogue winds up the 'serape' structure with the Death Day celebrations, in which the characters in the stories reappear and thus lend a metaphoric quality to the film as a whole.

Yet another variation, dated Moscow 1932, outlines a different dramatic structure: 'There are 7 parts or 5 episodes to the film. At the centre are 2 short novellas [each with 2 parts] . . . while the other 3 episodes serve as a framework for them.' In his *Afterword* of 1947, Eisenstein remarked on the incompleteness of this version compared with his original intention in that it lacked two episodes, *Fiesta* and *Soldadera*, which had not been filmed. It is thus difficult, even today, to form any precise picture of how the film might have turned out, not only because Eisenstein would no doubt have modified his ideas during the filming, and certainly at the editing stage, but also because not enough is known about all the documentary material relating to the film.

Shooting started on 13 December 1930, long before a script was sent to Sinclair. On 15 April 1931 Sinclair wrote to Kimbrough: 'We are not in the least worried about the design or story of the picture; we are quite cheerfully leaving that to him.'[12] The same day Eisenstein wrote to Sinclair: 'It is true that you are in the same position as was Sovkino when we were shooting *Potemkin* – we had such a lot to do, that nobody in Moscow knew *what* we were doing! . . . The more because it is very complicated for me to expose on paper what and how the film will become and is becoming. Still I'll try to do it on the next page, exposing you the basic moving ideas of the different parts which we want to visualize.' And the same letter continues: 'Two weeks later! I started heroically to expose the story . . . but stuck on the sixth page and could not continue – time, time!'[13] Finally he did send Sinclair the outline of the script (including the six stories) but this was only in a letter dated 2 October 1931.*

* It appears from the Sinclair archive that Eisenstein was uncertain about his precise intentions for some time, and this has given rise to the assumption that his filming was at first pure experimentation. My belief, however, is that the lack of clarifying material in the archive does not signify any imprecision on Eisenstein's part. I assume that, for some reason or other, he did not reveal his thoughts in detail to Sinclair (the scenario he sent the latter seems, in fact, to have been much vaguer than his actual conception of it at that stage). The evidence of all the documents and their correlation with what we know of his creative process (in both preceding and subsequent films) justify, I believe, my contention that Eisenstein's ideas had crystallized and that such experimentation as there was – and with Eisenstein there was always some – took place within the framework of these preliminary, well-defined intentions. Tallying with this viewpoint is Jay Leyda's film-study which clarifies Eisenstein's aims: they were not, it is quite evident, gropings, but persistent efforts to find the best plastic solutions for realizing certain precise ideas. The only fundamental change was the initial one when he decided against a travelogue in favour of a more complex cinematographic opus. What followed from that point onwards was not experimentation, but elaboration.

Que Viva Mexico! marked the apogee of Eisenstein's preoccupation with the composition within the 'frame'. Whether filming a statue or some swiftly moving action, Eisenstein went to infinite pains to find the most expressive angles and compositional arrangements. When shooting a bull-fight, for example, he exercised phenomenal patience in calculating the precise moment for the picador to make his thrust in order to catch the moment of impact in the very centre of the frame. (Jay Leyda's *Studies for Eisenstein's Mexican Film* – a work of outstanding importance in which he pieces together with scrupulous care, in the order of its filming, part of the negative not mutilated or sold by Sinclair – contains numerous examples illustrating Eisenstein's perseverance in pursuit of perfect plastic composition.) At the same time Eisenstein was equally engrossed with the question of composition in depth, on which he had worked while filming *The General Line*. At this point childhood memories of the lilac bough and Poe's story flooded back to him. The result was a series of shots of arrestingly bizarre composition, such as the close-up of a skull dominating a background scene of penitents on pilgrimage, or the profile of a young Mexican girl set against the distant silhouette of a pyramid. Montage, as a problem, Eisenstein now considered settled, and in this film he wanted to resolve the same problems at frame level. It was during this period, in fact, that he wrote the essay 'The Principles of Film Form' which as he commented in a note to his publishers, he believed to be 'one of the most serious and fundamental' expositions of his thinking about the cinema.[14]

As his centre for filming, Eisenstein picked on Tetlapayac, an old Spanish plantation owned by Don Julio Saldivar, situated eighty miles or so southeast of Mexico City. Between shooting sessions Eisenstein would retire to the monastic seclusion of his room and, while the smell of simmering pulque wafted to him from the courtyard below, bury himself in his studies and reading (which does not mean that he lost his good humour or ceased indulging in childish gunfights and general horseplay). Pavlov, Planck, Eddington, Jeans and other physicists were devoured; yet still he asked his friends in Moscow – with whom he kept in constant touch – to send more books, including Spinoza's *Ethics* and a history of the German language. Simultaneously he was working on his book of film aesthetics, *Direction* – a book started a long time before, which he feared he would never finish.

Meanwhile filming continued, although the original deadline – and the budget – had long since been exceeded. In the course of shooting, Eisenstein expanded his ideas in the scenario, sometimes developing brief passages into long and detailed scenes and transforming other episodes. Other delaying factors were the impossibly difficult filming conditions, the language barrier, and the *mañana* attitude both of the Mexican extras, who regularly turned up late or disappeared at crucial moments, and of the Mexican authorities whose

With an actor, overlooking the hacienda, Tetlapayac

permission to shoot certain scenes was required. Then there was the torrid heat that had members of the unit literally falling on their feet and frequently brought filming to a halt. This was followed by the rains and a new series of obstacles. Finally Eisenstein himself succumbed to an illness that immobilized him for a period.

All the time Eisenstein was working in the dark with the help of only a few simple rushes, since the filmed material was sent straight to California for processing. Meanwhile Leopold Stokowski, who had met Eisenstein at the end of January 1931 while travelling in Mexico with Mrs Frances Payne of the Rockefeller Foundation, had agreed to arrange the music for the film.

Still the filming was not finished and the time limit was extended again and again. The expenses too were mounting (though they remained ridiculously low compared with the usual costs of a production on this scale), and Sinclair once more sent his son-in-law, who had returned to the United States, to supervise the activities of Eisenstein and his team. Kimbrough's arrival was followed by a sharp clash with Eisenstein that gave rise to a whole crop of misunderstandings and arguments. In Hollywood, meanwhile, where Sinclair arranged a showing of some ten thousand metres of the rushes sent by Eisenstein, the film aroused the enthusiasm of everyone who saw it, including Seymour Stern, Chaplin and also, apparently, Albert Einstein. And on

177

With Don Julio Saldivar at Tetlapayac

26 October 1931, on the basis of the material filmed by Eisenstein so far, Sinclair wrote enthusiastically to Stalin: 'It is going to be an extraordinary work, and I think will be a revelation of the moving-picture art.'[15]

Yet in a letter written by Eisenstein to Salka Viertel only three months later, on 27 January 1932, we read:

I shall do everything he wants. . . . I accept Kimbrough, everything, anything . . . if only they let me finish this film. I have worked under most incredible harassment, no, not worked – fought. When I see you in Hollywood I will tell you what we had to go through and what probably is still ahead of us.

I myself am incapable of persuading these people, Zalka, you have already helped in this cause. We, all three of us, are convinced that this is our best film and that it must not be destroyed. I beg you, Zalka, go to Sinclair. As you were authorized to see all the rushes, he will certainly use the occasion to pour out to you everything which caused the present situation; or better, you could ask him and I am sure influence him. . . . A film is not a sausage which tastes the same if you eat three-quarters of it or the whole *Wurst*. . . . Our only hope is that meanwhile a miracle will happen and that the Soldadera episode will be filmed. Help us, Zalka! No, not us, help our work, save it from mutilation![16]

What had gone wrong? The tragic sequence of events has been documented in detail both by Marie Seton and by Harry M. Geduld and Ronald Gottesman. As they emerge from the documents, the facts, very briefly, are as follows.

Four days after Sinclair's enthusiastic comment quoted above, Eisenstein's loyal friend, the Mexican critic, Augustin Aragon Leiva, confided to Seymour Stern in a letter that Eisenstein was 'facing such troubles' that he was 'in danger of producing an unfinished symphony'. It appears that with no definite end of filming in sight, and the initial budget exceeded, Sinclair wanted to stop the film altogether. So began an ugly campaign against Eisenstein into which slander, intrigue and allegations about his private morals were thrown. Marie Seton, on the basis of convincing evidence, maintains that this campaign was motivated by a mixture of financial considerations and personal vindictiveness. Professor Gottesman, however, does not believe that a campaign, as such, existed. In the light of his researches with Professor Geduld, it appears that Eisenstein, on the one hand, had lost the confidence of the Soviet authorities, and that the Sinclairs, on the other, felt 'pressurized' into stopping the filming and refusing to forward the material to Russia 'by the broken promises of Eisenstein and Amkino'. Thus the *Que Viva Mexico!* affair is much more complicated than it seemed, and the guilt does not, apparently, lie entirely with the Sinclairs.

Nonetheless, one fact is incontestable: that Eisenstein would have given anything to realize this film, which would probably have proved a landmark in the history of the cinema, *but was prevented from doing so*. The basic issue was an artistic, not a financial one; and Sinclair was first and foremost an artist and not a businessman. Yet Sinclair, for whatever reasons, was guilty of the worst crime an artist can commit: the destruction of another's work of art.

Some of the documents show that Eisenstein was doing everything he could to complete the film and was not greatly concerned with doing so diplomatically. Kimbrough's actions undoubtedly worsened the trouble. But did Sinclair always act in good faith? On 21 November 1931 he received a dramatic cable from Stalin:

'EISENSTEIN LOOSE HIS COMRADES CONFIDENCE IN SOVIET UNION STOP HE IS THOUGHT TO BE DESERTER WHO BROKE OFF WITH HIS OWN COUNTRY STOP AM AFRAID THE PEOPLE HERE WOULD HAVE NO INTEREST IN HIM SOON STOP AM VERY SORRY BUT ALL ASSERT IT IS THE FACT'[17]

We all know today what Stalin meant by such a statement. It is correct to say that Sinclair defended Eisenstein. And yet he was clearly told, several times, that the USSR did not want Eisenstein's picture.[18] Moreover, the correspondence clearly shows that Sinclair acted with Moscow against Eisenstein. A wire from Ernest Greene (21 April 1932) demands Sinclair's silence about the decision to exclude Eisenstein from the final editing of the film:

'IF EISENSTEIN ENROUTE HEARS ABOUT SUCH TRANSACTION HE WOULD EXPLODE AND LIKELY RETURN HERE BUT AFTER ARRIVAL SOVIET SOIL WOULD BE UNDER THEIR GOVERNMENT AND COULD NOT TALK TO YOUR DETRIMENT THERE'[19]

In the next year, on 26 July, Sinclair wrote to Harry Dana that: 'the Russian Government got their great artist back and avoided having him turn in to a White, as Rachmaninov and Chaliapin have done. They owe this solely to our efforts. . . .'[20] It is ironic to look back in the correspondence to a letter of Sinclair's of December 1930, when he wrote: 'This will be the first time in Eisenstein's life that he has been entirely free to make a picture according to his own ideas.'[21]

In the meantime Eisenstein had concentrated all his efforts on completing the film, trying to come to some agreement with Sinclair while continuing the shooting – and, what is more, still finding the strength to laugh and joke, and, on 2 November 1931, to take part in the Death Day celebrations. In November he was working with his team on a picture for the Mexican government, which had to be, as Kimbrough states, 'a three-reel picture of the big athletic celebration' and which the President of Mexico asked them to make as 'the official picture of the celebration'. He was still hopeful. At the beginning of December, despite a flood of slanders that were inwardly telling on him, he wrote to Seymour Stern in very restrained terms:

I do not know what will be the future, but so far now I think it is the *most* serious (and I had many) situation I ever had. . . . Do not try to find out but wait when it will be over – I myself will let you know. And then you will believe in the reality of fairy-tales.... It is a pitty [sic] that neither you nor I do not believe in god.... We might pray to him to get some help in my situation. So far god seems the only one who could do something.[22]

Shortly before writing he had learned that one of his articles had been published in *Querschnitt*, a review in which he had, as a youth, dreamed of seeing his work in print. Now he asked Stern to send him a copy, adding a melancholy postscript that indicated the depth of his feelings: 'There are *so* few dreams made in the youth that become realized some day, even if some-what *too* late – like the one with "Q"!'

Though the prospects looked blacker and blacker, Eisenstein left for Mexico City, where he obtained General Callas's promise of the Army's help in filming the *Soldadera* novella. At that stage he needed a bare $7,000 or $8,000 to complete the filming. A comparatively trivial sum – but Sinclair could not be budged from his decision.

Eisenstein returned to Tetlapayac, where he spent Christmas alone, 'in the *best company I can imagine*', as he put it. Isolated in the hacienda with none to share his thoughts, his mood alternated with lightning speed,

like the wandering Jew, or Dante, touring through hell – getting out of one trouble only to get in another – and usually worse one! – out of one mess in another. 'Mass movement' – the glorious title accompanying my career should be really written 'mess movement' and mean a continuous and uninterrupted movement through 'messes'! But I am really getting desperate and continuing to have the most stupid optimism in the world! So, I expect to be out of [this] one in the soonest time.[23]

Shortly afterwards, in mid January 1932, just as Eisenstein was about to start shooting *Soldadera*, Sinclair announced his definitive refusal to back the film further. Entreaties and attempts to negotiate, then or later, all proved fruitless. Consequently, without money and with all the film shot to date in Sinclair's possession, Eisenstein was forced to leave Mexico for the United States – finding time, before doing so, to speak at the opening of an exhibition of Siqueiros's paintings. With Tisse and Alexandrov, he set off in their old run-about car, but got no further than the frontier crossing into Texas, where they were refused entry visas by the American authorities. For nearly four humiliating weeks they waited there until, following numerous interventions on their behalf, they received transit visas valid for one month. During this enforced stay Eisenstein tried through official Soviet channels in America to make arrangements for cutting the film in Moscow. Sinclair agreed to this in a telegram to Eisenstein in which he promised to ship both the film and his luggage via Bogdanov, the representative of Amtorg, the Soviet purchasing commission in America. In less conciliatory tones, Sinclair went on:

Your statements that picture incomplete are damaging. Insist you do not make such statements again. If New York papers question you hope you will be wise and explain it was your proposal to cut in Russia.[24]

For many years, even after the catastrophic cutting up of his film that made it impossible for him ever to complete it, Eisenstein kept this telegram, embodying the reassurance of all his hopes, pinned up on his wall.

On 14 March the interrupted journey was at last resumed. During the nineteen days on the road between the frontier and New York, Eisenstein diverted his thoughts with a study of American humour, accumulating a vast sheaf of comic strips from magazines and newspapers bought en route. Meanwhile Sinclair was simmering with anger and disgust over a new incident. In a letter of 19 March 1932, addressed – but never, apparently, sent – to Soviet officials, there is, among other accusations, one which reads:

It appears that Eisenstein spends all his leisure time in making very elaborate obscene drawings. I have a specimen of his work brought from Mexico. It is identified as Eisenstein's by his handwriting on it. Believe me, it is not an anatomy study nor a work of art nor anything of that sort; it is plain smut.[25]

This specimen was probably brought by Kimbrough and it may have been the one that Sinclair described to Marie Seton as being 'a parody of Christian paintings showing Jesus and the two thieves hanging on crosses; the penis of Jesus is elongated into a hose, and one of the thieves has the end in his mouth'.[26] Later, when shooting was halted, Eisenstein included in the trunks and boxes he was sending to Hollywood 'several portfolios containing many hundreds' of these drawings. They were found, Sinclair says, by Customs men who said 'they were the worst they had ever seen in their lives. They wanted to confiscate the whole shipment'[27] – which contained property of Sinclair's. The writer claimed that Eisenstein had put these pornographic drawings in the trunks in the hope of damaging him. This seems improbable; for according to Sinclair the Customs men 'declared that if this stuff had been opened in New York – which was Eisenstein's proposition made by telegraph to [the Amtorg official] Lambert – the whole shipment, including all the property of the Company, would have been confiscated and Eisenstein would have been liable to prosecution'[28] – and Eisenstein would surely have avoided trouble for himself, since his main purpose was clearly to be allowed to stay in Hollywood and edit the film.

Once in New York, problems over the film crowded in on Eisenstein. On one occasion he managed to see the processed film. Sinclair, while remaining totally inaccessible to direct contact, nonetheless promised in another telegram to ship the film 'on the next boat',[29] and Eisenstein consequently went ahead with arrangements for Stokowski to visit Russia at a later date. Meanwhile, according to Alexandrov, Eisenstein edited some forty Russian shorts made available to him in New York into a documentary on the Five Year

Plan, and tried – successfully, it seems – to forget his anxieties in a variety of other distractions. He continued to explore the city, dancing at nightclubs and visiting Harlem. He spent light-hearted hours with the dancer Sara Mildred Strauss, once improvising a ballet with her, Tisse and Alexandrov at her studio, and showing her his drawings from Mexico (which were exhibited in October that year at John Becker's gallery on Madison Avenue). In spite of everything he seems to have retained something of his old optimism – that naïve, childlike optimism, tinged with irony, that contrasted so strangely with his moods of despair and uncertainty about *Que Viva Mexico!*

Mexican tragedy

On 19 April 1932 Eisenstein left the United States for good on board the Europa. He had arrived there a young man full of enthusiasm; he departed an old and exhausted shadow of his former self.

After docking at Cherbourg, he stopped at Hamburg, which had earlier fêted him as a celebrity. Now, according to Alexandrov – though there appears to be no documentary evidence for his story – it witnessed a major scene of the Mexican tragedy: for here the cases in which, with Sinclair's approval, Alexandrov had packed the reels of film for despatch to Moscow, were stopped by Sinclair's cable and turned back to the United States.

From Hamburg to Berlin, which Eisenstein found overshadowed by the growing threat of Nazism; at the Golf Hotel where he put up, Adolf Hitler was rumoured to be occupying a suite two floors above him. During his brief stay in Berlin he talked of a number of new projects, including again his proposed *Götterdämmerung* film, and a travel film on the Soviet Union which he planned making on his arrival home.

It was 9 May 1932 when Eisenstein finally reached Moscow, only to find himself caught up in a new scene of the Mexican tragedy. Even after learning of vicious attacks made by Sinclair with the aim of blackening his reputation with the Soviet authorities, he still hoped to obtain the film. But during June, as Professors Geduld and Gottesman write, 'Sinclair had arranged for the picture to be cut in Hollywood and Eisenstein was to have no part in the matter. The novelist revealed this as a "confidential" aside in a letter to his son, David (4 June).'[30] In August Eisenstein heard of Sinclair's decision to allow Sol Lester – producer of Tarzan films – to cut the *Que Viva Mexico!* material for a film to be entitled *Thunder over Mexico.** When this distorted travesty of Eisenstein's intentions was previewed in May 1933, the contro-

---

* In a letter to Smirnov dated 22 July 1932, Sinclair wrote: 'Using about the half of the Eisenstein material, so far, we have made three complete pictures – the Hacienda story of nine reels; the Tehuantepec story and the Bullfight story of five reels each.'[35] The negatives of *Thunder over Mexico* and *Death Day* were destroyed later in a Hollywood fire.

versy, which had continued in a lower key over the intervening months, flared up anew, many prominent figures protesting to Sinclair over his action. An International Defence Committee for Eisenstein's Mexican Film was even set up. Yet the worldwide censure of Sinclair fell on deaf ears. Renewed attempts to negotiate on Eisenstein's behalf proved vain, and the following year a short second film, *Death Day*, was produced from the material originally intended by Eisenstein for his Epilogue. Sinclair's tactics varied: attempts to exonerate his actions alternated with further promises to forward the material to Moscow, only to be followed by new slanderous charges against Eisenstein. Worn out by the intense, prolonged and cumulative strain, Eisenstein finally broke down and was sent to the Kislovodsk Sanatorium with what Pera Attasheva described at the time as 'a serious nervous condition'.[32]

On his return home, Eisenstein received a letter from his friend Augustin Aragon Leiva relating the filming of a Hollywood production, *Viva Villa*, at the very hacienda in Tetlapayac which Eisenstein knew so well:

Where is Eisenstein? . . . Tetlapayac is waiting for him . . . that corner's room is filled with his thoughts and his tremendous devilish dreams . . . a strange light comes out from the room through the curtained windows. The light of his mind . . . but where is he? . . . Tetlapayac waits for him and when it is heard in the tinacal the counting song of the peones it seems like an invocation . . . Eisenstein, where are you? . . . are you dead . . . ?[33]

No, Eisenstein had recovered, but without regaining his zest for life, torn from him by the tragic destruction of his ' "chef d'oeuvre inconnu" – the film which no one will see', as he wrote about it in October 1932.[34] From that point until the end of his life the spectre of *Que Viva Mexico!* never left him. The Sinclairs never renounced what, on the basis of imprecise wording in the contract, they considered their sole rights to the negative; rather they continued to capitalize on it. Following *Thunder over Mexico* and *Death Day*, more negative was mutilated with the production of *Eisenstein in Mexico*.* Marie Seton, too, spoiled a large part of the negative in 1939 with her vain attempt to reconstruct Eisenstein's aims in her film *Time in the Sun*. Then in 1941–2 five or six educational shorts were made from the remaining footage.

* As early as September 1931 Sinclair had tried to have a separate picture made out of the hacienda episode, for 'this would be a real "story" in the Hollywood sense and could be sold at once'. As Geduld and Gottesman point out, this clearly anticipates the making of *Thunder Over Mexico*. Eisenstein's response to the suggestion also makes clear his ideas about the film: 'The project of making two pictures (one hacienda, and the other – other episodes) is not possible: if they have not *one* subject running through, that does not mean that the episodes are just heaping up of disconnected materials without forming a synthetic and symphonic whole. . . . The picture is *not* a "travellog" – (as was planned within the 75,000 feet!) in which scenes, bits and episodes are following just the railroad order of stations. Our picture is a strict Mexican "Menu" and cannot be sold "à la carte". Besides that it is not possible for the "hacienda" to overgrow the 3 reels she occupies in the whole of the picture.'[31]

Alas, poor Yorick

When Eisenstein eventually saw some of these films many years later, the experience reawakened all his bitter suffering:

Passer-by! Do not look for my thoughts here in cinematographic discordances cobbled together by the filthy hands of money-makers. Those films, which have been compiled from the material filmed by us on the wondrous soil of Mexico, do not belong to me! [36]

Never was this tragedy to be expunged from the depths of Eisenstein's soul, however much he tried 'to overcome death through irony – the death of my own child on whom I lavished so much love, work and passionate inspiration'.

9. 'Polemics Rage Around Me'

Où sont ces têtes que j'avais
Où est le Dieu de ma jeunesse
APOLLINAIRE

Back in Moscow, cramped in his uncomfortable bed-sitter with shared kitchen and lavatory on Chysti Prudi, Eisenstein soon found that neither this discomfort nor the problem of his Mexican film was his chief source of trouble. He was being subjected to attacks and derogatory comments as part of a campaign whose instigator, Boris Shumyatsky, recently appointed head of the Soviet cinema, nourished a lively antipathy towards Eisenstein that was probably augmented by envy on the part of a man who hankered after undisputed authority and who saw in Eisenstein's idolization a threat to his own importance. On Eisenstein's return home, Shumyatsky set out quite simply and deliberately, it seems, to destroy him. The first thrust against Eisenstein had come in 1931, while he was still abroad – during the period of correspondence between Sinclair and Stalin – in the form of an article by Ivan Anisimov,[1] analysing with patently malicious intent Eisenstein's creative work to date and questioning the value both of this and of his theoretical researches. Now the campaign was resumed and amplified in the press, where he was accused of having stayed abroad too long and acquired a taste for the exotic, neglecting meanwhile the transformations that had taken place in his own country. It was a paradoxical situation: while Eisenstein enjoyed enormous prestige both at home and abroad (about this time, for example, in July 1932, Pirandello sent him an outline scenario for a film which he begged him to make), polemical press articles were simultaneously trying to discredit him. And a particularly disconcerting aspect of the affair was that several of his former friends, including even Yutkevich, were joining in the attack.

All this, coming on top of the painful Mexican experience, might well have crushed a man of the strongest nerve. Yet Eisenstein, his characteristic sense of humour, perhaps, coming once more to his aid, turned his thoughts instead to new film projects.

Film projects

Soon after Eisenstein's return, it was suggested that he should make a musical comedy, a proposal totally unsuited to his artistic interests and one which he was bound to turn down. It was later taken up – without consulting Eisenstein – by Alexandrov, who arrived back in Moscow in June. Making use of his experience with *Romance Sentimentale* and his time with Eisenstein in the United States and Mexico, Alexandrov produced the film known abroad as *Jazz Comedy*. Eisenstein contributed to the production with scenographic ideas; sketches by him for comic musical instruments in the film, for instance, survive in the Eisenstein archive.

Eisenstein's fascination, dating from his Mexican period, with 'the play of time' now became channelled into two projects quite different in genre: a grotesque comedy, *M.M.M. (Maxim Maximovich Maximov)* and a historical pageant, *Moscow*. The first – on the theme of 'the Russian boyars projected into the conditions of contemporary Moscow, giving rise to various possibilities of comic *quid pro quo*'[2] – was intended to satirize the realities of everyday life by alternating them in a grotesque way with the fantasies of the hero. Eisenstein described *M.M.M.* in a letter of October 1932 as the next theoretical step to his discoveries and elaborations in *An American Tragedy*. He worked on it for several months, producing the scenario and shooting-script and even giving screen tests to potential actors. Simultaneously he was engaged in theoretical analyses and researches into the sources of comedy and, by 'combining logic with intuition', elaborated a complete theory relating to Soviet film comedy. But his ideas did not coincide with Shumyatsky's restrictive cultural policy, and the film had to be shelved.

The second project, *Moscow*, was begun the following year. It was conceived, as Eisenstein's sketches and notes graphically illustrate, as an epic treatment of Moscow's history over four centuries, and reflected in many ways Eisenstein's frustrated ideas for the panoramic portrayal of Mexico's history in *Que Viva Mexico!* Indeed, the compositional ideas for his abortive Mexican film obsessed him till the end of his life and continually resurfaced in various forms, without ever being realized. In this case the history of Moscow was to be unfolded in parallel with that of a representative member of a Muscovite working family whose successive generations provided continuity of theme.

His face changing from age to age, he must move through the film both as a personal descendant of one generation to the next, and as a unique character whose own life story unfolds beyond its normal limits, beyond those of the family history, of the generation, of class. . . . Compositionally, he must represent a new, original aspect of the wandering Jew, of the figure who, straddling time and space, has so often captured our fantasy and imagination.[3]

Eisenstein asked the novelist Fadeyev to collaborate with him on this project. But Fadeyev, though attracted by the idea, could not spare the time. In any case the project was soon quashed by Shumyatsky, and it was twelve years before Eisenstein took it up again.

In 1934, parallel with this project, Eisenstein was interested in staging Nathan Zarkhi's play *Moscow the Second*, which was written at the same time as the scenario for the film. The subject attracted him immediately: a Stakhanovite hero, whose outstanding work is recognized by the erection of a statue to him, develops a strange relationship with the ideal of himself personified in the statue. As Eisenstein described his ideas to Marie Seton, the statue arouses in the hero

a whole gamut of contradictory feelings and actions, which reflect the conflict between the old and new emotional concepts. Thus the theme of the play becomes the struggle for the new man, the new personality and new attitude towards labour and fame.[4]

There were six characters in all, including the statue, whose relationship to the hero was modified in Zarkhi's several variations on the theme. What the final variation might have been is not known, as this project also was vetoed by Shumyatsky; and in 1935 Zarkhi died.

There were other unrealized projects, including one with the title *Daughter of France* to which the archive list assigns no date. In July 1934 *Sovietskoye Iskusstvo* published – in reply to Shumyatsky, whom it also reported – the article, 'Eisenstein accepts the challenge' (of Shumyatsky): Eisenstein takes upon himself the duty of making a film about the *Chelyuskin* expedition. Then there was a reversion to Eisenstein's old dream of a film about China. This interest dating from his earliest years in the cinema had revived after Mexico, when he wanted to write a scenario about China and afterwards to go there. It was a project never far from his thoughts, continually nourished as it was by his reading and by the Chinese music in his record collection. At the beginning of 1935 his ideas took more definite shape as a result of discussions with André Malraux in September 1934 about the possibility of screening his *La Condition Humaine*. Then in March 1935, with Mei Lan-fang, he made an experiment in translating to film the art of this celebrated Chinese actor.

Parallel with his practical work, Eisenstein was absorbed, as always, in theoretical investigations. Since his appointment in October 1932 to conduct the directors' course at the Moscow State Institute of Cinematography, this had become a veritable laboratory for his ideas. His interests at this time took in the works of D. H. Lawrence, Lewis Carroll and Gogol, all of whom he studied exhaustively (discussing Gogol's use of colour at length with Andrei Bely, the author of an original work on the Russian writer, whose observations were to influence Eisenstein's later studies on colour). During that summer Eisenstein also met H. G. Wells, at Litvinov's villa, and Maxim Gorky, who read him his scenario for a film intended as a retort to Ekk's *Road to Life*, which he heartily disliked.

Meanwhile Eisenstein's health was again frail. In August 1934 he left for several weeks' rest in the Caucasus, afterwards going on to the Crimea as a production consultant. While staying at Yalta, he visited the Young Pioneers' camp at Artek, regaining his old spirits for a while as he played with the children. He revisited the Alupka Palace, where he stopped to contemplate the stone lions filmed for *Potemkin* (and fooled some American engineers by pretending to be an American tourist and joining his 'compatriots' in running down Eisenstein), and then Odessa itself. Finally he returned to Moscow with definite intentions, at last, of starting on a film.

Eisenstein had been interested in Haiti since March 1931, when he had proposed making a film about the struggle of the Haitian slaves against the French colonialists.* In Mexico the theme had recurred to his imagination, as a series of sketches made at the time attest; in 1932 his interest had been revived once again when A. K. Vinogradov suggested a screen version of his novel *The Black Consul*, and now, in the Soviet setting of 1935, the theme may have had a ring of actuality. He was particularly attracted by the figure of the revolutionary leader, J. J. Dessalines, and the thought of casting Paul Robeson in this role. For days and nights on end he elaborated the scenes, reading, sketching and making notes. He even devoted to *The Black Consul* a series of lectures at the Institute, where his pedagogic interests determined him to find not only the artistic solution for one scene, but also 'the method, the path which the director must take to arrive at the solution'.[5]

In December Robeson arrived in Moscow and spent much of his time with Eisenstein at his home, at Litvinov's villa, and sight-seeing in the capital.

* As Ivor Montagu recalls: 'It is true we got the book [John W. Vandercook's *Black Majesty*, Harper and Brothers, 1928] from the Hollywood bookstore while we were still at Paramount, and talked about it then, and corresponded with both the author (I think) and (certainly) with Paul Robeson. But it was simply as an attractive subject that might become possible under other circumstances. . . . The idea, and it did not get any further at that time than an attractive idea, was never put to Paramount, but only . . . came up again as a wild possibility for independent finance when we were clutching at straws after Paramount had given us the sack. But we did virtually nothing about it. There was not the time' (*With Eisenstein in Hollywood*, Berlin 1968, page 346).

Eisenstein was enchanted by this 'black Mayakovsky', as he nicknamed Robeson, and after Robeson's departure from Moscow in January 1935 looked forward to his intended return for filming. This project, however, eventually followed the familiar pattern, becoming just one more unrealized dream.

That January proved a particularly black month for Eisenstein when the All Union Conference of Cinematographic Workers, held from 8 to 13 January, developed into a forum for renewed attacks on him, with his 'friends' once again to the fore. Eisenstein himself presided over the conference on the opening day, in the course of which he made a brilliant speech, only to find himself the early target of an attack by Dovzhenko (Eisenstein's generosity towards whom we have seen) for his very erudition:

If I knew as much as he does I would literally die. [Laughter and applause.] I'm sorry you're laughing. I'm afraid ... I'm convinced that in more ways than one his erudition is killing him.

Other 'friends' joined in the chorus of mockery, including his former student, Sergei Vasiliev, and his close associate Yutkevich. (Yutkevich recently recalled the conference as 'an almighty battle between the generations',[6] and explained away his own action with 'as we were good friends of Eisenstein, we started with him'.) Only Kuleshov spoke up warmly in Eisenstein's defence:

You have talked about him here with very warm, touching, tearful smiles as if he were a corpse which you are burying ahead of time. I must say to him, to one who is very much alive, and to one whom I love and value greatly: ... Dear Sergei Mikhailovich, no one ever bursts from too much knowledge but from too much envy. That is all I have to say.

Eisenstein, who had, as Vishnevsky later revealed,* been deliberately presented with subjects that he would be forced to reject, was also maliciously attacked for not having produced a film since his return from Mexico. Jay Leyda, who was a student of Eisenstein's at that time, recalls the reaction when he broached the subject of Eisenstein's unrealized projects. 'He gave me the most genuinely anguished look I ever saw on his face and shouted at me: "What do you expect me to do! How can there be a new film when I haven't given birth to the last one!"' – meaning *Que Viva Mexico!*[7]

At the evening award-giving ceremony in the Bolshoi Theatre to mark the fifteenth anniversary of Soviet cinematography, Eisenstein's Calvary continued when he found himself the humiliated recipient of an award far inferior to those bestowed on his colleagues, Pudovkin, Dovzhenko, the Vasiliev brothers, Alexandrov. . . . The next day, again presiding over the conference, for which he made the closing speech, he replied in level-headed terms to some of the attacks.

* In a 39-page brochure on Eisenstein's life and work, published in June 1939.

Sketch for *The Black Consul*

And despite all the humiliating taunts – perhaps as the only form of resistance against them – Eisenstein threw himself once more into his creative work. Several years later he was to recall with irony the 'grey atmosphere' of the early 1930s and the attempt to force everyone into a straitjacket of creative conformity. His own apparent conformity at the time was thus clearly a surface one only.

Bezhin Meadow

Shortly after the conference, Eisenstein began work on a sound film, *Bezhin Meadow*. It meant interrupting his lectures, but four of his students joined him as apprentice directors, among them Jay Leyda, who kept a production diary throughout much of the protracted activity on the film until his return in 1936 to the United States, where he became an enthusiastic propagator of Eisenstein's theories and later translator and editor of his works.

The scenario, commissioned by the Communist Youth League on the theme of the Young Pioneers' contribution to collective farm work, was written by Alexander Rzheshevsky. Inspired by Turgenev's story set in the village of Bezhin Lug, Rzheshevsky had gone to stay there with the intention of drawing a comparison between the peasant children in the classic and those of his own time. After two years there he had written a script based on Turgenev's tale and on the true-life story of a young village hero, Pavlik Morozov. Morozov – who becomes the Stepok of the scenario – had organized the pioneers to keep a night watch over the collective farm harvest, thereby frustrating the plans of his kulak father to sabotage it. By so doing, Stepok provoked him to such a pitch of uncontrollable fury that he killed his son. In the scenario, the whole action takes place in twenty-four hours, from the morning of one day until the following day of harvesting.

Rzheshevsky's was an 'emotional scenario' – one, that is, which, as well as telling a story, aims more particularly to give the director an 'emotional stimulus'. It thus accorded with Eisenstein's ideas, recorded some years earlier, that

the scenario is not merely a dramatic narrative . . . nor does it represent the staging of a subject but one step in its processing. . . . The scenario is a cipher through which the transfer of one temperament to another is effected.[8]

Eisenstein now took Rzheshevsky's dramatic basis and, passing it through the filter of his own artistic temperament, gave it his own particular interpretation – recorded in a multitude of sketches of the compositional ideas, the costumes, settings, gestures and even abstract concepts relating to the film. All told, he was delighted with the scenario, especially its simplicity, which he intended preserving in his film, describing it as one 'about children and adults for adults and children'.[9] But, of course, Eisenstein's creative process was not a simple one: during the gestation period, his initial ideas always ramified as rapidly and uncontrollably as the luxuriant tropical Mexican vegetation. Or so it seemed; in point of fact, the apparently haphazard ideas fell strictly into place along the central guide lines of a mathematically precise conception that he followed through unwaveringly to the end. Even more amazingly, however total his apparent absorption in his idea for the film, he always had the energy – and indeed the need – simultaneously to pursue other, different interests, be they theoretical abstractions or quite simply other film projects.

As usual, Eisenstein set about casting with extreme thoroughness, particularly for the role of Stepok. From 2,000 boys his assistants selected 600 'possibles', whom Eisenstein personally whittled down to 200 in the course of twice-weekly sessions of four hours each. Still Stepok had not been found. Suddenly, at one of the final sessions, Eisenstein caught sight of Vitka Kartashov. 'He *is* Stepok,' he exclaimed to the astonishment of everyone present. The boy, as Jay Leyda relates,

seemed to have everything (and everyone, including Rzheshevsky) against him: his hair grew in the wrong way, insufficient pigmentation of the skin gave him great white blotches on his face and neck, and at the test his voice grew stiff and dull – until he was told to ask us riddles, when he produced a clear, fine, almost compelling voice. Only E. was able at once to see the positives, later clear to all.[10]

For some of the roles he chose actors, among them Boris Zakhava, director of the Vakhtangov Theatre, and four other theatre directors. In the main, however, he was faithful to his 'typage' concept, giving the role of grandmother, for instance, to an old woman found in an old people's home.

Parallel with the casting, a search was going on for suitable filming locations, as Bezhin Lug itself was unsatisfactory. Eisenstein drew up a map of a 'synthetic village' and sent out parties to scour for sites incorporating one or other of the various features required for the film. Meanwhile, on 5 May 1935, shooting began in Moscow on the film's prologue.

Eventually, on 15 June, at six in the morning, Eisenstein left Moscow by aeroplane with six of his team and all their equipment en route for Armavir and the Stalin State Farm near the Sea of Azov – their first location. As he set about filming, it was with precise ideas and a distinct vision of what he wanted to achieve. This was to be Eisenstein's first sound film and he was evidently bent on applying the fruits of his earlier theoretical meditations. Although without sound equipment at Armavir – it was to come into use only at the next location, Kharkov – he took meticulous account of the sound factor throughout the shooting. As he explained to his fellow workers:

On the editing table this episode will be handled in the same way a composer works on a fugue in four voices. The material we're filming here is only one of the voices.

Most of it will be used for rear-projection and transparencies when the second voice will be worked out – with figures and close-ups in the foreground. . . . The third and fourth voices (or motifs) are in sound – sound and speech.[11]

The whole audio-visual structure of the film was aimed at the ultimate realization of 'a sound film expressive of a specific artistic form and of a psychological interpretation of reality'. And every scene took account of this aim, as also did the décor: in the lines of exaggerated perspective for the interior of Stepok's home, for instance, or in the deliberately stylized, polished gold interior of the church.

'All the culture of the world', Jay Leyda relates, was brought into play for every new problem. For the compositions in which Eisenstein wanted to show '*how* Turgenev saw the things around him', he analysed Turgenev's literary style in minute detail, delving into his sources of inspiration and his creative method, for which he then sought suitable plastic equivalents. Consequently in one sequence 'the listening, waiting villagers assume the postures, even the sharp lighting of the listening, waiting disciples in the paintings of the late Spaniards'; elsewhere

the blanket arranged over the face of the dead mother reminds you of the death masks of Negro sculpture. A gorgeous embroidery brings along with it the composition of a Vermeer. Thus there are places in the film where an encyclopedic culture has been so integrally welded into cinematography that they remind you of nothing but Eisenstein.[12]

With this film, too, as with his Mexican film, Eisenstein aimed at 'a revival "in a new quality" of film poetry'.

The film also contained emotional echoes from Eisenstein's own life, not least in the basic theme itself – the father–son relationship that turns up again and again in Eisenstein's films (and projects), and whose emotional source is always patently clear. In this respect there was a grain of truth in Shumyatsky's later maliciously critical article in which he attempted to justify his brutal quashing of the film. From the first episodes filmed, according to Shumyatsky, Eisenstein had demonstrated that he was treating the events in a subjective and arbitrary way. But the real target of Shumyatsky's fury was Eisenstein's marvellously effective and widely admired techniques. Eisenstein's characterizations, for instance, depended on 'a metaphor concerning the centrifugal character of unleashed elemental forces', and Stepok's father, 'instead of being endowed with the features of the real enemy, appears like a mythological Pan from the paintings of the symbolist Vrubel'. Still more blasphemous from the Communist viewpoint, the central figure of Stepok was presented 'in luminously pale tones, with the face of a consecrated holy child. . . . In some of the shots, the source of light is placed behind Stepok so that this blond child in a white shirt seems to radiate a halo.'[13]

Generally speaking, the filming progressed well, Tisse, inspired by Eisenstein's plastic imagination, exploring the most expressive angles and compositions. Eisenstein's working relationship with the actors, however, was sometimes far from cordial, mainly because of his practice of keeping them in ignorance of the scene to be shot until just beforehand, and then only briefly outlining their movements. He used them as just one plastic element in the shot, without putting undue emphasis on their acting. This, and his deafness to the consequent complaints, was to be a frequent source of reproach. Meanwhile, in smoothing down frictions Eisenstein gratefully accepted the help of Elisabeta Teleshova, who was after to continue as his casting adviser and close personal friend.*

Work was intensive, with shooting from six in the morning till seven at night, when the unit retired to their hotel to discuss the day's work and plan the next. Eisenstein was determined to keep up to schedule and constantly recalled the experience of *Potemkin*:

'Well, have we come up to the record set during *Potemkin* when seventy-five shots were made in one day's filming on the steps?' 'No, but forty-five . . . is also pretty good.' 'Not good enough, not good enough. Don't let the old battleship shame us.'[14]

To film the acted sequences of the 'Highway' episode – only the biggest mass scenes were shot at Armavir – the unit later moved to Kharkov. During the move, Eisenstein paid what was intended to be a flying visit to Moscow, only to go down with ptomaine poisoning which delayed his return. This was the first of a series of misfortunes that were to dog the film from then onwards. On arriving at Kharkov, though only half recovered, he launched straight into the highway episode which, being the climax and the most complicated part of the film, he wanted to complete so as to construct the rest around it. In the episode two militiamen dislodge four incendiarists from their barricaded hide-out and lead them off to the city jail. On the highway the incendiarists attempt to escape but are recognized by the enraged farm-workers, who threaten to take the law into their own hands. At this point Stepok intervenes and relieves the tension of the situation with a joke, after which the saboteurs are again led off quietly. After the shooting of this episode one day the four incendiarists were hustled off to Kharkov airport

---

* The Teleshova in question was Elisabeta Sergeyevna Teleshova, often referred to in error as Elena. From one of Eisenstein's unpublished letters in the Elisabeta Teleshova archive at the Moscow Art Theatre Museum it clearly emerges that she was Eisenstein's mistress. In another, written to the local administration, he introduces Teleshova as 'my wife'. The apparent bigamy – for he had previously, it seems, married Pera Attasheva (Fogelman) – is explained by the fact that the matrimonial laws, which up to the 1940s were rather liberal, accepted as legal any *de facto* marital relation. Teleshova died during the war years (having appointed Eisenstein as her heir); and Attasheva remained Eisenstein's legal wife and, after his death, heiress – although they had always lived in separate places.

where, much to the astonishment of the onlooking unit, they were filmed in the slipstream from the propellers. But there was really no mystery: for, in the scene where the farm-workers recognize the saboteurs and express their fury in whistles and catcalls, Eisenstein envisaged the sound-track becoming progressively less realistic; he wanted gradually to eliminate all sound except for the whistling, which was to crescendo until finally merging into the wail of ships' sirens and factory whistles. The visual imagery had to keep pace with the sound-track, and so the script indicates filming the four first 'under a high wind' and then 'as in a hurricane'. The metaphor is sustained for some considerable time, and later in the scene, after Stepok has cracked his joke, the fields, sky and trees are shown reverberating under the gales of laughter.

Eisenstein also gave meticulously detailed attention to the frame compositions: sometimes, before allowing shooting to begin, he carefully arranged the position of each one of Stepok's fingers, the creases in his shirt, and even individual strands of hair.

During the spring Eisenstein had chosen a field near Moscow and had personally supervised its sowing with wheat in readiness for the filming due to begin there in the autumn. But heavy local rainfall had ruined the crops, and every time wheat grain was needed it had to be brought from the studio's properties store. The scene to be filmed there was Stepok's death. At the crack of dawn every morning, Stepok had to be lying stretched out, as if dead, in time for the cameras to catch the first few minutes of daybreak when the light was just right. In the eeriness of the morning mist, with Eisenstein issuing his instructions in a subdued whisper, Stepok's 'death' was sometimes so realistic that the onlookers were hushed into a tense silence. In view of their numbers, this was some achievement; for Eisenstein's friends and colleagues, including Kuleshov, Ermler, Savchenko, Barnet, Trauberg, Esther Shub and the Vasiliev brothers, as well as foreign visitors and tourists, all trooped out daily to the shooting. The veritable ballet enacted every time, under Eisenstein's magic direction, the equipment that had to be moved – and the crowd of onlookers with it – was a spectacle in itself.

Filming continued afterwards in the studio, the sound sequences by night. The first of these was the shooting of Stepok, in which the enraged father's hysterical madness mounts through a sort of animal dementia to a culminating violent paroxysm of fury. Again, the tension among the audience at times reached an unbearable pitch – until one of the perpetual jokes exchanged between Eisenstein and the young Stepok abruptly shattered the suspense. At other times, nothing would keep the boy awake, and the clearly recognizable snores that suddenly issued through the microphone would startle the unsuspecting sound operator out of his concentration.

In the course of filming, Eisenstein had at last been allocated new accommodation in a four-roomed flat at Potylika, which he finished furnishing by

September. At the same time a dacha was being built for him just outside Moscow.

Towards the end of October, when more than half of the filming had been completed, Eisenstein went down with smallpox, probably contracted while rummaging through the property boxes for old costumes. As the only known case in Moscow for two years, it represented yet another piece of atrocious bad luck. Three weeks of quarantine followed, during which daily radio bulletins on his health were issued, since his heart condition was also, apparently, causing concern. Nevertheless he kept up his spirits, as appears from a jocular letter to Marie Seton about 'them poxes'.[15] There followed a protracted convalescence, spent in a sanatorium in the Caucasus. Eisenstein nonetheless intended finishing the film by May 1936 – an intention soon frustrated when he caught a particularly virulent type of influenza that kept him in bed for his thirty-eighth saint's day.

After this second long absence, Eisenstein was forced to revise the scenario on orders from Shumyatsky, who had meanwhile expressed his dissatisfaction with the film so far shot. Thus his illnesses created new problems; for, in Jay Leyda's opinion, 'if his original schedule had been met the film might have been finished without major crisis and judged as a whole'.[16] As it was, Eisenstein now called on Isaac Babel's help for the revisions demanded by official policy changes. He greatly admired Babel and had invited him to speak to his students at the Institute – the same Babel who had once commented that 'to write a scenario is like summoning the midwife on the wedding night'.[17] Shooting was resumed in the autumn, but yet more revisions were to follow.

Despite a number of alterations to the plot, Eisenstein did not abandon his basic vision of the film. In its first form, the characters were – according to Shumyatsky –

not images of collective farmers, but biblical and mythological types. Eisenstein even hit upon the clever idea of portraying the chief of the political department as a man with an immobile face, enormous beard and the conduct of a biblical Saint.[18]

As for the 'smashing the church' episode, this was 'a veritable bacchanalia of destruction'. In the new version modified to meet Shumyatsky's demands, the history of the first production, in his opinion, repeated itself: the bacchanalia of destruction in the church was replaced by the bacchanalia of fire in the granary-firing episode, while the film's conception was again based on 'a clash of elemental forces of nature, on a struggle between "good" and "evil" '.

Lion Feuchtwanger, who saw the fire sequence soon after it was filmed, recalls Eisenstein's anxiety lest, even at that point, cuts would be demanded. Eisenstein also foresaw a number of other difficulties looming up in the future, which appeared even blacker as Babel gradually became marked down as a victim of the cultural purge.

In the meantime, however, filming continued. In January 1937 Eisenstein again succumbed to influenza, but in a letter to Leyda dated 1 February he expressed hopes of finishing the film in 'three–four weeks'. The same letter is interesting for revealing Eisenstein's continued interest in Western cultural life, despite the chilly political atmosphere. Even more revealing is the astonishing confession that with Leyda's departure he no longer had anyone with whom to discuss his theoretical ideas.

Most of the time with you I was petty and disagreeable – but that was a sort of self-protection against . . . oneself: against things that drive me mad – things I cannot put down in book form being chained to producing other things! You were allways [*sic*] provoking and touching my most secret wounds – *the* side of my work which is to my opinion the really most important of what I have to do – and which I am not doing . . . and when I by accident jump out of production for an hour or so, I feel like Peer Gynt in the scene where he watches the rush of leaves on the earth which happen to be his ideas that never got form.[19]

It was a strange confession, coming from an artist in the full fever of creation, that his *raison d'être* was to be a theoretician. Equally illuminating is the implication that he was now putting his theories into practice. The confession explains a lot about the genesis of his work and its experimental character. His creative fire linked up with his intellectual thinking and was nourished by it in a complex way that recalls Leonardo da Vinci.

After three weeks in bed, Eisenstein resumed work at the beginning of March 1937. On 17 March, however, Shumyatsky, who was to be deposed less than a year later as 'a tool of political enemies', finally vetoed the film, publishing the malicious article in *Pravda* which has already been quoted. At this point the film disappeared without trace, and was rumoured to have been destroyed without Eisenstein's knowledge.* Subsequently all reference to the film was forbidden; even a whispered mention of it was risky. Thus two years' creative work was brought to nothing, thanks, as Vishnevsky put it, to 'continued efforts of enemies and saboteurs'.

* Thanks to Eisenstein having saved a few frames from each shot, Naum Kleiman was able to reconstruct his main ideas for the film: not only the structure of the missing film, but also the modifications imposed on the second version. The official story is that the working-copy as well as the negatives were deposited in an underground shelter, and that during the war water penetrated into the shelter and destroyed all the films in it. There seems to be no concrete evidence, however, that the film was destroyed; it has been stated on good authority that Eisenstein's montage assistant handed it over one night to a chauffeur from the Ministry of Cinema, whence all trace of it was lost. The *montageuse*, however, whose good faith I have no reason to doubt, maintains that Eisenstein once told her that he had hidden a copy so thoroughly that no one would be able to find it; her supposition was that he had it buried in the grounds of his dacha, though no attempt to verify this has been made. A number of other indications – none of which may be revealed at the present time – lead me to believe that somewhere there exists a copy which will, I hope, one day come to light.

There followed, on 19–21 March, a conference staged with the evident purpose of condemning Eisenstein, the outcome of which was a long and complicated self-criticism published as a brochure along with other critical comment on the film. Esther Shub relates that on 20 July Eisenstein sent her a copy on which he had written in red ink 'to my dear friend, Esther', and sketched the palm of a hand.

The artistic line was traced on the palm with several breaks in it, and beside it the comment: 'ha, ha'. The line of destiny – an arrow and again 'ha, ha'.[20]

Bezhin Meadow was, in Eisenstein's own words, 'one of the most bitterly painful experiences in my creative life'.[21]

Meanwhile, in June, Léon Moussinac had found him greatly changed and resolutely unwilling to discuss the political climate, although at the same time keeping up an outward appearance of calm.

It was probably faith in himself and his artistic mission that kept Eisenstein going; that, and his opinion, committed to paper in connection with Meyerhold's fate, that 'a dose of philistinism ensures peace and stability, the in-rooting and pleasure of dedication, while the lack of it condemns a hyper-romantic nature to eternal anxieties, troubles, and ups and downs, to the vicissitudes of fate, to the destiny of Icarus, whose path through life is identical with that of the Flying Dutchman'.[22] This seems to provide a clue to what is otherwise something of a mystery: how Eisenstein survived when heads all around him were rolling, including those of his friends Tretyakov, Meyerhold and Babel. In 1936 and 1937 rumours of his arrest were rife abroad, though he himself denied them in an article in *Izvestia* of 8 February 1937. The most plausible explanation appears to be Stalin's arbitrariness when it came to deciding where the axe should fall next. His weakness for films is well known, and the cinema was apparently the only cultural sphere in which no outstanding figure was liquidated. In addition, Stalin seems to have had a special sympathy for Eisenstein himself, as their many meetings suggest and as Eisenstein's personal notebooks – which reportedly describe the exact nature of their relationship – may well be found to confirm. (Permission to publish or even consult them is persistently refused.) It thus seems likely that Eisenstein's abject self-criticisms represented that 'dose of philistinism' necessary to secure, not merely his 'peace and stability' but his actual physical survival. They were almost certainly not a sign of cowardice, his tortuous and sophisticated self-criticisms in connection with *Bezhin Meadow* having rather a ring of irony about them. In an article on his staging of *The Valkyrie*, published in 1940, he described 'the twilight of the Gods' as symbolizing 'the death of the whole "world of murder and plunder, legalized by falsehood, deceit and hypocrisy"'[23] – a somewhat gratuitous synopsis which many have interpreted as his comment on the contemporary Soviet scene. In any case the

Sketches for *The False Nero*

fact remains indisputable: that his compromises were restricted to words and did not affect his creative activities. They were, if you like, a form of struggle for the survival of his work.

Other Projects

Apart from his real friends, the only prominent cultural figure who stood by Eisenstein at this difficult period seems to have been Fadeyev, who sent an admiring and encouraging letter begging Eisenstein not to pay overmuch attention to the slanders and attacks, and ending up: 'I clasp you warmly, warmly by the hand.'[24] It did much to restore Eisenstein's morale, and marked the beginning of a close friendship between them; in moments of trouble Eisenstein was frequently to seek Fadeyev's company and to include him among the few people he addressed by the familiar form.

Far from giving way before the implacable onslaught which – almost like the recurrent theme of his films – threatened to crush him, Eisenstein, encouraged in all probability by Shumyatsky's removal, was, in fact, preparing new projects. Even while he was working on *Bezhin Meadow*, two projects were in the wind. One was the *Black Consul* idea, revived by Robeson's arrival in Moscow for a concert tour and his promise to be at Eisenstein's disposal for filming from July until October. Another was apparently suggested by Eisenstein's good friend Vsevolod Vishnevsky. Eisenstein often visited Vishnevsky for a meal, after which they would retire to the writer's study and spend long periods sitting looking at each other in silence. After *Bezhin Meadow* was stopped, Vishnevsky did his best to encourage Eisenstein, and out of this there eventually emerged the idea for a joint project entitled *We the Russian People*. Eisenstein was enthusiastic about the script and, after its favourable reception by a group of actors, scenographers and the artistic council of Mosfilm to whom Vishnevsky read it, looked forward to starting work on the film. But it proved to be, as Vishnevsky wrote two years later, yet another of 'all those films which Eisenstein's enemies obstructed'.

Another possibility was Feuchtwanger's historical novel *The Ugly Duchess*, which Eisenstein discussed with the author during his visit to Moscow in connection with the screening of his novel *The Oppenheim Family*. In March 1937 Feuchtwanger also sent a copy of another novel, *The False Nero*, to Eisenstein, who made a series of sketches and designs for it, possibly for a stage production. Then there was talk of a film based on V. V. Distler's scenario about gold-prospectors in Siberia.

Projects, projects and yet more projects. . . . But the next film was to be an entirely different proposition.

10. Pedagogic Respite

I hope to rob a couple of months out of my director's biography and still accomplish what I ought to do.
EISENSTEIN

'The Institute exhausts me,' Eisenstein often remarked. But it was a pleasurable exhaustion, his love – and perhaps need – to teach dating back to his days at the Proletkult Theatre. From 1928 until he went abroad in 1929 he lectured at the Technical School of Cinematography (GTK) – upgraded during this period to an Institute (GIK) – conducting, among other things, a seminar on Emile Zola and 'several purely cinematic elements in the plastic side of his creative work'[1]; and from his appointment to the Institute's Chair of Directing in October 1932 until the end of his life he was continuously engaged in lecturing.

Between the autumn of 1932 and early 1933, Eisenstein channelled his frustrated film-making energies into reorganizing the Institute and elaborating the programme for the Director's Course: 'Standard Course of Directing and Creative Methods in Cinematography'. 'It was,' he sadly recorded, 'some compensation in those years when, after the Mexican trauma, I was not able to make a single film.'[2] His ill-wishers made frequent pointed remarks to the effect that he who can, creates; he who can't, teaches. His retort – that 'to teach' at the present stage still meant really 'to create' – was no empty phrase: in line with the declared aim of his course – 'to penetrate the laboratory of creation' – his classes were indeed veritable creative sessions.

Eisenstein held extremely firm pedagogic principles. Plagiarism was ana-

Professor Eisenstein . . .

thema to him and if ever he caught his students imitating him he would bark out: 'So you've decided to rival the steps in *Potemkin*? You want to pinch from me? . . .'[3] Nor did he suffer mistakes lightly; but although he brought the full harshness of his judgement to bear in criticizing his students' work his sense of humour was never far away, and his classroom frequently resounded with hoots of laughter.

His first lecture in 1928 has been recalled by one of his students, Vladimir Nizhny. The first-year class was then held in the former hall of mirrors of the old Yar Restaurant and, as Eisenstein entered the room, his 'close-up' was reflected over and over again in the multiple mirrors. 'One thing at least is obvious,' he joked; 'as you perceive, you're going to have not one but a whole bunch of teachers.'

Later on Eisenstein came to be known as 'the twenty-headed director' – not because of the mirrors, but because in teaching he made a point of drawing all twenty of his students into discussions on any problem to be solved. In a lively exchange of question and answer, their different solutions were debated at length before Eisenstein would finally pronounce on it himself. At this point silence reigned supreme as the students took one more step in the direction of learning to think creatively. It was one of Eisenstein's basic tenets that

. . . blesses his pupil Vasiliev

the instructor is no more than *primus inter pares* – first among equals. The collective (and later each member of it individually) works its way through all the difficulties and torments of creative work, through the whole process of creative formation, from the first faint, glimmering hint of the theme, down to a decision on whether the buttons on the leather jacket of the last extra player are suitable for filming purposes.[5]

He demanded absolute precision from his students, sometimes snapping, 'Don't say "I think!" Until you *know*, I will not listen to you!' For his first and foremost aim was to get his students thinking, and thinking clearly; while his ultimate objective was that their minds should be receptive to all forms of culture.

Eisenstein invariably opened the course with a light-hearted discussion, listening to his students' tales and launching into reminiscences of his own travels. Each new section of the course began with his presentation of certain concrete problems to be solved. These entailed a continual dialogue during which he expounded clearly his line of thinking before throwing out dozens of questions, weighing up the answers, contradicting them. . . . These discussions would be supplemented by a vast variety of illustrative material produced from his enormous yellow briefcase: Hokusai sketches, Daumier engravings, reproductions of Serov, exotic ritual masks from all over the world, books, photographs. He stirred their imagination in every direction, sketching on the blackboard the while to convey his ideas with greater clarity. This pictorial clarification – 'always try to define things plastically'[6] – was a method he constantly urged his students to adopt. Further variety was added through his practice of inviting colleagues and specialists, among them Gorky and Babel, to speak to the students. Once he invited a member of the Kabuki Theatre to give a supplementary course on movement. Two of his friends, the actress Judith Glizer and the actor Maxim Strauch, were sometimes used as veritable guineapigs.

His lectures gave the impression of being improvisations. In fact, however, they were the fruit of long preparatory work, carried out with the same thoroughness and attention to detail as he put into his film-making. Not surprisingly, his methods produced some outstanding students – from the Vasiliev brothers to the young Rostotsky – who in turn became celebrities in their own right.

Eisenstein's lectures – running into thousands of pages – were stenographed, but only a handful, edited by Vladimir Nizhny, have yet been published. They constitute a mine of unimaginable wealth relating to that intimate 'laboratory of creation' of Eisenstein's, a mine that he intended drawing on one day for a series of books on film aesthetics.

11. *Alexander Nevsky*

To remove the barriers between sight and sound, between the seen world and the heard world! To bring about a unity and a harmonious relationship between these two opposite spheres. What an absorbing task!
EISENSTEIN

In 1937 Eisenstein was unexpectedly asked to make a historical film of considerable political significance in the context of the rising threat of Nazi Germany: the thirteenth-century story of the rout of the marauding Teutonic armies by Russians united in a sense of patriotism and national identity under Prince Alexander Nevsky. The request demonstrates the esteem which, in spite of everything, he still enjoyed, and was probably inspired less by benevolence than by a clear-sighted realization on the part of those who knew him well that a subject of such major importance could best be served – and perhaps be helped to achieve the biggest impact abroad – by Eisenstein.

The film at first held almost no appeal for Eisenstein, the theme having little in common with his current interests, while the precise demands involved were alien to his spontaneous free-roaming creative nature.

A difficult situation. The most difficult situation in our work, for a creative imagination. To 'invent' for the screen a character that would strictly conform to thematic 'demands' theoretically expressed with a mathematical exactitude in a formula! This was the formula – to create the images to accord with it! . . . But there are situations when you have no choice. And this was precisely the case as far as we were concerned.[1]

Given the precariousness of his position, it was, indeed, Hobson's choice, and he accepted. With his characteristic sense of irony, Eisenstein thought of 'the saint' — Alexander Nevsky had been canonized — whom he now 'had to make into a film hero, since his country had turned him into a national hero'.[2]

'With heroes from the past we discuss as man to man'

In making *Alexander Nevsky*, Eisenstein proposed resolving in practice a number of problems that had long preoccupied him in theory — in the first place, those of audio-visual composition.

Even before his celebrated manifesto on aural and visual counterpoint, published in the summer of 1928, Eisenstein had approached the problems of synthesizing sight and sound both in working with Meisel on the *Potemkin* score and in his plastic interpretation of sound effects in *October*. But 'the sweet poison of audio-visual montage attacked my organism only later'. There had been that 'humble piece of irony', *Romance Sentimentale*, his 1930 conference in Hollywood[3] — when he expressed his belief that 'the first powerful example of the perfectly cut and constructed sound film' had yet to materialize — and finally his experiments in making *Bezhin Meadow*. His experience had taken a step forward in this film, in which 'in one episode the audio-visual counterpoint was resolved in principle (and in practice)'.[4] And the solution found was now — tragically late in view of Eisenstein's pioneering theoretical work ten years earlier — to help create, in *Nevsky*, 'an organic cinematographic fusion of sound and image'.[5]

Another problem which he needed to solve was the presentation and structure of a historical film — which had also, as a primary official requirement, to be a contemporary film. The central question Eisenstein set about tackling back to front: not how to transpose the film's historical subject into the context of the critical contemporary situation, but how to elevate the *topics of the day* to the level of historical generalization *through the intermediary* of the subject. What means of expression would permit such inverted metaphorical treatment of this period of history? Was it more important to pay meticulous respect to historical detail or to bring out the contemporary significance of the events depicted? Should the characters be hieratically stylized as in the icons and art works of the period? Should the 'saint' Nevsky be portrayed as an exalted and revered figure or as 'a down-to-earth man even to his carpet slippers'?

The answers came to Eisenstein as he elaborated his plan for the film. History should be interpreted from the viewpoint of its topical relevance. The first essential was clarity, and as he analysed the characters he saw them as fundamentally 'the same as us', as heroes with whom 'we can talk as man to man'.[6] There was no need to debase the heroes of the past nor to elevate modern man to bring them to a common level. Any stylization of the characters must, he therefore concluded, be one of broad outline only; the same applied to the landscape and setting with which they had to blend. And so, in portraying the historic landscape, his guiding principle became to concentrate on the distant perspective, avoiding a 'multiplicity of detail' – a principle that attained its peak expression in the battle on the ice where only the ice and the vast expanse of grey sky are visible.

An apple for Nevsky

However alien to him was his rigorously established blueprint, Eisenstein found his creative passion fired anew the moment he started work. The theme of fatality, dating from his childhood and associated particularly with the memory of the trains at Smolensk, inspired the very first image, that of the attacking Teuton 'wild boar' gallop* – which he outlined in a montage sketch for the first frame 'even before coming to an agreement with Pavlenko'[7] (his co-scenarist) – and thus determined the film's prevailing emotional tone. The sinister nocturnal shrieks after the battle were also, as we have seen, evoked by the screeching of the changing signals in the inky darkness of Smolensk railway station.

These were Eisenstein's basic ideas when, together with his co-scenarist, Pyotr Pavlenko, he set about his documentary researches in preparation for writing the scenario.

In the first documentary record he delved into, an ancient biography of Nevsky, Eisenstein was amazed by the similarity between a description of the Crusaders' sacking of Gersik and an account in that day's newspaper of the barbaric destruction of Guernica by Fascist bombs. This strange coincidental similarity between past and contemporary events vindicated his choice of stylistic approach, as also did the museum exhibits he scrutinized in his familiar striving after the 'feel' of the period. A persistent 'leitmotiv pulsating through the dust of the documents and the rust of the museum antiquities' reinforced his belief that 'in spirit, if not in letter, the events of the thirteenth century are emotionally close to ours'.[8]

In defining the central figure of the scenario, the 'saintly' Alexander Nevsky, Eisenstein was at first led astray by his very sainthood. His initial idea was to endow him with superhuman qualities – with the colossal strength, for instance, to rip apart an apparently indestructible fishing-net – but this was eventually abandoned in favour of a real-life figure with both feet planted well and truly on the ground. Nevsky's essential feature Eisenstein saw as being his inspiring courage, which emanated from a deep intellectual wisdom; in trying to synthesize these two facets of his character in plastic terms, he hit on the two figures of his comrades-in-arms: the Novgorod heroes, Buslai the brave and Gavrilo the wise.

---

* A battle tactic of the ancient Teuton cavalry which advanced in closed formation to pierce the enemy ranks like the thrusting snout of a wild boar.

A major problem proved to be how to give plastic expression to the genius of Nevsky's battle stratagem. What could make Nevsky hit on the idea for defeating the Teutons by cutting their advancing forces in two? Having long been fascinated by the triviality of the incident that inspired Newton's theory of gravitation, Eisenstein proposed making Nevsky's inspiration dependent upon an equally simple happening on the eve of battle. The problem was to find the 'apple'. For days on end he and Pavlenko racked their brains. Pavlenko's first solution was a wood-chopping scene in which an axe becomes immovably stuck in a knot of wood, inspiring Nevsky to thoughts of a 'wedge' trap for the enemy. Then the fact that the battle took place on ice suggested the idea of Nevsky watching the ice break beneath the weight of a cat. After many sleepless nights in a row, Eisenstein eventually hit on a solution derived from folklore: the story of the vixen and the hare, in which the hare leads the pursuing vixen into a narrow cleft between two birch trees, where she sticks fast, and then rapes her.

Eisenstein and Pavlenko discussed this idea, and after various modifications of detail it was written into the scenario. 'If we had had more time to work on it, a month say, we would have come up with a more complete solution. But there was no time.' In fact, Eisenstein later realized that a sound image would have been far more effective. Nevertheless, he was sufficiently pleased with the solution adopted to give Victor Shklovsky – who had given him the book containing the folktale – a drawing of its climax.

The next problem was to find an actor talented and forceful enough to narrate this story convincingly, and also to provide a role sufficiently tempting to attract him in the first place. Dmitri Orlov was eventually chosen and given the 'vacant' role of the Novgorod armourer, Ignat – a role till that point completely undefined – which then developed around him. Thus the originally minor figure of Ignat filled out into the colourful figure we know from the film as new ideas cropped up and were woven round him. One idea was to make him the person in Novgorod responsible for summoning Nevsky to head the Russian soldiers. Next, Ignat was given the role of handing out the suits of armour he had forged – leaving himself with one that was too small for him. Ignat would comment: 'It's a bit short!' The idea fitted in with another desideratum: a character entrenched in the sympathies of the audience, whose death would symbolize and intensify the tragedy of the Russian losses in battle. Ignat, therefore, would die – and as a result of the suit of armour. It would leave his neck unprotected, an inviting target for a traitor's knife. The comic remark, 'It's a bit short!', repeated as he dies, would be rich in pathos.

And so the abstract ideas, the prescribed theoretical demands, took on shape in flesh-and-blood images. The reins of what Eisenstein called 'the two coursers – logical thinking and imagination'[9] – were both firmly grasped and the two steeds set galloping side by side.

For the settings Eisenstein followed his customary practice of visiting the actual historic scenes of the action: Pereyaslavl, the Nevsky Heights, the banks of Lake Pleshchayev and other places trodden by the feet of the real Alexander Nevsky. Mentally Eisenstein relived the events of the period. The siege of Novgorod, the battle on the ice, the Pskov fire, characters with clearly defined features and clothing – all those were so vivid for him during October and November 1937 that he recorded them in precise detail in his sketches.

In November the first version of the scenario, entitled *Russ*, was completed and published – after the incorporation of a series of suggestions volunteered by Vishnevsky at the galley-proof stage – in *Znamya* (No. 12, 1937). Following publication, a whole avalanche of suggestions flooded in from historians, teachers, students and even schoolchildren. But along with the friendly advice came the predictable carping criticisms – this time to no avail, as the official go-ahead for shooting had already been given.

For the moment, however, Eisenstein was still engrossed in preparatory research; and the winter of early 1938 saw him contemplating the ancient buildings of Novgorod, 'fondling the theme that sang in every stone'. He tried to imagine the inhabitants of seven centuries before – how they talked, how they ate, how they walked. He climbed the crumbling walls and tower and looked out over the scarcely changed landscape; he touched the things they had touched, endeavouring to make them come alive for himself. But apart from the twelfth-century Church of Spas-Nereditsa, little remained of the town, and Eisenstein experienced intense difficulty in conjuring up the period scene until he noticed the plaque recording the starting and finishing dates for the building of Santa Sophia cathedral. This did the trick, evoking for Eisenstein a picture of thirteenth-century workers toiling at their task – ordinary workers, just like those of modern Russia and bearing no resemblance to the stylized silhouettes in the icons and miniatures of the period.

Eisenstein's visit to Novgorod revealed, however, the impossibility of filming there. As he wrote to Vishnevsky: 'Almost nothing remains. . . . There are architectural remains, but they have sunk so deeply into the earth that their proportions are ruined.'[10] Instead Eisenstein designed a new Novgorod with gleaming white walls, that may have owed something to his indignation at the décor for a production of *Prince Igor* he saw with Jay Leyda: 'Imagine assuming that the buildings then looked like the same buildings today – ruined and grey!'

Outside Novgorod, on the ice of Lake Ilmen, he could scarcely record the sensations inspired in him by the vast icy stretches, so bitterly cold was it.

The scenario was still undergoing modifications when, on 2 February 1938, Pavlenko wrote despairingly to Eisenstein:

The main thing is that neither you nor I prolong [the work] too long. I've a feeling that you've a tendency in that direction, have you not? If so − I beg you on my knees, don't prolong things too much. Let's hurry − this is one of the factors of success![12]

Of course Eisenstein wanted to hurry; but with the scenario still unfinished it seemed inevitable that the winter scenes − in other words, sixty per cent of the film − would have to wait till the following winter. It was at this point that Dmitri Vasiliev, who had been appointed by the studio as Eisenstein's co-director, with the obvious though unstated object of keeping a check on him − suggested shooting these scenes during the summer. The idea was tempting, but the problem of creating an illusion of winter that would not appear obviously faked seemed insurmountable. Happily the only feasible solution − to concentrate on the essential features of winter, 'its dimensions of sound and light', eliminating all extraneous detail that would be difficult to reproduce, coincided with Eisenstein's original ideas for a stylized landscape, and he eventually accepted the risk. Between March and May intensive preparations were made for the filming, as numerous sketches from this period illustrate.

The shooting-script was written in twelve days and, as is clear from Teleshova's unpublished diary, filming started in June. Shooting for the battle scenes began under a blazing hot sun, and for once luck was on Eisenstein's side: forty days of continuous sunshine allowed the battle on the lake to be filmed without interruption − in an apple orchard near the Mosfilm studios which had been cleared of trees and covered over an area of about seven acres with a layer of artificial snow. For the spectacular ice-trap episode, the location was a lake near Moscow, one shore of which was carpeted with 'snow', while the boughs of the trees were painted white and dotted with cotton wool to give an effect of hoarfrost; the actors themselves were liberally sprinkled with salt. The 'ice', weighing well over seventeen tons, was supported by air-filled pontoons from which the air could be released at a given signal for the 'ice' to give way.

To counteract the strong sunlight and summer sky effects, hand-operated cameras and special filters were used throughout for the winter scenes. The slow shooting-speed this necessitated served coincidentally to accentuate the dynamic quality of the battle episodes.

During filming various acting problems arose which Teleshova again helped Eisenstein to sort out. She had already assisted in the casting and it was she, in fact, who insisted on Nikolai Cherkasov for Alexander − a role which, ironically in view of his initial refusal, later brought him the Order of Lenin.

Eisenstein personally supervised every detail, from make-up to the manufacture of Nevsky's armour, reproduced from thirteenth-century armour in the Hermitage Museum. He was even present at fittings, once spending a full hour in the sweltering heat adjusting part of Cherkasov's costume.

Work proceeded at an intensive pace, studio filming − according to

Alexander Nevsky: publicity picture with (below) a parody of it, with Tisse (left), Eisenstein and Prokofiev

Teleshova's diary — going on parallel with shooting for the outside battle scenes.

At the editing stage, Eisenstein began his familiar improvisations. Certain shortcomings in the film's structure, for which he himself was to blame, became evident at this point. The montage composition for the battle seemed lacking in clarity, for example: general shots clearly showing one mass of combatants charging into another were needed to supplement the near shots. And so he was obliged to film a whole new mass scene. Even this did not do the trick and he simplified and modified further, cutting out some characters (Nevsky's wife, for instance) altogether. Yet still the definition of each phase of the battle was not sufficiently clear, and he proposed shortening part of the scene by some 200 metres. Permission to do so was, however, refused, so that the final version — universally hailed for its compositional perfection — was in fact 200 metres too long in the estimation of its creator! (According to Jean Mitry, 600 metres.)

In his montage for the 'wedge' attack by the Teutonic Knights, Eisenstein strove to attain particularly emotive compositional effects:

This episode passes through all the shades of an experience of increasing terror, where approaching danger makes the heart contract and the breathing irregular. The structure of this 'leaping wedge' in *Alexander Nevsky* is, with variations, exactly modelled on the inner process of such an experience. This dictated all the rhythms of the sequence — cumulative, disjunctive, the speeding up and slowing down of the movement. The boiling pulsing of an excited heart dictated the rhythm of the leaping hoofs: pictorially — the *leap* of the galloping knights; compositionally — the *beat* to the bursting point of an excited heart.

To produce the success of this sequence, both the pictorial and compositional structures are fused in the welded unity of a terrifying image — the beginning of the battle that is to be a fight to the finish.

And the event, as it is unfolded on the screen according to a timetable of the running of this or that passion . . . involves the emotions of the spectator according to the same timetable, arousing in him the same tangle of passions which originally designed the compositional scheme of the work. [An echo of the 'montage of attractions' is here discernible.]

This is the secret of the genuinely emotional affect [*sic*] of real composition. Employing for source *the structure of human emotion, it unmistakably appeals to emotion*, unmistakably arouses the complex of those feelings that gave birth to the composition.[13]

Meanwhile there still remained the central problem of the audio-visual montage, for which Eisenstein would have liked to be able 'to experiment in peace, systematically and with control, with so many thoughts and hopes accumulated during years of meditating on sound cinematography!' But he was already under pressure of time: even after the shift from winter to summer filming the schedule had been cut three times, and one entire scene that had been filmed with great difficulty, the scene of the bridge over the Volkhov, had to be jettisoned for a remarkable reason. According to Victor Shklovsky, the editing was almost completed when a nocturnal telephone call announced that Stalin wanted to view the film at once. It was rushed round to the Kremlin, but the reel containing the Volkhov bridge sequence was forgotten: Eisenstein, putting some finishing touches to it, had fallen asleep over it in the cutting room. Stalin did not notice that a reel was missing and afterwards nobody dared to tell him that he had viewed – and enjoyed – an incomplete film. Thus *Nevsky* was released without this sequence, a sequence nobody has seen. It seems probable that Eisenstein preserved the reel; if so, I cannot help wondering where it is now.

The pace of work was telling on Eisenstein. (For months after the first night he still could not concentrate properly on his theoretical work, so exhausted was he.) And now, in the early summer of 1938, with his deadline of 7 November looming ever nearer, he foresaw the crowning tragedy of having to abandon all his ideas on the sound film completely. At precisely this point, however, he had the stroke of fortune to encounter the extraordinary qualities of Sergei Prokofiev.

Meeting with Prokofiev [14]

The collaboration between Eisenstein and Prokofiev constitutes a notable phenomenon in art history: two artists of genius synchronizing their talents so perfectly that a single mind might have been at work.

Some of Prokofiev's less well-known characteristics will help to explain the basis for this successful collaboration. He had, according to Heinrich Neuhaus (Richter's piano teacher), an 'astounding capacity for work, letting nothing – time, place or mood – deter him'. His punctuality, too, was proverbial: he would give prospective visitors appointments precise to the minute, and would be irritated if the visitor was the slightest bit late. Eisenstein's remark that he 'functioned like a clock' (he was referring in this instance to the precision that characterized Prokofiev's creative work) was confirmed by Prokofiev's neighbour, the cellist Rostropovich, who claimed to tell the time to the minute by the whir from Prokofiev's razor.

Yet, despite his punctiliousness and extraordinary self-discipline, he liked dancing and tennis, finding common ground here with Eisenstein. And this most cerebral of contemporary composers – as Eisenstein characterized him – also had a 'very warm heart'. His wife recalls his extreme sensitivity and identification with the sufferings of others, while Ehrenburg relates how he was overwhelmingly saddened by 'those dreadful years' of political persecution, in connection with which he once said: 'Today one must work. Work's the only thing, the only salvation.' [15]

Eisenstein held Prokofiev's work in the highest esteem, comparing it with 'the precise and laconic style of Stendhal'; and he was soon to be impressed and intrigued by the composer's ability to penetrate to the very essence of a film image.

Their collaboration began in May 1938. From their first meeting, they needed few words to understand each other; both were ready to start work immediately. Prokofiev had already studied examples of medieval music sent by Eisenstein and had spent several days thinking about the film, so that in all probability he arrived at the meeting having – in conformity with his principle – 'the basic theme material in mind, which means that the principal element for setting about the work is ready'.[16] Eisenstein, for his part, had prepared numerous sketches incorporating his ideas for the score. After discussing the overall character of the music, they turned in greater detail to the battle on the ice, for which Eisenstein asked Prokofiev to compose the music before filming. Showing his sketches for the shots and explaining his emotional and structural ideas for the episode, he suggested that Prokofiev should use ancient Catholic canticles for the Teutonic knights' attack. But Prokofiev found these left him cold and came up with an alternative proposal which coincided with Eisenstein's own basic stylistic ideas for the film: to arrange the music 'not in the form in which it sounded at the time of the battle on the ice, but as we would imagine it sounding today'. Similarly with the Russian theme music. Thus there was from the beginning perfect emotional and conceptual accord between the two artists.

Elaborating further, Prokofiev explained the need to divide the music into that for the Russians and that for the Teutons. The latter should, he thought, jar on the ear of the Russian listener, and he proposed experimenting with the microphones to produce deliberately distorted sounds. Between them they established where special sound effects should be added so that the music for the attack should tail off into the sounds of battle, from which the triumphant Russian theme would later emerge. After several days Prokofiev produced the music for the whole episode, which was then recorded as a basis for the filming.

Thereafter, since neither was keen to 'go first' and set the rhythm for a scene, there was a constant toss-up as to who should do so. Sometimes Eisenstein started, completing the montage for a sequence and running it through several times for Prokofiev in the evening. The composer demanded absolute silence throughout, as he watched with intense concentration while simultaneously beating rhythmically on the edge of the armchair. Eisenstein looked on fascinated, curious to fathom the secret of the composer's creative process. On one occasion Prokofiev exclaimed 'Marvellous!' over a montage sequence in which, as Eisenstein recalled, there was 'cleverly interwoven a counterpoint of three distinct movements of rhythm, cadence and direction:

the protagonist, the group making up the background, and the column of men cutting in close-up into the view of the panning camera.'

These run-throughs usually ended at midnight, when, having noted only the timing of the sequence, Prokofiev would leave, promising the music for the following day at 12 o'clock. And Eisenstein could always be certain that on the dot of 11.55 Prokofiev would turn up in his little blue car bringing music that harmonized perfectly, not only with the general rhythm of the action but with all the emotional and structural subtleties of the montage.[17] Rare were the occasions when the composer failed to 'feel' the intimate emotional structure of each sequence and attune his own sensibility. His only serious clash with Eisenstein came after the score was completed, over the proposed overture for the film. This he refused to write, since the music for the tragic opening scenes was irreconcilable with his own ideas for a triumphal-heroic introduction; while Eisenstein regarded as impossible at this late stage any further changes to the montage structure. The overture never materialized; hence the projection of the credit titles in silence – which many commentators have interpreted as a specially intended effect on Eisenstein's part.

Eisenstein employed a number of ingenious methods for conveying to Prokofiev the nature of the music required for a given scene – for the part of the battle scene, for instance, where pipes and drums are played for the victorious Russian soldiers.

I couldn't find a way to explain to Prokofiev what precise effect should be 'seen' in his music for this joyful moment. Seeing that we were getting nowhere, I ordered some 'prop' instruments constructed, shot these being played (without sound) *visually*, and projected the results for Prokofiev – who almost immediately handed me an exact 'musical equivalent' to that visual image of pipers and drummers which I had shown him.[18]

Although Eisenstein frequently denied any understanding of music, he did on one occasion write: 'I think it's only by chance that I am not a composer. For nothing excites me more than compositional problems.'[19] Prokofiev, for his part, considered that the symphonic character of Eisenstein's montage constructions implied a subtle appreciation of the nuances of music and consequently respected his opinions on the music; it was not unknown for him to rewrite a passage as many as six times until it met with Eisenstein's unqualified approval. Once he abandoned an attempt to introduce some previously composed themes on seeing that Eisenstein 'would not let any rusty old horseshoe slip by him'.

Sometimes the process was reversed, when the music inspired Eisenstein to entirely new plastic interpretations. This happened for the scene of Gavrilo's farewell embrace with Vaska and likewise for the sequence of the cavalry charge, in both of which the revised visual effects harmonize perfectly with

Visual sound

the tonal structure of the film. The same was true whenever Prokofiev composed the music before the editing. In these cases Eisenstein began by thoroughly assimilating all the plastic material available for a scene until his picture of it was limpidly clear. Then he looked for a perfect match for a particular image in a certain snatch of music, 'an "intimate consonance", defying rational explanation, between the musical and the pictorial fragments'.

When it came to recording the sound-track, Prokofiev again demonstrated his characteristic thoroughness, first familiarizing himself with all the technical problems and with the studio's sound-effect equipment. Some of this he used in the score. The 'square formation' sequence, for example, is scored for five percussion instruments – and the Mosfilm bath-tub. (The cantata *Alexander Nevsky* differs considerably from the film music of which it is an adaptation.) He experimented with microphone distortions, recording the Teuton trumpets, for example, so close to the microphone as to amplify the distortions and thus achieve 'an immensely dramatic effect'. Other experiments even put to use defects in the apparatus to obtain special effects. One technique which he pioneered was to record the orchestra and choir separately, mixing them afterwards to synchronize with the dramatic requirements.

After each final rehearsal, the composer would invite Eisenstein to be present at the recording. Invariably the latter found some tiny detail that needed attention, some dramatic effect that needed highlighting, with the result that, as Prokofiev agreed, 'we greatly improved the musical effects'.[20]

Both Eisenstein and Prokofiev were delighted with the result of their collaboration – as, indeed, they were with the whole creative experience it provided. For Eisenstein it was to mean the discovery of the laws for harmonizing sound with picture. Prokofiev, for his part, was shortly afterwards to declare: 'I consider cinematography to be the most modern of the arts.'[21]

The Rigours of Composition

The completed *Alexander Nevsky* was remarkable for its forcefulness and concise and unified character. Eisenstein himself attributed this to the fact that '*everything* revolves round a *single* idea . . . the enemy and the need to defeat him'.[22] And in another unpublished note he defines *Alexander Nevsky* as 'a fugue on the theme of patriotism', the montage method for which is also 'the method of the fugue'.

Equally remarkable is Eisenstein's stylistic precision, which reaches a new height in the exactitude of the plastic compositions (often echoing in more developed form techniques used in *Que Viva Mexico!* and *Bezhin Meadow*) and the expressiveness of form. In the compositional groupings of characters, for instance, the unity of the foreground figures is invariably balanced by symmetrically – or ostentatiously asymmetrically – arranged groupings in the background. As Jean Mitry pointed out in illustrating this, if there is a tower in the foreground and a flight of three steps in the background, then there will be three figures on the tower balanced by a lone figure on the steps. A feature of the arrangements is their graphic linearity or geometric form. Jean Mitry and Gaston Bounoure even distinguish geometrical formulae corresponding with particular emotions or psychological states. Colour, too, plays a vital role in heightening the emotional intensity: the brutality and death associated with the Teutons are – paradoxically – expressed in terms of white, the heroism of the Russians in black. The dynamic of all the shots is subordinated to these plastic characteristics. The Teutonic knights always appear in strictly geometrical formation, contrasting with the irregularity and disarray of the Russian troops who advance in successive waves. By alternating the movements of the 'white' Teutons and the 'black' Russians, Eisenstein creates what Mitry describes as 'plastic rhymes incorporated in a symphony of lines, forms and colours which unfold a single symphony of movement'. The ice theme, too, is linked symbolically with the Teutons – like fire with the Russians – while a whole series of plastic themes, such as the rows of helmets behind the lances, metaphorically convey certain ideas or emotions.

Topping all these accomplishments in *Alexander Nevsky* was, of course,

Alexander Nevsky: sketch and realization

Eisenstein's outstanding success in combining sound and pictorial images. On the basis of his solutions to this complex compositional problem, he subsequently theorized at length and in minute mathematical detail on the 'key to the measured matching of a strip of music and a strip of picture'.[23]

To what extent was *Alexander Nevsky* pre-planned and to what extent a spontaneous creation? In describing his methods of preparing for a film at this stage of his artistic development, Eisenstein spoke of his 'strictly academical' approach:

I make use of all available scientific data; I discuss with myself problems of programme and principle, I make calculations and draw inferences. I 'dissect music' in the course of its progress, and sometimes anticipating its progress, with the result that its elements are buried in my drawers among heaps of material relating to principle. I stop writing the scenario and instead plunge into research work, filling pages and pages with it. I don't know which is more useful, but abandoning creative work for scientific analysis is what I am often guilty of. Very often I settle a particular problem of principle only to lose all interest in its practical application.[24]

This was not, however, the case with *Alexander Nevsky*; such calculations, equations and deductions as he made were but a prelude to the act of creation. Even the shooting-script represented only a preliminary stage in the creative process. In the heat of creation, he no longer thought about the 'hows' and 'whys', no longer translated his basic selection 'into *logical evaluation* . . . but into *direct action*'. In other words, his thinking was no longer expressed in abstract theorizing, but projected directly and spontaneously into pictorial images.

The back is straightened
The film had its première on 23 November 1938, when Eisenstein sat in the place of honour with Prokofiev and Cherkasov on either side of him. He was amused by the composer's almost immediate whispered query as to who was on his other side, and gratified by the implicit tribute to Cherkasov's make-up. Cherkasov himself recalls another amusing incident during the summer filming of the battle on the ice when, exhausted by rehearsals and the scorching heat, he drove back to the film studios for a short rest before filming. There, however, the gate-keeper would not let him in, refusing to believe that he was Cherkasov. Only after the actor threateningly drew his sword with a princely flourish did the poor man give way, fleeing in terror from this madman.

The première was a festive occasion, following which Eisenstein was once more restored to his previous place of honour in the Soviet cinema. On 1 February 1939 he at last received the Order of Lenin, and the following March he was accorded the title of Doctor of the Science of Art Studies. With

Alexander Nevsky

the public, too, the film had an enormous success, reflected in the besieging of stationery shops by children clamouring for paper clips to make suits of mail like Nevsky's.

After the effort and rush of making the film, which, as he commented in a letter to Jay Leyda, had been 'a hell of a job', Eisenstein felt exhausted and looked forward to devoting the expected respite from film-making to his theoretical writings. 'Like Michelangelo, let us, too straighten our backs . . . diverting our gaze from the laboratory vessels, the filters, projectors, diffusers, dialogues and scores.'[25]

Not very long after, *Alexander Nevsky* was released in France and the United States, where, as Eisenstein learned, President Roosevelt arranged to have a private showing. Once again an Eisenstein film had conquered the world.

221

12. The Path towards *Ivan*

Primo avulso, non deficit alter.
VIRGIL

By the early months of 1939, though not yet fully recovered from the exhaustion induced by *Alexander Nevsky*, Eisenstein was nonetheless immersed in the next film project, *Perekop* (sometimes referred to as *Frunze*). In April, however, he complained of continuing fatigue and indicated that the film was not likely to start materializing before the summer of 1939.

Perekop, the scenario for which Eisenstein began writing with Fadeyev, was to retell the story of Frunze's 1920 campaign against the White forces concentrated in the Crimea. His ideas moved in the realm of the monumental, the Battle of Perekop being envisaged as a struggle between two titans. Through it Eisenstein intended re-elevating the Civil War to the pedestal from which the Vasiliev brothers' film, *Chapayev*, had, he considered, toppled it five years previously.

In the midst of his researches into the period, an insignificant press item about his forthcoming film brought an avalanche of documentary material cascading in from historians and participants in the Civil War.

Parallel with this he was still engaged on the books he was 'constantly writing'. In April an idea from a chapter of one of these books suffered 'a certain elephantiasis', as he himself put it, and set him off writing an article on 'El Greco y El Cinema', which he envisaged running to some 26,000 words solely on 'how cinematic in all directions that old Spaniard behaves!'[1]

In May the painful question of his Mexican film was once more revived and

222

a new exchange of letters ensued. At first optimistic about the renewed possibility of editing the film, Eisenstein soon lost heart, turning his attentions instead to a new film project for which – temporarily as he then thought – he meanwhile abandoned *Perekop*.

Ferghana Canal

In May, Pavlenko returned from a trip to Uzbekistan and enthused to Eisenstein about the construction of the Ferghana Canal. Eisenstein, in turn, discussed the subject with Tisse early in June, when the decision seems to have been taken to make a film about it. At this point Eisenstein thought in terms of a film 'that would be half documentary, half acted'. On 18 June, with the official blessing – indeed at the suggestion – of the Committee for Cinematographic Matters, Eisenstein, with Tisse and Pavlenko, set off by plane for Tashkent to look into the filming possibilities. The next few weeks he spent touring the area by car, covering some thousand miles, visiting the historic cities of Bukhara and Samarkand, studying manuscripts and miniatures, and tracing the course of the future canal.

Stimulated by this direct contact with the historic sites, his imagination once more began to work overtime, torrents of ideas streaming forth nonstop. Particularly intriguing was the mixture of ancient and modern, which revived his desire to make an epic film spanning several stages of history: this time three stages in the history of Central Asia from antiquity to the present. Pavlenko was wary about the magnitude of Eisenstein's ideas, foreseeing problems over the unity of composition, and agreed, with reservations, only to a simple diptych (before and after the Revolution); but Eisenstein's mind was already made up.

Meanwhile he eagerly continued his explorations. Iranian miniatures had always intrigued him, despite what he considered their exaggerated stylization. Now, however, he was amazed to see with his own eyes silhouettes of people, trees, and even half-white, half-black rams and piebald horses with geometrically spaced patches of colour, identical with those depicted by the miniaturists. All this, together with local legends, folktales and songs, became inextricably interwoven with the documentary and emotional material from which the scenario was to be conceived.

Eisenstein's visions for the shooting developed parallel with his ideas for the script. He was not hampered by conventional views on scenario construction, believing that 'the director should break down the "holy of holies" relating to the specific ingredients of the literary scenario'[2] – something he had, in fact, been doing all his life.

At this point Eisenstein rejected all thought of a semi-documentary film. He now saw the film's theme as the life-and-death struggle for water in that arid area. It would unfold in three stages, beginning with the Central Asia of antiquity thriving under its miraculous irrigation system. But man loses his control over the water during the fratricidal wars and the invasion of Tamerlane – and the desert sands sweep over everything. Then comes the misery of the desert wastes during the time of the Tsars, when every stray drop of water has to be wrung from canals where once the world's most perfect irrigation system flourished. And, finally, the miracle of the first victory of the collective: the Ferghana Canal, constructed by the collective farmers of Uzbekistan as an enduring witness to fraternity and socialism.

Eisenstein's interest in a vast, time-spanning epic had been revived a few months previously on reading Priestley's plays and discovering his 'extremely fascinating solutions' for coping with the time-span problem. A phrase from *Hamlet* – 'The time is out of joint' – had also been nagging persistently at his mind. Then there were the things he came upon in Uzbekistan, and the many associations with Mexico they evoked. All these things played a contributory role in Eisenstein's ideas for the structure of *Ferghana Canal*.

The basic structure settled, there still remained the complex problem of a unifying thread for the film. Eisenstein thought back to his earlier films in which the time question had been tackled: *Strike* represented the accumulated experience of recurrent strikes in history, i.e. time; *Potemkin* had concentrated a whole revolutionary period into one representative episode; *The General Line* had dealt with two conflicting stages in the history of mankind; the time-span theme had been broached in several projects, including the proposed films about America's history and the growth of Moscow into Russia's capital. But only in *Que Viva Mexico!* had he seriously tackled the problem of a vast structure embracing the entire history of humanity, as summed up in the various civilizations of one particular country. His proposed solution for this had, however, had the major flaw of providing the unifying factor only in the final episode when all the characters scattered throughout the different stories were to be brought together on Death Day. For *Ferghana Canal* the solution was found in the figure of the aged singer, Tokhtasin, who was to span its whole epic structure: at the beginning by singing about the days of old; in the second part by singing about his own lifetime; and in final scenes by participating directly in the action. This basic idea gradually took on more detailed shape. A solution for spanning the gap of thirty-three years between the second and final parts was suggested by a book that fell into Eisenstein's hands by chance, on the compositional devices used by Tolstoy in *Hadji Murad* and *Kholstomer*, where everything is portrayed through the retarded memory of one of the characters. Tokhtasin's conscious memory, too, could stand still during a thirty-year period of isolated withdrawal from the world. Another problem was to find a pictorial way of expressing the mirage that had to appear to Tokhtasin to set him

In Uzbekistan

singing about the olden times. Several ideas were dismissed before, from out of that 'vast assortment of visual images' within him, there flashed into Eisenstein's mind an image associated with one of Pushkin's poems: an inverted image of trees reflected in water like a mirage. By further association he thought of a desert oasis reflected in water, then he recalled a film seen in childhood: Marie Antoinette on the scaffold reflected in Cagliostro's mirror . . . water and mirrors. The waters could therefore act as a mirror reflecting Tokhtasin's vision of the past: cupolas, mosques, a sheik from Bukhara. . . . Detail by detail, and with much greater complexity than this account may suggest, Eisenstein's montage ideas for this sequence took shape.

Gradually the scenario filled out with details as they occurred to Eisenstein through a continuous associative process. During a farewell visit to the dancer, Tamara Khanum, on the eve of his departure from Tashkent, for instance, he saw her small daughter Lola dancing. This at once set new thoughts racing through his mind which he recounted to Pavlenko at the first opportunity: Tokhtasin, too, would have a daughter who danced, and her dance would be linked with the drama of the water shortage and the old man's thirst. Furthermore, it would be the girl's death that drove him in anguished despair out into the desert to the mountains, far from the bitter struggle for water. His period of wanderings would provide a natural hiatus for the thirty-three years that must pass before his return for the final part of the film. So the thoughts set in motion by a small child served to weld together the last two sections of the scenario. It was she also who suggested the symbolical likening of water to life blood.

Eisenstein and his colleagues returned to Moscow on 12 July and the next day verbally outlined the ideas for the scenario to the studio leadership. Pavlenko agreed to them, at Peredelkino, on 16 July, urging Eisenstein, however, to try to simplify parts of the scenario. On 21 July the project received official approval.

Next came the editing of the scenario and – contrary to Eisenstein's normal practice – the simultaneous elaboration of the shooting-script. At this stage Eisenstein also tried to resolve the problems of the stylistic approach. He proposed employing three styles for presenting the factual material, three forms which would coalesce and link up – epic, dramatic, psychological.

Ferghana Canal, like *Que Viva Mexico!*, was to open in an atmosphere of death until Tokhtasin's first song conjures up the flourishing scene of ancient times – reflected pictorially in the waters of an artificial lake. Then more death and destruction as Tokhtasin sings of the dreaded Tamerlane's siege of the city of Urganj: 'Tamerlane quietly speaks : "Water is the strength of that city." After a moment of silence, he adds: "Take away the water from Urganj . . ."' Meanwhile the Emir of Kharesm kneels at prayer in the besieged city while prisoners toiling at the repairs to the walled defences cry out: ' "Water! water! . . . No water to mix the mortar! What are we to do?" . . . The Emir tersely commands: "Mix the mortar with their blood." '[3] And he resumes his prayers as the scimitars flash in response to his order and a bloodbath ensues.

Thus the 'ocean of cruelty' that appears in *Que Viva Mexico!* and all Eisenstein's films abounds in this project too. And, just as the Mexican film ends on a victorious note with the triumph of life over death, so too *Ferghana Canal* closes on a note of triumphant optimism. Indeed, all the familiar themes that crop up obsessively again and again in Eisenstein's works are woven into the epic structure of *Ferghana Canal*.

The scenario was completed in the last three days of July, and the first form of the shooting-script was edited in record time at Kratovo in the course of the first three days of August. Meanwhile, on 30 July, Eisenstein had received a letter from Prokofiev regretting that lack of time prevented him from accepting Eisenstein's invitation to collaborate over the score for the film.

At this point Eisenstein gave some thought to the question of colour. After his brief experiments in *Potemkin* and *The General Line* and the use of two contrasting tones in *Nevsky*, he now saw colour entering his work as 'a natural problem' integral to it.

The scenario was delivered on 23 August and the film unit left for

Uzbekistan. By October Eisenstein had designed part of the décor and costumes and even begun casting. On the eve of shooting, however, a halt was suddenly called, leaving everything in mid-air. Eisenstein returned home with only the preliminary footage (later edited into a short documentary) to show for months of minutely detailed and laborious work. Shortly after there followed an official order to abandon the whole project – whether on grounds of economy or for 'organizational reasons' is not clear. On learning that yet another dream had ended in dust, Eisenstein wanted to jump out of the window, and was only saved by his students.

The Valkyrie

Among the honours bestowed on Eisenstein following the triumph of *Alexander Nevsky* – which until the Nazi–Soviet Pact, and again after Hitler's invasion, became a patriotic rallying-point – was his appointment in 1940 as artistic head of Mosfilm. Never content unless hard at work, Eisenstein threw himself enthusiastically into the job, determined that his name should not appear as a mere formality on the credit titles of films emanating from his studio.

He attended discussions on scenarios submitted, sparing no criticism of the less good:

Why is there an automobile called *Zis-101*? Because there had been 100 models before it! And that's the point. Before publishing *Anna Karenina* Tolstoy wrote a trunkful of drafts! And what has this author submitted to us today? The first thing that came from his pen.[4]

But he urged wider publication of outstanding scripts, articles and analytical studies, and insisted on detailed criticism of rejected scripts. He attended filming sessions and trial run-throughs and generally interested himself in everything down to the make-up. For some people his tyrannical presence must have been thoroughly irksome. Others he helped to produce their best work.

While immersed in this work, Eisenstein was surprised by an invitation to produce Wagner's *Die Walküre* at the Bolshoi Theatre. Immediately attracted by aspects of the opera – 'the epic quality of the theme, the romanticism of the subject, and the surprising pictorial nature of the music, which calls for plastic and visual embodiment' – which coincided with his interests at this time, Eisenstein accepted and set to work 'with indescribable enthusiasm and inspiration'. He was absorbed in the direct apprehension of the music and its appropriate staging:

But what most attracted me in Wagner were his opinions on synthetic spectacle which are to be found scattered throughout the great composer's theoretical works. And the very nature of Wagner's music dramas confronts producers with the task of creating internal unity of sound and sight in the production.[5]

But he also regarded the experience as invaluable for his future film-making as a testing-ground for his ideas on the unity of sound and image and on the dramatic function of colour. In the last act, for instance, he attempted to interpret Wagner's orchestration in terms of colour, with 'a triple alternation of lighting (silver, copper and blue) over the whole stage background . . . and in tone with the Magic Fire music, brought into play nuances of sky-blue and flame-purple lighting'.

Every part of the opera – a piano version of which is annotated in Eisenstein's handwriting – passed through the filter of Eisenstein's grandiose vision, the hyperbolic dimensions of Wagner's myth and music thus finding singularly appropriate expression. Eisenstein's conception for the décor, for instance, was on a monumental scale, added to which, in accordance with his view that the music's 'visual embodiment must be incisively clear-cut, impalpable, frequently shifting material',[6] the mountain scenery was made to oscillate in a rising and falling motion in rhythm with the performers' movements. A further original element was the integration of pantomime choruses into the organic structure of the drama to reflect and accentuate the thoughts and emotions of the characters.

Our aim was to convey through them the feeling that is typical of the period of epics, legends and myths. That is, the feeling that man is not yet cognizant of himself as an independent unit set apart from nature, as an individual that has already acquired independence within the collective body.

For this reason, in our production many of the characters are at certain moments enfolded, as it were, by these choruses, from which they seem inseparable, which vibrate with one emotion, one and the same feeling with them. Thus Hunding, the representative of the crudest, atavistic stage of the tribe – when the tribe is still nothing more than a horde close to the flock, the herd or the pack – appears surrounded by the myriopod, shaggy body of his pack, a body which on falling to the earth appears to be the hunting pack of a leader, and which on rising to its feet reveals itself as Hunding's entourage – kinsfolk, armour-bearers, servants.[7]

Eisenstein also wanted to create a special rapport between spectator and spectacle; not through physical propinquity as in his early stage productions, but through an original interplay of space, sound and lighting. But his ideas came up against the conservatism of the Bolshoi traditionalists and were never put into effect. (It may have been their frustration on this occasion that prompted Eisenstein's later interest in producing Prokofiev's *War and Peace*, for which he believed he would be allowed a freer hand.)

The Valkyrie opened at the Bolshoi on 21 November 1940, exactly two years after the first night of *Alexander Nevsky*. On the copy of the programme that he sent to Jay Leyda, Eisenstein commented among other things that he had 'had great fun in doing the production'.[8] But much more than having been fun, *The Valkyrie*, through the musical and visual techniques he used, represented a step towards *Ivan the Terrible* – though another four years lay ahead before the latter's première.

'The Poet's Love'

In retrospect, other experiences accumulated during these 'unproductive years' were also to be seen as essential steps on Eisenstein's road towards *Ivan*. There were, as usual, many projects that were abandoned, readily or reluctantly: a film about Lomonosov; *The Prestige of an Empire*, based on a play about the Beilis case* by Lev Sheinin, on which Eisenstein worked between May and December 1940; a colour film about Giordano Bruno, proposed by his studio during the period of his work on *The Valkyrie*. This last attracted Eisenstein – 'Italy . . . Renaissance costumes. . . . Burning at the stake' – but got no further than the proposal stage. Nonetheless the studio committee was determined that Eisenstein should make a big colour film, and so the search for suitably picturesque subjects went on. Following Giordano Bruno came a suggestion about Tommaso Campanella: as Eisenstein later remarked, 'the colourful past was inevitably sought on the border between the Middle Ages and the Renaissance'.[9]

Possibly on this principle, a colour film about the Black Death was suggested. To Eisenstein this seemed self-contradictory. He was fascinated, nonetheless, by one episode – a banquet held in the midst of the raging plague – and gave further thought to the project. It would not be a film in colour but a film about the colour black: the blackness of the plague inexorably spreading everywhere, swallowing everything in its wake, the engulfing blackness of the funeral cortège smothering the motley colours of the carnival. He soon abandoned the project, however, in favour of a theme in which the colour was not merely an ornamental appendage but an essential requirement of the theme's inner dramatic content. But what sort of theme? Sound films, he reasoned, had introduced the lives of musicians as an obvious theme; and colour films those of painters. For sound and colour combined? 'What about the biography of a poet? This is how the idea was born for a film on Pushkin.

'And from it rose *Ivan Grozny*.'[10]

But the idea of *black*, linked with his obsession about blind inexorability, still stayed with him. He also recalled the powerful impression left by his discussion with Andrei Bely in 1933: an analysis of the recurring chromatic waves in Gogol's works had shown them to echo exactly the tragic advance of

* Mendel Beilis, a Jew from Kiev, had suffered a long trial for the charge of the ritual murder of a Russian boy. Some references to this title identify it as concerning T. E. Lawrence.

the madness that took possession of the writer's mind. These were the thoughts that led Eisenstein to the subject of Pushkin's life.

Pushkin had fascinated Eisenstein ever since he had seen an amateur performance of *Eugene Onegin* during his childhood in Riga. Later he had read and re-read Pushkin's poems, analysed many of them in minute detail with his students at the Institute, and, in 1939, actually outlined ideas for a book, *Pushkin and Cinema*. (Pushkin it was who in 1940 provided the epigraph and the title to an autobiographical fragment which Eisenstein called 'An Inexhaustible Theme'.) Now all his studies and lucid analyses helped to feed the fire of creative inspiration.

The Pushkin theme first appears in notes (some of them in English, French or German) and sketches made in March 1940 for the rough shooting-script for a scene from *Boris Godunov*. In them certain features of *Ivan the Terrible* are also clearly foreshadowed: the themes of the candles, the exaggerated shadows, the significant hypertrophic plastic quality of the frescoes, and the Tsar's lunatic arabesque through the great hall of the palace; the scenic atmosphere; and even certain frame compositions. But the notes petered out, as though Eisenstein's imagination had dried up.

Later in the year, after the other projects had fallen through, scenes from Pushkin's life again burst upon Eisenstein's imagination in a succession of chromatic explosions in which the colour constituted an integral part, not only of each individual image as it arose, but of the film's dramatic structure as a whole.

Besides the marvellous play of the musical leitmotifs, the *outline* of his life is, as it were, totally ripe for colour. These leitmotifs are of a purely Wagnerian kind – and at that period I produced Wagner at the Bolshoi; his method amused me for its resemblance to what Chekhov had done, in *The Three Sisters*, for instance.[11]

Tinyanov's hypothesis about Pushkin's 'unknown love' being Karamzina became the central dramatic pivot, Eisenstein considering the love theme to be 'the most beautiful of all the possible themes of the poet's life'. And around this focal point the other scenes grew up, the scene from *Boris Godunov* being incorporated in the form of a nightmare.

Once again the theme of fatality, of a dreadful implacable force, cropped up. This time, however, it found expression not in black, but – as with the inexorably advancing Teutons in *Nevsky* – in white. For the colour white signified for Eisenstein 'something tragic, something wasted'[12] and it turns up again and again in his vision of the film as a leitmotif conveying a sense of impending doom: the young Pushkin is warned by a gipsy to beware of white; Natalia loses her wedding ring – a sign of bad luck – while arranging her white bridal veil; Dantes's uniform is white, while he himself is blond; the white snow stretches as a shroud-like background to the duellists. This theme of an all-engulfing white threat would probably have reached its highest dramatic expression in the scene of Pushkin's sleigh ride over the colourful Saint Petersburg promenade on his way to the duel and death; for here Eisenstein envisaged not merely a forceful colour metaphor, but also a harmonious synthesis of colour and sound. Beneath the happy dance music of the promenade scene the grave note of the distant strains of Prokofiev's requiem would have been intermittently insinuated. And, as the gaiety of the aristocratic Saint Petersburg revelries increases, so too the strains of the requiem would swell all the more insistently. As Pushkin leaves the scene behind, the motley of colour becomes blurred, then gradually pales before being swallowed up in the frosty blueness of the atmosphere; hoarfrost gradually blots out the splashes of colour of hair, moustaches and side-whiskers; and finally the snow falls, 'extinguishing beneath its all-engulfing mantle the firework display of colour'.[13] There is one more explosion of colour in Natalia's cherry-red muff – suggestive of the theme of blood – as the sleighs of the two lovers pass each other without her recognizing Pushkin. After this everything is inundated in whiteness, culminating in the background shroud of snow in the duel scene, against which the black silhouettes of the duellers stand out in stark relief.

Eisenstein envisaged employing this selective colour technique, in which the chromatic interplay dramatically echoes the unfolding action, throughout the film. Blood red appears as the theme colour for moments of high drama: Tsar Boris's monologue takes on an incandescent quality through the red and pink tones sprinkling every detail; Pushkin's vision is conjured up out of the crimson flames of the hearth; 'the first spot of blood of the rekindled flames glows in the reflection of the gendarme's helmet' with sinister portent; and in the requiem the red theme, symbolizing blood itself, 'penetrates the peak of Dantes's cap'; while in the scene of the poet's death a crimson bloodstain appears, not on the snow but in a superb metaphor of 'the sun's blood-red orb' suspended in the sky.[14]

Similarly the colour tones and textures throughout correspond with the dramatic line and structure. An early episode showing the poet in a dusty landscape is expressed in pale, pastel tones. As he moves south and comes upon the gipsy encampment, there is an explosion of strident colours not unlike the chromatic effects of the Russian historical painter Bryullov, or the colourful costumes of the nineteenth-century oriental aquarellists. 'The grizzly motifs, expressed in pale blue, of the blizzard, the fiends – foreshadowing both musically and visually the duel to come – and the mantle of snow . . . are picked up in the tinkling of the bells' as Pushkin is banished to Mikhailovskoye. After the snow storm, stroked in with 'a thick colour brush' in the flame in the hearth, comes the period of creative maturity with *Boris*. The mist of the south disperses, giving way to the picturesque in all the colours of the spectrum. Instead of watercolour tones, the images take on 'the brilliant quality of paintings in oils'. In Moscow, the 'magic of love' is tonally conveyed through a 'symphony of bluish violet', while, conversely, moments of dramatic conflict have their intensity heightened by a chromatic dissonance. The multi-coloured exuberance of the Saint Petersburg revelries, for instance, is swamped in clashing tones of 'blue-black and indigo' as the emotional atmosphere becomes increasingly charged with jealousy. Eisenstein's inspiration for this came from his solution for the Black Death theme, where the encroaching blackness of the plague was to obliterate all gaiety of colour. Similarly inspired was his chromatic treatment of the final episodes in the poet's life, in which black again becomes synonymous with death: for the silhouettes of the duellists, the stark, bare trees, the coffin and so on. All this adds up to a chromatic rhapsody following and interpreting the dramatic content:

Water colours. A delicate scale. Oil. Saturation. Again a delicate, lyrical scale. Then the motley gamut of the aristocracy. A black and white engraving, with a splash of colour. The repetition of the multi-coloured aristocracy. A black graphic relief against the background whiteness. Blackness relieved by stripes of light and the stains in the finale [the colour stains of the green card-table cloth, and the yellow candles at Princess Golitsina's nocturnal receptions].[15]

In short, the poet's life described in the language of colour.

Eisenstein worked on the film with total absorption, preoccupied with Pushkin to the exclusion of all else for days on end, during which he produced numerous sketches and a draft outline for the scenario. Simultaneously he was clarifying his thinking on colour-film techniques in a series of theoretical studies which he was to pursue till the end of his life. (The last line he ever wrote was for a new study on colour.) His archive includes twenty-two different manuscripts incorporating hundreds of close-filled pages of notes on what he termed 'the dramatic function of colour'.

Apart from representing a milestone in Eisenstein's colour thinking, the Pushkin film, *The Poet's Love*, was also a landmark as his first portrayal of an erotic theme in all its psychological aspects and nuances. After his previous caustically metaphoric (*The General Line*), caricatured (*Romance Sentimentale*), cynical (*An American Tragedy*), biological (*Que Viva Mexico!*), or mineralogically stylized (*Alexander Nevsky*) treatments of love, Eisenstein now for the first time took it as his theme and presented it in all its subtleties. Esther Shub recalls his telling her how he wanted to make a film about 'a great, lasting and wonderful love',[16] and simultaneously to rehabilitate Pushkin by killing off once and for all the Don Juan image and replacing it with that of a genuine, intensely passionate lover. The cold, lucid Eisenstein was consumed, it would appear, with the desire to create a psychological

Sketch for *The Poet's Love*

poem about love. Tinyanov's interpretation, in which he had 'immediate psychological faith', was supplemented by 'remembered scraps of Freudian interpretation'. To these were added concrete recollections connected with Chaplin's love life, which Eisenstein had observed at close quarters ('there are many points in common between Chaplin in his everyday life and Pushkin as we picture him from those characteristics of his that are known').

But the film proved impossible to make because of the inadequacy of the technical equipment available for colour filming. Laconic though Eisenstein's comment – 'we were not prepared from the technical point of view' – may sound, it hid a depth of bitter disappointment, infatuated with colour as he had always been. In fact, he never quite abandoned his ideas for the film: during an illness which several years later, in 1943, forced him to interrupt work on *Ivan the Terrible*, an article by Tinyanov revived all his former enthusiasm and passion for the theme. As he wrote in 1943:

I hope that our leaders will have the idea of concluding something like a 'colour convention' with the U.S.A., so that we shall be able to use their techniques for our subjects. However that may be . . . I beg you to 'hang on to your Pushkin' as 'my preserve'.[17]

But never, tragically, was he to make this film.

233

13. *Ivan the Terrible*

. . . he made a note reaffirming his belief that art always serves beauty, and beauty is the joy of possessing form, and form is the key to organic life since no living thing can exist without it, so that every work of art, including tragedy, witnesses to the joy of existence. And his own ideas and notes also brought him joy, a joy so tragic and filled with tears that it made his head ache and wore him out.

<small>PASTERNAK</small>

'The most important thing is to have the vision,' Eisenstein wrote while working on *Ivan the Terrible*.[1] Such was his first vision for this monumental creation that, from his initial draft notes, dated 26 January 1941, over two years were to pass before it was to take precise shape in all its minute and intricate detail and filming was to start on 22 April 1943. And even then, throughout the course of making the film, ideas and details were to be added or modified in Eisenstein's persistent and unrelenting striving after perfection.

The Vision

In January 1941 Eisenstein, prompted apparently by his reading, did some sketches of a number of mythological figures. Four of these depicted Apollo, Dionysus, Poseidon and a faun, each holding something in the hand: a lizard, a staff, a mermaid and a flute respectively. Characteristic of all of them was the lyricism of the artistic vision. All four showed an adolescent form (even Poseidon, whose beard alone, in colour, lent him a certain dignity) of an exceptional translucency: one melancholic, another innocent, a third sardonically meditative. . . . While the mermaid in the hands of the innocent-looking Poseidon had the hard-bitten face of a tart, the lizard held by Apollo took on the latter's lithe form and graceful elegance. They summed up a legendary world stripped of all mystery and every trace of force or brutality, and

234

Apollo

chai acterized by purity and transparency. These sketches were dated
25 January. The next day Eisenstein was drafting the first lines of his scenario
for *Ivan the Terrible* -- a film which, like those preceding it, abounds in extremes of violent savagery.

In approaching the subject, Eisenstein's initial idea was to 'rehabilitate' the
much-maligned Tsar, whose barbarous acts of cruelty had been painted in
such lurid tones as to obscure the single, gigantic passion that motivated
them: the creation of a great and united Russia. Eisenstein's intention was not
to whitewash him, to turn Ivan the Terrible into Ivan the Gentle, but rather to
show objectively the full scope and range of his activities so that 'this image,
fearful and wonderful, attractive and repellent, utterly tragic in his inner
struggle along with his struggle against the enemies of his country, can be
made comprehensible to the man of our own day'.[2] The treatment was to be
monumental to match the monumental figure portrayed.

In the complex and detailed elaboration of the basic initial idea,
Eisenstein's inspiration came from the most unexpected directions. The gestation period was an apparently chaotic one in which the various disparate
elements flashed into his head with no obvious rhyme or reason: fragmented
episodes from the hero's life together with ideas for illustrating them; ideas
about the acting, the music, or the lighting for a particular scene; the vision of

one corner of the décor for a completely different scene. His fantasy played on every one of the instruments in that inner orchestra of his own peculiar artistic universe as he summoned up the scenes:

> One you may visualize as a vivid slice of life. A second you act. A third you hear. For a fourth you see a shot. A fifth you feel as an already edited sequence. A sixth as a chaos of coloured blotches.[3]

All this he feverishly tried to commit to paper. The sheets rapidly filled with notes and sketches: a fragment of dialogue; diagrams for the positioning of the actors; precise instructions about the design, and even the materials, for a piece of décor; suggestions for the composer, or an odd one for the lyric writer about the right tone for a ribald song. . . . The sketches – hundreds and thousands of them – captured a myriad of details:

> You suddenly see the outline of a whole scene and, rising simultaneously before this same inner eye, a close-up in full detail: a head nesting on a great white ruff.
>
> Just as you are seizing from the passing figures in your imagination a characteristic bend of Tsar Ivan's back in the confessional, you must drop your pencil and take up your pen to sketch the dialogue for this scene, and before the ink of this is dry, your pencil is once more making a note of an image that came to you during the dialogue – of the priest's long white hair descending like a canopy over the Tsar's graying head. Before this mood has finished, you find yourself drawing with your pen and pencilling notes for the dialogue – on the sheets of drawings.
>
> Directions become drawings; the voices and intonations of various characters are drawn as series of facial expressions. Whole scenes first take shape as batches of drawings before they take on the clothing of words.[4]

The first scene to take shape in Eisenstein's imagination – though it eventually appeared towards the end of the film – was the confessional scene. And it was this scene that set the stylistic and emotional tone for the film as a whole. (The scenario was subsequently written in stylized Church Slavonic Russian and blank verse.) In this scene Ivan is in the Uspensky Cathedral where years earlier, before the coffin of his poisoned Tsarina, he had first questioned his justification for all the dreadful deeds he was committing in his struggle against the traitors – in having many of them put to death, in sacking Kazan. Fixing his gaze on her dead countenance, he had then asked: 'Am I right in this hard struggle of mine?' And in what he imagined to be a softening of her features he had read an answer of approval. Now this earlier scene is reinvoked, the same basic structure based on the same principle of counterpoint being used, but this time with powerful apocalyptic effect:

> The angry countenance of the Tsar of Heaven,
> Sabaoth,
> in a fresco of the Last Judgement.

The Tsar of Heaven is holding the Last Judgement:
he is calling the righteous to himself,
casting sinners into fiery Gehenna.

   . . .

Around the Heavenly Tsar
are ranged fiery circles:
the hierarchy of Heaven painted.
Fiery swords are directed downward
by the winged Tsar's Men of the Tsar of Heaven.
Down,
thither, where, in eternal flames,
sinners are burned by eternal fires.[5]

Throughout the entire scene — as throughout that of the Tsarina's burial service — is heard the intoning voice of a monk; only this time he reads from an endlessly unwinding scroll the interminable list of those killed on Ivan's order.

In the darkness below the fresco of the Last Judgement
in a corner,
where most insatiably of all
the eternal fires devour sinners,
lies prostrate
Tsar Ivan.

   . . .

Prostrate in the dust lies Tsar Ivan.
Above him hangs the Last Judgement.
On a throne above the Tsars sits the Heavenly Judge.
The eyes of Sabaoth flash lightning.
And his face is dark with wrath . . .

At his feet the sinners burn in eternal fire.
But, more fearfully than hellfire, remorse
tortures, scorches, gnaws
at the soul of the Tsar of Earth —
of Muscovy.
He accounts as his a fearful responsibility.
Sweat pours in streams from his forehead.
Scorching tears stream from his closed eyes.

   . . .

And Ivan's lips whisper,
as though he were justifying the terrible deed:
Not from malice. Not from wrath. Not from savagery. For treason.
For betrayal of the cause of the whole people . . .

He awaits an answer from Sabaoth.
But the wall is silent.

Says Ivan in anguish:
Thou art silent? . . .
He has waited. No answer.

Angrily, with defiance,
the Earthly Tsar to the Heavenly Tsar
has repeated threateningly:
Thou art silent, Tsar of Heaven?!
The Figure is silent.

Then flings, as a mighty gage,
the Earthly Tsar at the Heavenly Tsar
his jewel-studded staff.

The staff shatters on the smooth wall.
It smashes to splinters.
The scintillating stones fly through the air.
Scattered like Ivan's prayers, to Heaven addressed in vain . . .[6]

And so Ivan alone must give his own stamp of approval; alone, though seared by the flames of his goal, he will unwaveringly carry on the dreadful struggle, defiant of the Tsar of Heaven and of His earthly servants alike.

Some critics have found a parallel between Eisenstein's vision in this scene and contemporary events in Russia, identifying the Tsar's ruthlessness with that of Stalin. And indeed, in a letter from the period when he was working on the film, Eisenstein made the following admission:

At the present moment I am, on the *human* level of my *Ivan the Terrible*, striving to convey the theme of autocracy as the tragic fate of the solitude of the absolute ruler. As one man, standing apart, as one abandoned by all and utterly alone. You will appreciate that this is what is being attempted in the scenario, as also in the film, first and foremost *to provide a substitute.*[7]

But to return to Eisenstein's original moments of inspiration. The next scene – the early one of Tsarina Glinskaya's death – came to him as he sat in a box at the Bolshoi Theatre during the Lenin commemoration ceremony. Rapidly he sketched it on the back of his invitation card. Next, inspired by a song about Kazan, appeared the episode 'Candle over Kazan', and along with it 'the epic colour of the script'. Other ideas, as they occurred to him, Eisenstein frantically committed to scraps of paper, notebooks, envelopes, the back of telegrams, anything, fearful of losing the ideas that poured in disarray into his imagination. For these drawings – more than 500 according to the archive list – were like 'those Japanese paper toys that, when cast into warm water, unfold and develop stems, leaves and flowers of fantastic and surprising shape'.[8]

Sometimes long intervals elapsed between the appearance of various ideas

'The characteristic position of fingers and hands in El Greco paintings' and the 'tall dark figure in the foreground'.

that went into one and the same scene. Sketches, for instance, for the scene in the cathedral when Ivan first makes known his resolve to become 'the Terrible', are dated February, March and May – then a long gap – and finally November 1942.

Out of these successive eruptions of inspiration, the outline of the future film gradually took on a coherent form, all the disparate elements falling into order along the central guideline established for the scenario. Other influences that came into play, widely differing though they were, also converged along this same line and found their place in the overall pattern.

First among these influences were Eisenstein's theoretical studies. Till the late summer of 1941 he was still intermittently engaged on the El Greco article, and his sketches for the film echo 'the characteristic position of fingers and hands in El Greco paintings' and the 'tall dark figure in the foreground'.[9] Then there were biographical influences, as well as the cumulative influence of all his previous creative work and the familiar themes that permeated them.

Throughout the period of working on *Ivan* Eisenstein seems, from his sketches, to have been flooded with memories: from his travels in Europe and Mexico, from New York, above all from his childhood and youth. A series of sketches dated 28 November 1942, for instance, depicts various of his

'Georges, maître de mes pensées' and 'souvenir d'enfance'

'friends' the clowns, who had brought him so much comfort in his childhood. Other sketches from 1942, such as 'the grandfather', also reflect the same obsessive recurrence of earlier memories; and it is no coincidence that on 17 October of that year Eisenstein wrote a foreword to projected memoirs of, apparently, his Western travels. In these he acknowledges that

the scenario for *Ivan the Terrible* in certain respects contains the author's own *apologia*. . . . A series of forceful childhood impressions and the emotions that accompanied them . . . determined that blend of passion and emotion that went into the deeds which the adult Ivan was bound to commit in the future. If a series of childhood traumas coincide, in an emotional context, with the burdens facing the adult, well and good. Such was the case with Ivan. I consider that in this respect I, too, have been lucky with my life. In my own sphere, I have proved essential to my times.[10]

Among these dominating childhood impressions is that of Ivan's old nurse singing the song of Russia's yearning for her lost seaboard territories:

> Ocean Sea,
> Azure Sea,
> Azure Sea,
> Russian Sea.

The song haunts Ivan thereafter until, crushing all who oppose the aspirations which the song represents, he finally succeeds in extending Russian power to the sea.

Eisenstein further remarks in his memoirs on the paradox that every ordinary 'good' child goes through a destructive phase, pulling watches to pieces to see what makes them work, disembowelling butterflies or torturing animals. By contrast, he considered himself a 'bad child' simply because he had never done these things, adding that 'it was probably for this very reason' that he had 'had to become a film director'. For, he reasoned, instincts of aggressiveness and brutality that are not vented in the inquisitive naughtiness of childhood tend to burst out in later life. Thus the experience of pulling a watch apart found its substitute in his passion for probing the mechanics of creation, destructiveness in his defiance of authority and tradition, the torturing of animals in the cruelty that characterized his films. It is an intriguing idea, though not an entirely convincing one. A more plausible explanation does, however, exist. Having submitted obediently as a child to the discipline of his martinet of a father, Eisenstein had, as we have seen, revolted against this authority at the first opportunity, adopting an iconoclastic attitude towards tradition in general. And the theme of revolt against traditional authority, and the accompanying need to destroy in order to assert a personal credo, reappears in *Ivan*, as, equally clearly, do other themes relevant to Eisenstein's own experience: the hero's betrayal by those closest to him, who neither understand nor wish to understand his actions; the hesitations, inner conflicts and final overcoming of incertitudes. A photograph of Eisenstein as a child – the child brought up under 'the tyrannical temperament' of his father and the 'uncompromising educational system' of his governesses – shows him with 'hair parted to one side, and feet in the third position'. In the film, the child Ivan sits on the throne, unable to touch the ground, with his feet dangling in exactly this position. Meanwhile a photograph of Eisenstein during the filming of *October* (reproduced in Marie Seton's biography) had caught him sitting on the Tsars' throne, with his legs again hanging in the same way. The facts call for no further comment, except perhaps that made by Eisenstein himself: 'Is not the coronation of the *young* Tsar really the determination of the heir to free himself from the shadow of the prototype of the father?!'

For his part, Eisenstein's determination to free himself from his father's shadow subsequently took, as one of its forms, a need to assert and distinguish himself – a need that persisted throughout his life. While abroad, for example, it was doubtless partly a desire to impress – as indeed he did – that led him to lecture, often, in the language of the country. Then again, he had been profoundly impressed, at the start of his artistic career, by the theatrical director and theoretician Nikolai Evreinov's four huge scrapbooks of press-cuttings on his productions; all his life he remembered them, even recalling their exact position on the shelf, their size, and their bindings.

I had no peace until my own album of cuttings on my own works could more than vie with those gray albums. Nor did I have any peace until my book *The Film Sense* had appeared [in the U.S.A. in 1942].

Thus the entire period of creative work on *Ivan* was, as Eisenstein put it in his memoirs, a period of

the struggle with phantoms . . . to liberate yourself from something emanating from an outside force that has provoked you at some time. No . . . by no means are they forces from another world, but, on the contrary, forces which almost always have an address and certainly a name and surname!

In this sense *Ivan* is an autobiographical work. And it is interesting that so powerful were these forces from which Eisenstein felt compelled to free himself that in *Ivan*, quite contrary to form, the omnipresent theme of fatality, here represented by the black cloaks and hoods of Ivan's bodyguards, the *oprichniki*, was chronologically the last basic sequence to take shape in his imagination.

Likewise, *Ivan* embodies a refined distillation of all Eisenstein's previous creative experience. Numerous techniques elaborated during work on earlier films are echoed in superior form. There is a basic similarity, for example, between the contrapuntal, polyphonic compositional structure of the fog sequence in *Potemkin* and the cathedral scene in *Ivan* around the coffin of the dead Tsarina Anastasia, poisoned by Ivan's enemies. Just as three compositional elements – the mist, the water and the surrounding objects – enter into the fog sequence, in *Ivan* three 'voice' lines are interwoven into a polyphonic tapestry of sound and image: the line of Ivan's consciously voiced thoughts (and his outward actions); his 'interior monologue', voiced by the monk intoning the psalm; and the line of worldly affairs spoken by Malyuta. The scene centres round the coffin containing Anastasia's corpse:

A voice in the darkness is reading in whispers a psalm – a psalm of David, the 69th:

> *Save me, O God;*
> *for the waters are come in unto my soul . . .*
>   . . .
> *I sink in deep mire*
> *where there is no standing:*
> *I am come into deep waters,*
> *where the floods overflow me . . .*

Ivan in deep sorrow beside the coffin.
                    . . .
The words of the psalm intermingle with words spoken by Malyuta.
Malyuta is reading a dispatch.

Ivan's eyes are fixed on Anastasia.
He has no ears for either the dispatch or the prayer.

But the dispatch is disturbing:
Prince Ivan Shuisky
has taken refuge on Lithuanian soil . . .

                    . . .

In a whisper, the monk:

> *They that hate me without a cause*
> *Are more than the hairs of mine head . . .*

Calm is the countenance of the dead.
Ivan gazes at her with yearning.
In his misery he flings himself on the ground.

In a whisper, Ivan:
Am I right in what I am doing?
Am I right?
Is this not the chastisement of God?

The monk continues:

> *I am become a stranger unto my brethren,*
> *and an alien unto my mother's children . . .*

Malyuta continues:
Prince Ivan Turuntay-Pronsky
has been captured in flight . . .

                    . . .

Ivan rises from the ground.
He fixes his gaze on the dead countenance.
Am I right in this hard struggle of mine?

The dead countenance of Anastasia is silent.
And Tsar Ivan strikes his forehead on the edge of the coffin.

> *When I wept, and chastened my soul with fasting,*
> *that was to my reproach . . .*[11]

The scene continues along these lines. More bad news arrives, while the monk goes on intoning the Psalm of David — reflecting Ivan's inner emotions. In a whisper, Malyuta tells the Tsar of the growing number of traitors.

The monk, in a whisper:

> *Reproach hath broken my heart;*
> *and I am full of heaviness . . .*
> *And I looked for some to take pity,*
> *but there was none;*
> *and for comforters,*
> *but I found none . . .*

And then, suddenly,

Ivan has turned his head.

And he roars, like a wounded beast, to the whole Cathedral:
Thou liest!

Through the whole Cathedral rings the proclamation:
The Moscow Tsar is not broken yet![12]

This is the moment of explosion, the moment when Ivan suddenly releases all the emotion that has been building up inside him throughout the scene. It also marks his moment of decision – the decision to set up his 'iron brotherhood' of *oprichniki*, whose 'iron abbot' he will be, and to leave for the Alexandrov Monastery. He confers with those who have remained faithful to him. Those who wish to follow him must make up their minds. He rushes up to the coffin again and looks at the frozen features of his wife. They seem to him to soften as if in approval. His hand over her, he swears the mighty vow:

> *Into my hands I shall take the Lord's avenging sword.*
> *The great task I shall accomplish:*
> a Sovereign almighty upon earth shall I become!
>
> . . .
>
> Two Romes fell,
> but the third –
> *MOSCOW –*
> shall stand.
> And a fourth Rome
> shall never be![13]

In analysing the similarities between this scene and the fog sequence in *Potemkin* – in each of which the mourning of a victim unleashes an outburst of fury – Eisenstein equated the lone figure of Ivan, shown as he is in so many different postures, with the whole multitude of mourners around Vakulinchuk's body. But whereas in *Potemkin* it is the different images of suffering among the crowd that constitute the polyphony, in *Ivan* a complex polyphonic composition is built up from the Tsar's whispers, groans and close-ups of his face, each expressively different – as also are the variety of postures in which he is shown before the coffin: kneeling, prostrate on the ground, slowly circling the coffin, overturning the candlesticks in his fury as he cries out the piercing 'Thou liest!', and so on. These different postures are reproduced abruptly, one after the other, without transition between them, 'almost as if a series of separate, self-contained characters were being presented, selected by the camera, not according to criteria of physical or spatial presence but according to the degree of emotion as it mounts in intensity with the action'.[14] (It is difficult not to regard this as foreshadowing the artistic techniques used many years later by Alain Resnais and Jean-Luc Godard.) This contrapuntal construction dominates the entire scene and subjects every-

Ivan the Terrible: preliminary sketches

thing in it – acting, costumes and all – to its laws, just as the polyphonic construction of the mist sequence in *Potemkin* had done.

This was how the scene appeared to Eisenstein in his 'vision', which he strove to reproduce faithfully when it came to the filming. Hence the strictest of instructions to the technicians. At that moment when Ivan seems absolutely alone with the body of his poisoned wife,

Nothing of the sort. The fearful steel cameras are recording his every movement, every trace of emotion on his face.

Eyes are watching him intently from every corner of the sound-stage: to make sure that he does not slide out of the compositional margins, that he does not slip out of focus, or out of the laboriously set lighting, that he does not raise his voice beyond the level that the sound-engineers have prepared for. . . .[15]

Equally exacting were his demands on the actors, and especially on Cherkasov, playing Ivan. Years later, Cherkasov still retained bitter memories of the impossible positions he had forced himself into at Eisenstein's insistence:

The décor scarcely allowed me room alongside the coffin. . . . Because of this I had to act out the scene in such a cramped position that anyone seeing me from another angle would have burst out laughing. . . . During innumerable rehearsals and filming sessions trying to reproduce Ivan's painful emotions, all I was conscious of was the physical discomfort, which made me thoroughly ill-tempered.[16]

This insistence on exactitude was, of course, nothing new. Another element in this scene reminiscent of Eisenstein's earlier films and film projects – and also of his own personal preoccupations as both child and adult – was the recurrent 'good and evil' conflict, the inner struggle for the soul of the hero. And linked with this was the theme of vengeance, which had turned up with unfailing regularity, and with varying degrees of sophistication, in every film and project from *Strike* onwards.

Then other long-standing compositional themes and obsessions make their appearance again in *Ivan*. There is a revival, for instance, of his youthful pantomime about the tragedy of the young man who unknowingly treads the clearly defined trajectory of his own destiny, which intersects those of others like him. (In connection with this pantomime, Eisenstein at one point noted: 'One thing is clear: the geometrical facet, abstract in appearance, was the first attempt to serve the idea and emotion of the theme.') The pantomime had cropped up once more, unexpectedly, in 1932, in connection with a comedy on which Eisenstein was then working:

At one of the most crucial points, the thread of the human relationships and of the situations becomes so hopelessly tangled that a dramaturgical way out no longer exists. The camera pulls back. The black and white tiled floor is, in fact, a chess

Nikolai Cherkasov as Ivan

board. And standing haphazardly on it, the tormented characters are seeking a way out of the general confusion of the action. Bent over the chess board, head in hands, the author and director attempt to unravel the labyrinth of the human relationships. The solution is found! The action is resumed. The paths of the characters interweave and disentangle smoothly. . . . The comedy unfolds further.

But with the folding up of the comedy the chess idea was left in suspension – to turn up again now in *Ivan*. As Eisenstein described it after the film's completion:

The Tsar of Muscovy's canny plan to bypass the Baltic Sea blockade by way of the White Sea is illustrated in the movement of chess men on a chess board. The chess set that Ivan sends as a gift to 'Ginger Bess', Queen of England. [An echo, from the methodological viewpoint, of the solution found some years before for illustrating the birth of Nevsky's stratagem.] But the chess men, of course, demonstrate the development of the drama much more comprehensively. At every move by the boyars, a counter-move by the Terrible. At every measure of the Terrible's, a counter-move from the boyars.

Eisenstein went on to add that it struck him as amusing that he had never in his life played chess, and had no aptitude for the game.

As regards frame composition, *Ivan* embodied all Eisenstein's experience to date. Over the years of enforced non-productivity his ideas had crystallized and clarified; so that, far from being an experimental film in this respect, *Ivan* represented a direct application of precisely defined, complex ideas.

From *the point of view of the object and the composition*, I strove never to limit the shot to a mere *visual* presentation of what appeared on the screen. The object must be so *chosen*, so *arranged* and so *placed* within the shot as to produce, in addition to the pictorial image, a complex of associations corresponding to the emotional and substantive content of the scene. In this way the *dramaturgy* of the shot is created. In this way the *drama* is integrated into the *work's overall structure*. The lighting, foreshortening and framing – all these are subordinated to the aim not only of *presenting* the object, but also of *highlighting* its emotional content, which is embodied at different moments in the respective objects placed before the lens.

Eisenstein quotes as an example the shot of Ivan projected against a background fan of vertical clouds in Kazan, where the clouds are significant, not as a meteorological fact but as a symbol of majesty. Again,

the giant, distorted shadow of the astrolabe encircling the head of the Tsar of Muscovy is perceived not so much as a lighting effect; the intersections of the bands make you involuntarily associate it with a cardiogram, reproducing this politician's flow of thoughts.

But the analysis of any shot chosen at random from *Ivan* would, Eisenstein maintained, reveal how the 'intersection of graphic images, the play of tonal effects, the actions and the shadows of the objects' all play a symbolic role which is of far greater significance than any 'purely plastic' effect.

The dream becomes reality

And now the story, if only in brief, of the years over which *Ivan the Terrible* was made.

On 26 January 1941, as we have seen, Eisenstein made his first notes for the scenario. On 21 March a film about Ivan was announced in the press. Then began a gigantic work of research into the chronicles of the period, into historical records and vast piles of documents, into folk songs and legends about Tsar Ivan – in short, into any relevant material available. The image of Ivan with which Eisenstein had grown familiar from his early reading and later research in preparation for the film about Moscow now changed as he probed more deeply into the period, and Ivan began to emerge as 'a poet of sixteenth-century ideas of statescraft'.

Later in 1941 Eisenstein received a Stalin Prize for *Alexander Nevsky*; but at the award-giving ceremony his personal satisfaction was tempered with sadness as he noted that eight out of ten of the recipients of top awards were former students of Meyerhold – of that great personality who had so senselessly and tragically been wiped out of existence.

During that summer Eisenstein was staying at Kratovo, just outside Moscow, when, on the hot sunny morning of 22 June, news came through of the German attack on Russia. Shortly afterwards Prokofiev, who was also in the vicinity working on *Cinderella*, arrived with his wife to confirm the dreaded news. Both artists were profoundly disturbed; their inner creative worlds that normally preoccupied them to the exclusion of all else were now suddenly and brutally assaulted by the harsh events in the outside world. Overwhelming emotions of patriotism stirred them both.

Eisenstein's nightmare theme of an implacably advancing alien force soon turned into reality as the German armies moved relentlessly forward over Soviet territory towards Moscow, where Eisenstein, who had meanwhile returned home, was, like everyone else, busily preparing for resistance. Barrels of sand, a wooden shovel and other fire-fighting equipment were brought into the house as precautionary measures against incendiary bombs – and subsequently kept as souvenirs.

As for the film studios, propaganda films quickly became the order of the day, and Eisenstein was appointed consultant for a documentary on the war effort. Together with four other prominent Jewish intellectuals and artists – the writer Ilya Ehrenburg, the playwright Perets Markish, the actor Solomon Michoels and the physicist Peter Kapitza – he also took part in an anti-Fascist meeting broadcast over the American radio network, calling for United States intervention in the war. Later he appeared in a film in which, speaking in English, he urged a united struggle against Fascism in the cause of a 'bright future for all humanity, irrespective of nationality'.

Meanwhile Eisenstein was still immersed in work on *Ivan*; for, as the violence of war intensified, he saw his own role with increasing clarity as a guardian of Russian culture. Every new act of barbarism saddened him: the destruction of the priceless medieval frescoes of Pskov and Novgorod, of the eighteenth-century palaces and fountains of Leningrad, and of the cathedrals around Moscow. Above all, the senseless sacrifice of human life pained him deeply. At the same time, even from the first days of the war, he thought about the 'culture and art of tomorrow', and hardened his resolve to make 'any sacrifice to hasten its coming'. By August that year he was finishing the article on El Greco and working on an English version of a study on Griffith and the history of montage in the arts, as well as thinking about an article to follow the close-up through art history.

That autumn Moscow came under heavy bombardment, and one midnight in mid-October Eisenstein and other film workers received instructions to evacuate the capital. The very next morning the exodus began by the train which was to take them for twelve days and nights – like 'a modern Noah's Ark', in Eisenstein's imagination – into the heart of Central Asia, to Alma Ata.

Alma Ata, 'a town of wide streets, lined by double rows of flowering trees', as Prokofiev described it, impressed Eisenstein with its view of 'gigantic mountains leaning their snow-covered peaks against the blue of the sky'.[17] Here the Mosfilm workers, evacuated as a body, gradually settled down to work along with other film-makers, including Pudovkin, Ermler and the Vasilievs, in the chaotic conditions reigning at the former Palace of Culture – now converted into a makeshift studio. It took many months before a normal working routine could be resumed. The size of the rooms allowed for only the most cramped of stage sets – sets totally unsuited for the monumental filming envisaged by Eisenstein for *Ivan*. Eisenstein was not given separate living accommodation, but had to make do with 'eleven square metres', as he wrote to Elisabeta Teleshova in an unpublished letter dated 3 March 1942; if she were to come, they could have a room to themselves of twice the size. An added problem he commented on was his 'completely catastrophic' financial situation.

Yet, despite the impossibly Heath Robinson conditions prevailing, Eisenstein persisted stubbornly in his original ideas, and insisted on personally supervising everything connected with the realization of his 'vision'. Every detail had to be right, even to the exact thickness of clay for the church vessels and the correct weight of the wax seals for letters presented by foreign ambassadors at Ivan's court.

Eisenstein's first preoccupation, however, was the scenario, for which he initially tried to enrol the help of the writer Leonov. But at the very last moment, with his bags packed and ready, Leonov suddenly withdrew his promised collaboration, so that the entire script, including the dialogue, was eventually produced by Eisenstein single-handed. He found it 'wildly interesting', long-drawn-out though the process of writing it proved, occupying him for many months, even during filming.[18] (After rehearsals had started he again revised 'the line of the characters'.) More and more autobiographical elements crept in: his fear of becoming addicted to games of chance, for instance, in the scene in Kurbsky's tent where 'the rational game of strategy' is contrasted with 'strewn gaming cards and gambling dice' symptomatic of 'crazy games of hazard'. It is in this same tent that Malyuta comes upon Kurbsky's empty armour, which Eisenstein thought so reminiscent of 'Daddy's hollow statues'. The violence of the war raging to the west also found powerful echoes in the scenario: in Ivan's resolve that 'like our forebear, the great Prince Alexander Nevsky, we shall show no mercy in driving the Germans from our land'; or in the scene, strangely prophetic of the taking of the Reichstag, in which Malyuta appears almost to fly as he bears the flag in the attack against Weissenstein Castle.

Eisenstein was also excited by the variety of the work and particularly by the novel complexity of the characters, as compared with the relatively straightforward heroes of his previous films. 'I myself am amazed at my skill in portraying the evolution of the characters, the inner forces motivating them and "the reciprocal interplay of passions", as well as other things with which I had never previously concerned myself.'[19] A case in point is the scene in which both Basmanovs, father and son, meet their death for betraying Ivan; here Eisenstein's superb handling of the conflicting thoughts and emotions constitutes a brilliant piece of psychological analysis.

The scenario seems to have met with the unanimous approval of its many readers. Ranevskaya, the actress whom Eisenstein proposed casting as Euphrosinia, was so taken with the role that she is reported to have told Eisenstein 'you could play it and then die'; in the event the part was played by Serafima Birman. Eisenstein also wanted to cast Galina Ulanova as the Tsarina Anastasia; Ulanova herself was enthusiastic and the screen and make-up tests proved an outstanding success. Travelling difficulties, however, forced her to decline and Ludmila Tselikovskaya was given the part instead.

At this stage Eisenstein was awaiting Teleshova's arrival to help him with casting and allied problems. Meanwhile he invited Cherkasov, then evacuated with the Pushkin Theatre in Novo Sibirsk, to play Ivan – a role familiar to him from the stage.

Rehearsals began on 1 February 1942 for filming scheduled to start in June.

In March Eisenstein wrote asking Prokofiev, whom he had not seen since the outbreak of war, to compose the music for *Ivan*. Prokofiev's warm telegram of acceptance arrived from his evacuation address in Tbilisi (Tiflis) on 29 March, and he himself arrived. Their methods of work were the same as for *Nevsky*.

Filming eventually started, long after its originally scheduled date, on 22 April 1943. There were some ingeniously improvised sets; and for the outdoor scenes of the Kazan Fortress – a plywood dummy was erected on the precipitous, sun-scorched terrain of Kazakhstan. For these scenes an overcast sky was a compositional necessity; but, as fate would have it, a freak heatwave prevailed, and for sixteen days on end, in a temperature alleged to have stood at over 140 degrees fahrenheit, Cherkasov stifled under his padded costume and heavy metal armour – not to mention his scorching helmet which made him cry out in pain whenever it touched his ears – waiting for the clouds to appear.

Studio filming could only take place at night (when the electricity was not needed for industrial purposes), following on a day spent in rehearsals and work on the costume and décor. At dawn, when shooting ended, Eisenstein started preparing for the next session, poring, for example, over a Michelangelo reproduction with the make-up artist, Gorunov, showing him the example of 'the flowing curve of Moses's beard', or pointing out how the hairs 'grew' on the faces of El Greco's figures.[20] Yet never once did he appear tired on set; nor did his equanimity or sense of humour desert him. No one could have guessed just how much each filming session taxed his already strained mental and physical resources. Normally he saw that there was a relaxed and happy atmosphere on the set, and shooting went on without any of the fuss normally associated with studio filming. Occasionally, however, when a distinctly solemn atmosphere was called for – for the coronation scene, for instance – Eisenstein became extremely severe and demanding. But even then he never raised his voice; an occasional frown or slight harshness of tone was enough to bring the whole unit hastily back to a regular rhythm of work.

During these years of working on the film, Eisenstein drove himself at 'a madman's pace'; the film apart, in September 1942 he resumed his teaching work at the Institute of Cinematography, which had also been evacuated to Alma Ata. He was, he complained in a letter to Elisabeta Teleshova, snowed under with work – the administrative chaos landing him with 'a mountain of trivial tasks quite foreign to directing'. Needless to say, he added to his burdens by his perfectionism. Cherkasov recalls examples of this, and the fact that he treated the actors 'like wax dummies', making Cherkasov himself 'practise long and tiringly to produce the tragic bend of Tsar Ivan's figure' exactly as he had imagined it in his sketches. And when, at one of the first make-up sessions, Cherkasov fell asleep after an exhausting journey from

Novo Sibirsk, Eisenstein was overjoyed that Gorunov could experiment at leisure. The minutest nuances of expression were tried out, Gorunov dutifully applying layer after layer of plasticine at Eisenstein's insistence; as he did so he jokingly recalled articles from Eisenstein's 'typage' period in which he had castigated the use of plasticine, false beards or wigs. Having made his *volte-face*, Eisenstein now demanded with equal dogmatism that the make-up should be absolutely flawless — remorselessly insisting, for instance, on Serafima Birman's eyelids being drawn upwards at a particular (and particularly painful) angle towards her temples, and remaining apparently unmoved when ugly bruising appeared after several days' filming.

There was the same meticulousness over the costumes: Ivan's bearskin coat had to be adjusted eight times in succession to 'sit on his shoulders' convincingly, the headdress of Metropolitan Pimen no less than forty times. Every detail — even at the risk of 'a state of dementia' ensuing — had to accord with Eisenstein's stylistic conception: 'For days we will struggle with the stubborn cloth, cutting and draping it to capture that rhythm of folds that suddenly struck me when I closed my eyes over that bit of brocade and envisioned a procession of boyars in heavy robes moving slowly to the chambers of the dying Tsar.'[21]

Concomitantly with all this Eisenstein worked on at his theoretical re searches as well as keeping in touch, as far as was possible, with his cultural contacts abroad. In August 1942 his first book, *The Film Sense*, was published in the United States, and a year later in England. During 1943 he exchanged letters with Leopold Stokowski, whom he invited to Russia after the war to discuss 'an idea for a musical film'. He and Pudovkin were, in turn, jointly approached by Alexander Korda about a projected screening of *War and Peace* (for which Orson Welles was suggested as Pierre Bezukhov); both were enthusiastic and sent a detailed summary of their ideas for the film. During the same year Eisenstein reread another Russian classic, *The Brothers Karamazov*, noting in his diary ideas for a possible screen version.

All these efforts — including thirty-two consecutive nights of filming — gradually took their toll, and during 1943 Eisenstein was forced to take time off to recuperate at a rest home close to the Soviet–Chinese frontier. Late in the year he wrote to Yuri Tinyanov expressing a very strong desire to escape from Alma Ata.

Meanwhile Eisenstein had taken the decision to expand *Ivan* from a diptych into a trilogy. Continual alterations in the film's structure ensued: on 17 February 1944 he made several changes in the character of Prince Kurbsky, only to see the whole scene in a different light on 27 March, when he dispensed with verbal descriptions in the text in favour of a much clearer exposition of the scene's tension and dynamism through changes in the action. New notes, drawings showing the positioning of the actors, and diagrams

Ivan the Terrible: page from the shooting script

— ♂ —

Неукло... ментох — князь Владимир Андреевич —
добрьго уямядяется. *[illegible handwriting]*

И кроли ... о викьм: .укалря. !
"Царэ замочмару крест ~~......~~."

...ни передернуло.
Но д...ит лапи, меч мертвый.

Курбски" вдгаядон прост...льный глядят ~~......~~
Над Иваном наклоняется:

Кам-нно-мертвое лицо Ивана.
Только кнаяа холодного пота на лбу...

~~[crossed out block]~~ △△

Как удаленный, подымается на локоть Иван, глядя
им вслед.
Он в лихорадке, но ядена в его вагляде, по крайной
мере, на тэдах.
~~......~~

Анастасия ..ддоня к Ивану. *[handwriting]*
Улыбка.
Сами выскользнули в дверь. *[handwriting]*
Пятях Чвадть, погаддшая на Ивана. *[handwriting]*

Мирно дакт ~~......~~ матери. *уМалсоры иа Jврках*

, мляэльнэ-прохожа в ~~......~~ Курбски".
~~......~~ смирно *[handwriting]*

Га э — сама толпа: *Посяедний а...*
умиляется Иванн визнани. *complete... п...*
Но не так тол уст са из — Андрей Михайлович:
вдомьеи обяз штно.ль, думат, вывоич.

,оро...отся князь на колени перед царицо:
,мэ:: будешь — от ...р Замяду. Т...
,мэ:: будешь — ~~......~~ (на престол возведу.)
,мэ:: будешь — ~~......~~ Тебя царством править буду!"

,ироко раскрыты, полны сляз царицины глаза,
,зумленно на Курбского гяядит.

,орвать князя хочет.
,о д...т ж" князь слова-вымолвить:
: ход и вскакивают; з. руку берет; к царице наклоняется
,а стеною гул боярский втот.

,дон-но слышали, мэлотом пяэменным гэордит:
Воя твоя — ядянь на я жизнь.
С тобой вместе — смерть на смерть.
С тобой на престол и плаху —
все одно! *[handwriting]*
Царица моя... Московски!.."

elucidating their movements appeared in the scenario. Part of the old text was scrapped and replaced by another version.

In the autumn of 1944 Mosfilm returned to Moscow, Eisenstein taking with him a huge, metal-lined wooden crate filled with his sketches and carefully bound folders. At this stage practically the whole of Part I and some shots for Parts II and III had been filmed.

Back in the old, familiar Moscow surroundings, Eisenstein led his now well-ordered and harmonious unit in the work on the montage and sound synchronization for Part I. During the montage he made considerable modifications, cutting whole scenes and orchestrating the entire film as a succession of huge tableaux, each generally starting at a slow tempo and gradually working up to a dramatic climax. Meanwhile collaboration with Prokofiev over the score continued. Both artists worked rapidly and in perfect harmony – though the start to their collaboration in Alma Ata had been anything but auspicious when Eisenstein had rejected outright the very first piece of music produced by Prokofiev. This was for the sequence of the oath-taking, which Eisenstein had asked Prokofiev to compose before the filming. Tempers on both sides became frayed, and Prokofiev refused to compose another note until Eisenstein had clarified his ideas in detailed sketches. After Eisenstein had done so the new music was a great success, as were Prokofiev's next compositions: for the nurse's song and for the lullaby which Euphrosinia sings to her murdered son Vladimir. In the former, Eisenstein declared,

Each instrument, each group of instruments, presents in motion one or another aspect of the ocean, and together they re-create, call to life (but not copy from life) a wonderful image of the vast and boundless ocean . . . as the builder of the Russian state sees it in his dream.[22]

And for the latter Eisenstein conveyed his ideas with such precision that, as Serafima Birman commented, 'Prokofiev intuitively understood what was going on in the troubled soul of Euphrosinia Staritskaya'.

The more usual practice, however, was for Prokofiev to compose his music for a sequence that had already been filmed. There were eight distinct stages in the process. First Eisenstein showed him the montage for the sequence, then its length was noted and Eisenstein explained his requirements – often enchanting Prokofiev with his vivid images: 'Here it should sound as though someone were tearing a child from his mother's arms,' or 'Make it sound like a cork rubbed down a pane of glass.' Back at his hotel Prokofiev would assiduously calculate, from the allotted time, the corresponding number of bars at the intended tempo. Then, with metronome and chronometer on top of the piano, and his otherwise virgin manuscript marked out into bars and scrawled over with cryptic notes intelligible only to himself, he would start composing

On the set of *Ivan the Terrible*

within this framework. Kabalevsky, who witnessed one of these sessions, recorded his amazement that Prokofiev's extremely logical and precise way of working 'in no way hampers his creative thinking; he writes film music with the same inspiration and passion that goes into his other compositions'. The next step was for Prokofiev to play the music on the piano to Eisenstein while the corresponding sequences were screened. As he did so he would join in with the choral parts – badly, to Eisenstein's amusement. This trial run-through was simultaneously recorded and, if both were satisfied that the music synchronized perfectly with the visual images, Prokofiev then wrote the orchestral score. Finally, after exacting rehearsals with the orchestra, the full score and sound effects were recorded.

At the end of December 1944 Eisenstein completed Part I of *Ivan*. It had its first showing in January 1945 and was instantly hailed as a triumph (receiving a Stalin Prize a year later). Congratulatory telephone calls poured in and a eulogistic article by Vishnevsky appeared in *Pravda*. Eisenstein was delighted. On its subsequent release abroad, *Ivan* had a mixed reception, though again congratulations flooded in from his friends. These included Feuchtwanger and Chaplin, who, in a telegram dated 4 January 1946, acclaimed it as 'the greatest historic film that has ever been made'.

But Eisenstein's happiness was to be short-lived: for *Ivan the Terrible*, Part II, a very different fate was in store.

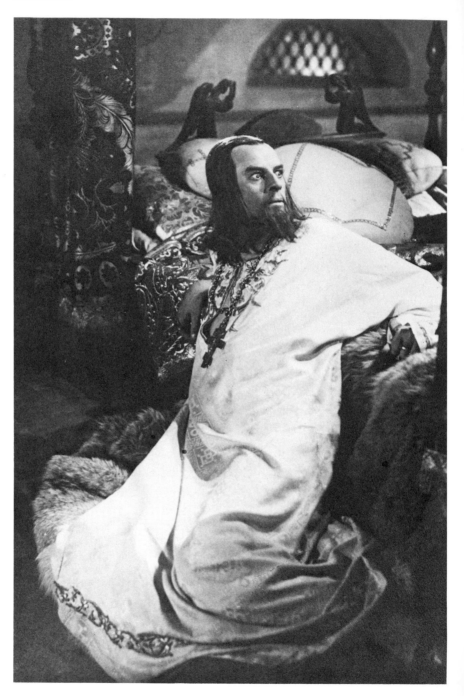

Cherkasov as Ivan in Part I

Erik Pyriev as the young Ivan

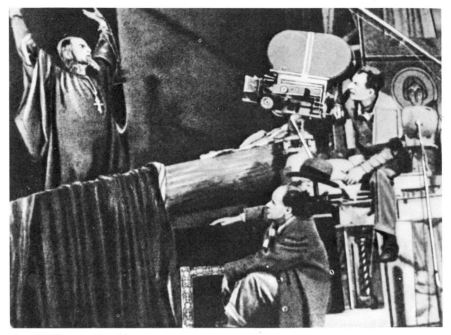

Shooting *Ivan the Terrible*

The fading of a dream

Following the success of Part I, Eisenstein resumed work on Part II and the projected Part III. At the same time he was absorbed, as ever, in a variety of other interests: in a new book that he was hoping to publish in the United States, and, it appears, in plans to produce a magazine of detective stories.

Throughout 1945 Eisenstein worked intensively on Part II, especially towards the end of the year and the beginning of 1946, when both filming and montage were nearing completion. The prologue shows scenes from Ivan's childhood. And, perhaps recalling his experiences twenty years earlier at Esther Shub's cutting-table, Eisenstein composed it as a *pot-pourri* of plastic and dramatic themes from Part I. As always, the montage was enormously complicated and demanded infinite pains and patience. At this stage, although a start had barely been made on Part III, the elaborate structure of the trilogy as a whole – scarcely discernible in Part I – began to take on a coherent outline. When the two parts of the film are seen together, it becomes evident, as Jay Leyda has observed, how 'the majestic, ceremonial qualities of Part One, growing more passionate towards its conclusion, are transformed into the flaming bitterness and physical violence of Part Two'.[23] This 'calculated stylistic growth' that Leyda noted also struck Jean Mitry:

There is a progressive movement from the static to the dynamic. . . . Most extraordinary of all,' in my opinion, is that this movement . . . runs counter to the dramatic development. The *first* part, with an epic character, is the more static; the *second*, essentially psychological, is the more dynamic.[24]

It was this complex structural coordination and the dramatic composition of each episode that was preoccupying Eisenstein at this stage. One particular problem was that he had yet to film the complicated sequence of Ivan's banquet and the dance of the *oprichniki*, for which he considered the inspiration of Prokofiev's music essential; but Prokofiev had left Alma Ata before Eisenstein, and in Moscow an illness had prevented the composer from working for several months and the music did not seem likely to materialize. As winter approached, however, chance came to Eisenstein's aid in the form of a conference held at the Ministry of Cinema. The conference discussions, revealing a generally unimaginative approach to colour, greatly irritated Eisenstein, just as did the facile use of colour – a 'coloured catastrophe', he called it – in the American and German films shown as illustrative material. But during a coloured documentary film of the Potsdam Conference certain shots suddenly aroused his imagination along the lines of his own earlier ideas on colour. The shots – of the interior of the Charlottenhof Palace – showed an expanse of red carpet stretching the width of the screen, while diagonally across it ran a line of white and red upholstered armchairs. Eisenstein was immediately struck by the 'functional' effect of the colour, as he was also, in a later shot of the Chinese Pavilion at Sans Souci, by the way the gilded oriental decorations powerfully reflected the surrounding green and the white of the stairs. The most effective colours, he concluded by the end of the session, were red, gold and black. Blue, too, he thought could be effective. It was a temptation to risk trying them out himself. And the sequence still to be filmed provided him there and then with the opportunity of doing so. He envisaged the episode as an explosion coming between the sombre preceding sequence of the conspiracy against the Tsar (already filmed at Alma Ata) and the equally lugubrious following sequence of the abortive attempt on his life.

Why couldn't this explosion be – in colour? Colour would participate in the explosion of the dance. And then, at the end of the feast, imperceptibly flowing back into black and white photography, the tragic tone of the accidental death of Prince Vladimir Andreyevich, killed by the murderer sent by his mother to kill the Tsar.[25]

Particularly effective, both stylistically and emotionally, would be the contrast between the golden robes of the *oprichniki* at the banquet and their sombre black garb in the scenes before and after.

These ideas were in line with Eisenstein's thinking about the use of colour—thinking formulated as far back as 1937, when he had advocated that in their search for a colour formula film-makers should address themselves not to paintings, as was usually done, but to '*gallant* literature and . . . the monochrome film'.

Eisenstein's basic principle was 'to dissociate the colours from the particular objects to which they were attached and make them lead on to a generalized mood or emotion, which afterwards links up once again with the object'. It is interesting, in view of its quite fortuitous application (apart from the chance stimulus of the conference, it was also sheer chance that Eisenstein managed to lay hands on a small quantity of colour negative captured among other spoils of war), that this complicated chromatic solution merged perfectly into the film's structure. But in the main body of the film already shot Eisenstein had – certainly not with future colour films in mind, but only the demand for colour in this film – used objects embodying a notion of colour: burning candles and the *oprichniki*'s costumes, embodying the colour red; the ceremonial vestments, gold; the cloaks of the *oprichniki* and of the Tsar, black. Thus the first stage of his basic principle preceded his intention of using actual colours. In the second stage, the colours came to stand for a generalized idea: red for the theme of plottings and vengeance, gold for orgies, black for death. In the third stage, through a contrapuntal construction which Eisenstein elsewhere called 'the dramaturgy of colour', the colour was again linked up with the object. Used in this way in *Ivan the Terrible*, the colours became a means of penetrating Ivan's inner world, and hence a dynamic instrument of psychological investigation. And it is precisely Ivan's psychological state, and not the *spectacle* of the dance, that is the essential feature of the sequence; and with the dynamic of the colour echoing Ivan's inner turmoil this is presented much more clearly.

In September 1945 Eisenstein's longing to get possession of his Mexican film suddenly revived, as happened every now and then, often at the most unlikely moments – as now, in the midst of creative work on *Ivan*. There followed a new flood of telegrams to and fro across the Atlantic; but again to no avail.

The beginning of January 1946 found Eisenstein immersed in the final stages of *Ivan*. Simultaneously he was still busy on his book – now three-quarters ready for typing – which he intended finishing during the holiday he planned to take immediately after the film's completion. He was also engaged in drawing up a theoretical balance-sheet of his twenty years of creative work, in which he detected an intimate link stretching from *Ivan* back to *Potemkin*.

Ivan the Terrible, Part II, was completed in February. During the evening of 2 February Eisenstcin put the final touches to it before leaving at 10.30 for the celebration given in honour of his Stalin Prize for Part I. There, in a jubilant mood, he joined in the dancing. At about 2 o'clock, however, in the middle of a dance with Vera Maretskaya, he suddenly collapsed from a heart attack: the dance of jubilation had, without warning, turned into a *danse macabre.*

But the attack – a myocardial infarction – did not kill him then and there. That incredible vitality that had seen him through so many critical moments in his life was now to pull him through this nearly fatal crisis.

14. Years of Meditation

*The fields of vision in a rabbit's eyes overlap behind the back of
his head. He sees behind him. . . . In front of the rabbit is a
piece of space it does not see. . . .*
*The rabbit's outlook on the world is different from ours. The
sheep's eyes are placed in such a way that its fields of vision do
not overlap at all. The sheep sees two worlds – the right and the
left, which do not merge into a visual whole.*
*Thus a different kind of vision produces a different kind of
picture-image.*
Not to speak of the higher transformation of vision into a
perception *and then to a point of view which comes about the
moment we rise from the sheep and rabbit to Man, with all his
accompanying social factors. Till finally all this is synthesized
into a world-outlook, a philosophy of life.*
How those eyes see. . . .
That is what excites me.
That is what interests me.
That is what I wish to find out.
EISENSTEIN

Despite the doctor's warning that if he moved he was 'a dead man', Eisenstein
exerted his enormous willpower to walk unaided to the car which took him to
the Kremlin Hospital. When he described the fateful evening to friends who
visited him in hospital after the first few critical weeks of total immobility,
Eisenstein jokingly added: 'I'm dead right now. The doctors say that, according to all rules, I cannot possibly be alive. So this is a postscript for me, and
it's wonderful. Now I can do anything I like.'[1]

When not wrapped up in his own thoughts he read voraciously. In March
he was allowed to sit up in an armchair and several days later to take his first
steps. At the end of May he was able to leave hospital to convalesce in a
sanatorium, and by June to return to his dacha outside Moscow. (Since the
previous year he had been in correspondence with people in Riga; now, in
1946, he wrote of his wish to see his native city again and applied for a villa
in that area.) Throughout his period of convalescence Eisenstein spent much
time meditating. Though with most visitors he invariably joked about his
illness, to Prokofiev, who visited him while still in hospital, he sadly complained that 'when life is finished, all that remains is a postscript'. Prokofiev

understood perfectly the bitterness of this active man now condemned to inactivity. He suggested a useful postscript would be the publication of his memoirs. Whether as a result of this advice or not, Eisenstein once more turned to a venture that he had toyed with in 1940, in 1942 at Alma Ata, and again in 1943–4; and most of his memoirs date from 1946.

He also resumed work on his book, commenting in an interview recorded in July for broadcasting in the United States: 'I use my time, and I have a lot of it now, in working on two of my books.'[2] On this occasion he was happy to hear that the English and American editions of his earlier book had sold 'like hot cakes', and he was subsequently to learn that it had also been published in Spanish (Argentinian) and Japanese editions. But, despite Eisenstein's apparent satisfaction at the news, Louis Aragon, who visited him about that time, was left with an impression that his health caused him profound anxiety.

Meanwhile, during Eisenstein's convalescence, criticisms of a number of recent Soviet films, including *Ivan the Terrible*, Part II, had been steadily mounting. Stalin had viewed the film and had disliked it intensely. Eisenstein's friend Victor Shklovsky, who has pointed out the film's allusions to contemporary history, states that Stalin saw Cherkasov (the actor who had played Ivan), Eisenstein being excluded from the meeting, and expressed displeasure at the fact that the boyars executed by Ivan aroused sympathy, adding that Ivan put to death fewer boyars than he should have done. On 4 September 1946 the storm burst with the publication of a Party Central Committee resolution castigating Soviet film-makers for not being 'sufficiently serious and responsible in their attitude to their work'. It claimed that Eisenstein had 'betrayed his ignorance of historical fact by showing the progressive bodyguard of Ivan the Terrible as a degenerate band rather like the Klu Klux Klan, and Ivan the Terrible himself, who was a man of strong will and character, as weak and indecisive, somewhat like Hamlet'.[3] As a consequence, the film was eventually banned – only twelve years later was the ban lifted – while the material that had been shot and edited for Part III was entirely destroyed.

Some time later, Eisenstein and Cherkasov were summoned – at Eisenstein's request – to a secret meeting with Stalin, as a result of which permission was apparently given for work to continue on the film provided that it was modified to comply with official demands. On 14 March 1947, Eisenstein sent a telegram to Jay Leyda claiming: 'Everything okay continue working Ivan.'[4]

But even before this Eisenstein had summoned up the necessary resources to resume his creative work. On 30 September his vitality, though gravely undermined by the serious heart condition, asserted itself once more; that very day he made the first notes for a new film planned as an epic poem in colour about Moscow.

Moscow 800, genealogy in colour

It is colour, colour and again colour to the very end, which can solve the problems of proportion and adduction in producing a general unity of sound and visual factors[5]
EISENSTEIN

The projected film, entitled *Moscow 800*, marked a fresh and final revival of Eisenstein's interest in a time-spanning, historical theme. Eisenstein's first vision of the film, as it emerges from his notes, was of a vast colour symphony incorporating the sum total of his emotional and artistic experiences, and crowning a lifetime's work. Under the heading 'Initial Impression', the notes begin with a description of those early impressions imprinted on Eisenstein's mind by the night trains in Smolensk station in 1920, which he saw as 'the starting-point for a generalized sensation threading, like Proteus, through the most unexpected imagistic effects and isolated situations'.[6] There follows a brief history of this theme of fatality as it crops up in all his films, and an outline of his use of colour (beginning with *Potemkin*). His conception of *Moscow 800* also corresponded with his expansive vision of the cinematography of the future: it was to synthesize in one single work sound, colour and literary, musical and plastic images, thus creating a new instrument of art and, at the same time, the first masterpiece composed for this instrument.

Particularly expansive was Eisenstein's vision for the use of colour. All the colours of the spectrum were to come into play – first individually, then in a polychromatic ensemble. Black would be the theme colour representing the dark moments of struggle in the city's 800 year history. For the basic theme, treated as it was to be from a 'cosmic' viewpoint, 'a basic, general spectrum common to all nature, the "eternal" spectrum' – that is all the seven colours of the rainbow – were to be brought into use. Figuring alongside these primary colours would be the elements – the Chinese five: fire, water, air, earth and wood. Linked with air would be 'the steel birds of aviation'; with wood the ancient buildings of Moscow; and so on. Colours and elements would then combine, the colour red becoming synonymous with fire – the fire of 1812, the Red Army, the Kremlin Star; green with the earth – the struggle for the defence of 'our land'; blue with the sea – the sea of Moscow 'spilling over, like the ocean of plenty, under the impetus of the Five Year Plan'; but new colours would be introduced by 'association of reciprocal transitions' – the gilded cupolas or the sparks flying from the flowing molten metal making the transition to the orange colour associated with industrialized Moscow.

Other techniques and themes developed by Eisenstein throughout his creative life converged on this one work. Old, familiar themes turned up again in modified form: now, for example, the all-pervading light would banish the darkness, whereas in *Bezhin Meadow* the light surrounding Stepok had been extinguished in the world of darkness. The projected seven-part structure of

Que Viva Mexico! reappears in the seven parts – corresponding with the colours of the rainbow – envisaged for *Moscow 800*. These were to be framed by a prologue (in which the rainbow symbolizes the patriarchal character of the city's beginnings) and an epilogue (where again the colours of the rainbow blaze forth in the firework display of V-Day). The rainbow of the prologue becomes engulfed by the black smoke of the enemy Tartars, while, conversely in the epilogue, 'the rainbow of victory' triumphantly swamps 'the black of the Fascist hordes'. In the seven intervening episodes a succession of conflicts between black and the appropriate colour of the rainbow are played out.

As in *Que Viva Mexico!*, Eisenstein envisaged the characters spanning the entire history of the film. The heroine, for example – first seen at her spindle and finally at her mechanized loom in a textile plant – personifies Moscow through the ages just as the Soldadera personified Mexico. Similarly the other characters, played as they are down the ages by the same actors, remain recognizable throughout, however much their features and outlook on life differ from generation to generation; they thus symbolically represent both the individual and mankind in general.

And so, for the moment, Eisenstein was freely improvising with all these themes. The project, however, never got beyond this preliminary stage; for, with permission to resume work on *Ivan*, Eisenstein's prime concern once again became the completion of that film. This he contemplated doing after a further period of convalescence. *Moscow 800* (Eisenstein's notes to which are dated 30 September and 29 November 1946) was to remain a fantastic unrealized dream.

Through the swirl of dry leaves

The author of the present work is the author of 'his own theme'.
And though the theme of his works over two decades may
appear to gallop through a variety of totally different spheres
. . . he is, nonetheless, the author of a single theme.
EISENSTEIN

Frustrated though he naturally felt at the period of inactivity enforced on him by his illness, Eisenstein was at the same time grateful for the unique opportunity it afforded him of taking stock of his life. As he looked back over his forty-eight years, however, he was at first saddened by the apparent pointlessness of it all:

I have understood nothing. Neither about life. Nor myself. . . . Nothing, except perhaps one single thing. That I have rushed through life. That I have glanced neither to right nor left. . . . My attention was always concentrated upon the moment. As if I had been hurrying somewhere. As if I had been anxious not to be late. As if my aim had been to arrive there. As if I had immediately wanted to rush on again further. Fleetingly, as from a train window, I see the images of my childhood, my youthful adventures and the events of my adult life. . . . And suddenly I am struck by the dreadful realization. Everything has slipped through my fingers! I did not know how to grasp hold and cling on.[7]

But as his recollections poured in on him in an avalanche of images, provoking him to speculate gloomily on whether he had 'really lived . . . or merely rushed on incessantly', he knew that he had indeed lived: through happiness and torment, but he had lived. And he would not have exchanged with anyone that life which now seemed so full that he felt a mad desire to make time stand still while he recorded it all. But memories eluded him in the attempt; he experienced the sensation of time disappearing. At the same time, he probed into his work and meditated on it; but still, I believe, with the aim of finding himself. During this period, for instance, he remarked that the genesis of one's work reflects 'not simply facts, but also the dynamic of the creative process'.

Thoughts of death and immortality began to preoccupy him. He traced back the theme of death in his own works, wondering whether that blind, implacable force that had stalked through all his films had now caught up with him in person. His heart condition, which, equally implacable, had already struck at him several times, now seemed to be closing in to deal the final deathblow. Obsessively the prophecy that he would die at fifty kept recurring to him – and his fiftieth birthday was now steadily approaching.

The idea of death and immortality became linked with that of unity between man and matter, with the theme of harmony. And as he looked back over his own works he saw them as dominated by this single idea of harmonious unity. Irrespective of time and place – the Middle Ages, the Renaissance, modern times; Moscow, Mexico, Uzbekistan, America – the theme was ever present. It might be the unity of a nation – as in *Alexander Nevsky* or *Ivan* – or of some smaller group. Sometimes it appeared in inverted form – the tragedy of individualism – as in *An American Tragedy* or *Black Majesty*. But whatever the treatment, the theme was essentially one and the same: that of unity and harmony.

His thinking led him on to examine the psychological and emotional stimuli in his own development, and in this he now recognized personal vanity – a form of Don Juanism – to have been an important factor. Life, which had 'slipped through his fingers' and through which he had wandered, like Peer Gynt through the swirl of dry leaves, while so many of his aims never came to fruition – that same life also included many undeniable triumphs.

For the moment, however, it was the tragedy of the banned *Ivan* that was uppermost in his thoughts.

'You must hurry'

*This is what will bring about my destruction, if anything does;
not Meletus nor Anytus, but the slander and jealousy of a very
large section of the people. They have been fatal to a great
many other innocent men.*
SOCRATES

Although Eisenstein had often complained bitterly that his whole life had been nothing but rush, now, as his days were drawing to an end, he constantly repeated to himself, 'You must hurry! Hurry! Hurry!' But this time the race was against death – a race to make the optimum use of his last remaining days, even hours.

By January 1947 he felt a little better, although the slightest effort was enough to force him back to bed. Even so, he obstinately refused to give up lecturing, and that month he arranged for his students to sit their examinations at his house. Amazingly, he continued teaching for several months more, during which time, as Professor A. R. Luria recalls, he also prepared a course of lectures on the psychology of creative work; but his death prevented him from presenting it at Moscow University.

A painful experience at this time was that of seeing at last, after fifteen long years, part of the material shot in Mexico – but in the cut and mutilated form of *Thunder over Mexico* and *Time in the Sun.* For an artist whose grandiose vision had been to edit this material – this 'child' of his – in such a totally different way, the shock of viewing these travesties must have taken a considerable toll on his ebbing spirits.

Nonetheless his characteristic vitality helped him to endure the torment of his physical condition that now confined him to bed. Again he planned to resume work on *Ivan*, this time in September and October. Each time his target date for starting work proved illusory, so he set a new one. Meanwhile he carried on with his theoretical writings, approving a second book of essays, for which he chose the title *Film Form*, for publication in America. The organization of a cinematographic section at the Academy's Institute of the History of the Arts (of which he was appointed head) simultaneously occupied his energies, as did plans for a projected trip abroad in the following months. He was also fascinated at this time by the idea of television. And all the time he felt impelled to record the fruits of his researches for posterity, racked by the thought 'how little aesthetics has achieved in mastering the means and potentialities of the cinema!'[9]

But throughout this time his illness had slowly been closing in on him. One day he was frantically writing when his pen slipped in his weakened hand, leaving a strange zigzag on the page. Deliberately taking up a red crayon, he arrowed the offending scrawl and added the comment: 'This is the graph of my illness.'

On 23 January 1948 he celebrated his fiftieth birthday. Had the fortune-teller's prediction perhaps been nonsense? He had placed a monkey-wrench near the radiator, so that in an emergency he could strike the radiator and summon Tisse from the flat below. A few days later, on 10 February, he was again immersed in his writings on the theory of colour. He broke off for a moment to doodle on the paper – a strangely prophetic doodle of a maze, like a children's puzzle in which the problem is to find the way out from the centre; then he continued writing. But the writing suddenly petered out . . . to be followed by a single word in red crayon: 'attack'. It was a heart attack, followed soon after by a second. Yet still he went on working into the night, till, in the early hours of the next morning, the fateful morning of 11 February 1948, his heart beat for the last time.

Many are the versions of Eisenstein's death. According to Victor Shklovsky and Marie Seton, he died alone in the house, while going to open the door to Maxim Strauch, or while going to the radiator to signal Eduard Tisse. Strauch himself maintains that Eisenstein was accompanied by the woman who nùrsed him. Some say that he was crossing the room when he fell from the attack; others that he slumped over the radio in the act of switching it on. Recently I was told a fourth and subsequently a fifth version – each totally different – by alleged eye-witnesses of the event. . . . The truth about the circumstances cannot yet be told. Even over his death, controversy continued to rage round Eisenstein.

15. Requiem

Poor, poor Uncle Vanya! . . . Your life has known no peace . . .
CHEKHOV

An accusation frequently levelled against Eisenstein was that his work was dispassionately cold, as icily cold as the coolly conceived and complicated ideas that lay behind it. When not motivated by sheer malice, this criticism generally arose from a simple lack of understanding – the sort of lack of understanding that greeted Whitman's assertion that he both embodied, and at the same time was, every human, earthly or cosmic experience. For Eisenstein's work – despite its defects, its proneness to over-cerebral, and not always successful, experimentation – pulsates with passion.

Yet, in the blinkered eyes of officialdom – the representatives of that set-up that time and time again condemned Eisenstein to artistic sterility – he was an ice-cold 'formalist'. Eisenstein replied with a sublime irony that was quite lost on his critics; slaves to formalism as they were, they were content with what they saw only as Eisenstein's self-critical recognition of his 'mistakes'.

What soul-destroying tragedy was Eisenstein forced to live through, prevented as he so often and so brutally was from creating! Even ordinary everyday events were experienced by him with extraordinary intensity; even the smallest incident took on dramatic proportions.

The light is turned off to economize on electricity. For me it's not just that. The switching off of a light means being plunged in darkness. The telephone gets unplugged and it means all contact with the world is lost. A delay in pay (how often!)

271

means the spectre of misery. And everything is magnified. Everything is experienced with extreme intensity. Every trivial event tends to be magnified almost instantaneously into a general calamity. You lose a button – suddenly you feel a tramp. . . . You forget a name – you feel as though 'senile decay and loss of memory' has set in, etc. Seen from the outside, all this appears highly amusing. But to live with it is the greatest possible torment.[1]

What hell, then, must such blows – not 'trivial events', but artistic deathblows – have caused Eisenstein to suffer!

In his films Eisenstein always aimed at reducing everything to its essence. (He often declared jokingly that the director had first to consider what *not* to show – after which it became clear exactly what *must* be shown.) Hence the ever-present three basic elements: water (the sea in *Potemkin*; the rains invoked in *The General Line*; the snow and the lake into which the Teutons fall in *Alexander Nevsky*; the snow in *The Poet's Love*; the sea-theme in *Ivan the Terrible*; the water in *Ferghana Canal*); fire (the gun salvoes and the candle held by Vakulinchuk in *Potemkin*; the fires in *Bezhin Meadow* and *Alexander Nevsky*, and the torches in the latter; the minutely orchestrated tapers in *Ivan*); earth (the shore in *Potemkin*; the land question in *The General Line*; the fight for territorial integrity in *Alexander Nevsky* and for territorial expansion in *Ivan*). Another basic theme that recurs constantly is that of life and death.

It is argued today that the contemporary film has qualitatively outstripped Eisenstein's cinematographic theory and practice. But let us examine a few facts. Orson Welles kept up a long and serious correspondence with Eisenstein on basic principles (unpublished to date) and still speaks of him with reverence; Elia Kazan admits to being profoundly influenced by Eisenstein; Jean-Luc Godard included in his *Les Carabiniers* an entire sequence in avowed homage to *Potemkin*; in Italy his works have influenced Umberto Barbaro and become set study material for students of the film; Henri Colpi acknowledges Eisenstein's clearly discernible influence in several of his fundamental artistic techniques in *Une Aussi Longue Absence* and *Codine*, stating in a letter to me that 'in detail as well as in the most general aspects' he recognizes 'an immense debt to Eisenstein'; Alain Resnais has declared not only his admiration for, but also his kinship with, Eisenstein, and spoken of his ambition to create a cinematographic opus 'à la *Nevsky*' or 'à la *Ivan*'; Antonioni, on a different level, pursues the same rigorous laws of film construction as Eisenstein, so that it is not surprising to detect an echo of the montage of attractions in *L'Avventura* (when the train passes through the shot of Sandro and Claudia kissing), or of Eisenstein's ideas on colour in *Il Deserto Rosso*.

And what homage could be more impressive than that perennially paid to his films, including the silent ones, by the revivals which, even today, continue to attract capacity audiences? Or the fact that commercial television channels have actually used excerpts from *Potemkin* for plugging advertisements? No doubt such sacrilege is viewed with apoplectic indignation by certain of Eisenstein's devotees. But he himself, I am convinced, would have been amused and delighted by this eloquent tribute to the undying success of his masterpiece.

The tragedy of Eisenstein's life unfolds like the legends of Sisyphus and the Danaids rolled into one. It is the story of one man's superhuman and ceaseless endeavour to accomplish his particular mission in life, only to see his attempt constantly frustrated by circumstances beyond his control. The torments of a Tantalus, too, were perpetually experienced by this insatiable artist. Yet, though unfulfilled in his chosen creative sphere thanks to the destruction of so many cherished dreams, he was, and remains today, a giant – the supreme exponent of the seventh art. The creator of so many legends, he was himself the hero of one, the embodiment of tragic myth and of the invincibility of the human spirit.

Notes and References

Note: For convenience, reference is made, in the following notes, to any known published English translations of the various Russian and other foreign sources. Not all these translations have, however, been used for the quotations in this book.

Introduction
1. Thomas Mann: *Letters, 1889–1955*, selected and translated by Richard and Clara Winston, London and New York 1970. Vol. 1, 1889–1942, page 185.

1. Sketch for a Portrait
1. Léon Moussinac: *Serge Eisenstein*, Paris 1964; Eng. trans. D. Sandy Petrey, New York 1970, page 21.
2. *Meyerhold on Theatre*, trans. Edward Braun, London 1969, New York 1970, page 321.

2. The Path towards Art
1. Eisenstein 'Colour and Music. The colour genealogy of "Moscow 800"'. First published in the collection *Mosfilm: Articles* etc., Moscow 1961
2. Eisenstein: *Film Form*, Essays in Film Theory, edited and translated by Jay Leyda. New York 1949, London 1951, page 88.
3. Eisenstein, first published in *Voprosyi Kinodramaturgi*, 3, Moscow 1959.
4. Eisenstein: 'Autobiographical Note'. *International Literature*, 4, Moscow 1933.
5. Eisenstein: *Notes of a Film Director*, London 1959, page 9.
6, 7. 'Autobiographical Note', as 4 above.
8. *Film Form*, as 2 above, page 28.

3. Through Theatre to Film
1. Eisenstein: *Notes of a Film Director*, London 1959, page 14.
2. *Notes*, as above, pages 12–14.
3. *Notes*, page 16.
4. Eisenstein: *Film Form*, Essays in Film Theory, edited and translated by Jay Leyda. New York 1949, London 1951, pages 14–15.
5. *Meyerhold on Theatre*, trans. Edward Braun, London 1969 and New York 1970, pages 311–12.

6. Eisenstein: 'Autobiographical Note'. *International Literature*, 4, Moscow 1933.
7. Eisenstein: *The Film Sense*, trans. and ed. Jay Leyda, New York 1942, London 1943, pages 166–7.
8. 'Autobiographical Note', as 6 above.
9. *Film Form*, as 4 above, pages 7–8.
10, 11, 12. *Film Form*, pages 9–12.
13, 14. *Film Form*, pages 175–6.
15. *Notes*, as 2 above, page 17.
16. *Film Form*, page 13.
17. *Film Form*, pages 15–16.
18. *Film Form*, page 3.

4. Strike
1. Eisenstein: *Film Form*, Essays in Film Theory, ed. and trans. Jay Leyda, New York 1949, London 1951, pages 261–5.
2. Eisenstein: *Film Essays*, ed. Jay Leyda, London 1968, page 19.
3. *Film Essays*, pages 96–7.
4. *Film Form*, page 16.
5. Jean Mitry: *S. M. Eisenstein*, Paris 1955.

5. Battleship Potemkin
1. Eisenstein: *Notes of a Film Director*, London 1959, pages 18–19.
2. *Notes*, page 21.
3. *Notes*, page 24.
4. See Vladimir Nizhny: *Lessons with Eisenstein*, trans. and ed. Ivor Montagu and Jay Leyda, London 1962, chapter 4.
5. Eisenstein's memoir on the making of *Potemkin* published posthumously in *Iskusstvo Kino*, 4, Moscow 1950; Eng. trans. *The Cinema 1952*, ed. Roger Manvell, Harmondsworth, 1952, page 168.
6. Eisenstein: *Film Form*, Essays in Film Theory ed. and trans. Jay Leyda, New York 1949, London 1951, pages 170–1.
7. Béla Illés: *Anekdoták Könyve*, Budapest 1960.

8. Mayakovsky: Speech at Sovkino discussion, 15 October 1927. *Kino*, Moscow 1946.
9. *Notes*, as 1 above, page 53.
10. Eisenstein: 'Nature Is Not Indifferent'. *Iskusstvo Kino*, Moscow 1962.
11. *Film Form*, as 6 above, page 49.
12. Eisenstein: Memoirs (MS, unpublished, in Eisenstein archive, Moscow).
13. *Film Form*, page 238.
14. Eisenstein: 'Our October'. *Kino*, 13 March 1928.
15. Rostovtsev: 'The Battleship Potemkin'. *Iskusstvo Kino*, Moscow 1962.
16. Ivor Montagu: *With Eisenstein in Hollywood*, Berlin 1968, page 32.
17. Eisenstein: *Film Essays*, ed. Jay Leyda, London 1968, pages 16–17.

6. Searchings: From October to The General Line

1. Ilya Ehrenburg, *Men, Years, Life*, London 1961–6. Vol. 3, *Truce 1921–33*, trans. Tatiana Shebunina and Yvonne Kapp, page 104.
2. Eisenstein: *Film Form*, New York 1949, London 1951, pages 37–8.
3. Léon Moussinac: *Serge Eisenstein*, Paris 1964; Eng. trans. D. Sandy Petrey, New York 1970, page 24.
4. Harry M. Geduld and Ronald Gottesman, eds. *Sergei Eisenstein and Upton Sinclair: The Making and Unmaking of Que Viva Mexico!* Bloomington and London 1970, pages 260–1.
5. Told to Ivor Montagu. *Eisenstein 1898–1948*, memorial brochure, London 1949, page 7.
6. Eisenstein: *The Film Sense*, trans. and ed. Jay Leyda, New York 1942, London 1943, page 28.
7. *Iskusstvo Kino*, 10, Moscow 1957.
8. Eisenstein: 'Die Schöpfungsgeschichte unseres "Oktober"-Films', *Das Neue Russland*, 4–5, 1928.
9. *Film Form*, as 2 above, page 56.
10. Eisenstein: *Film Essays*, ed. Jay Leyda, London 1968, pages 44–45.
11. *Film Form*, page 58.
12. *Film Form*, page 184.

13. Esther Shub: *In Close-Up*, Moscow 1959.
14. Quoted by Moussinac, as 3 above, pages 149–53.
15. Ivor Montagu: *With Eisenstein in Hollywood*, Berlin 1968, page 123.
16. Jean Mitry: *S. M. Eisenstein*, Paris 1961, page 114.
17. Eisenstein: Memoirs (MS, unpublished, in Eisenstein archive, Moscow).
18. Eisenstein: 'Der Siegeszug des russischen Films "Die Hauptlinie",' *Das Neue Russland*, 1–2, 1927.
19. Jay Leyda: *Kino*, London 1960, page 260.
20. *Kino*, page 267.
21. *Film Form*, page 21.
22. *Film Form*, page 64.
23. *The Film Sense*, as 6 above, page 62.
24. *Film Form*, page 80.
25. *Film Form*, page 258.
26. From the first volume of the Russian edition of Eisenstein's writings. See Bibliographical Note.
27. Moussinac, as 3 above, page 147.

7. Abroad

1. Marie Seton, *Sergei M. Eisenstein*, London 1952, page 130.
2. Ivor Montagu: *With Eisenstein in Hollywood*, Berlin 1968, page 29.
3. Jean Mitry: *S. M. Eisenstein*, Paris 1961, pages 121–3.
4. Eisenstein: *Film Form* ed. and trans. Jay Leyda, New York 1949, London 1951, pages 184–5.
5. *Film Form*, page 105.
6. Eisenstein: Memoirs (MS. unpublished, in Eisenstein archive, Moscow).
7. Eisenstein's memory is less than perfect. The relevant passage from the letter in question reads: '. . . je suis ennuyé de la nature humaine. J'ai besoin de solitude et d'isolement; les grandeurs m'ennuient; le sentiment est desseché. La gloire est fade à vingt-neuf ans; j'ai tout epuisé: il ne me reste plus qu'à devenir bien vraiment égoiste.' (British Museum Additional MS. 23,003: letter to Joseph Bonaparte from Cairo, 25 July 1798, as cited by A. du

Casse in *Mémoires et Correspondance Politique et Militaire du Roi Joseph*, tome 1, Paris 1855, page 189.)
8. Letter to author, 17 July 1964.
9. Memoirs, as 6 above.
10. Vladimir Nizhny: *Lessons with Eisenstein*, trans. and ed. by Ivor Montagu and Jay Leyda, London 1962, page 60.
11. Seton, as 1 above, page 160.
12. *Film Form*, page 98.
13. Nizhny, as 10 above, pages 10–11.
14. *Film Form*, page 103.
15. Eisenstein: *The Film Sense*, trans. and ed. Jay Leyda, New York 1942, London 1943, page 24.
16, 17. Memoirs, as 6 above.
18. Montagu, as 2 above, page 102.
19. Montagu, page 342.
20. *Film Form*, page 106.
21. *Film Form*, page 96.
22. *Film Form*, pages 97–101.
23. *Film Form*, page 96.
24. Léon Moussinac: *Serge Eisenstein*, Paris 1964; Eng. trans. D. Sandy Petrey, New York 1970, page 52.
25. Carbon copy of original in Eisenstein Collection, Museum of Modern Art Film Library, New York.
26. Montagu, page 120.
27. Esther Shub: *In Close-Up*, Moscow, 1959.
28. Memoirs, as 6 above.
29. Letter from Seymour Stern to Marie Seton, quoted in *Eisenstein*, as 1 above, page 191.

8. Que Viva Mexico!
1. Harry M. Geduld and Ronald Gottesman, eds.: *Sergei Eisenstein and Upton Sinclair: The Making and Unmaking of Que Viva Mexico!*, Bloomington and London 1970.
2. Eisenstein: Memoirs (MS. unpublished, in Eisenstein archive, Moscow).
3. Esther Shub: *In Close-Up*, Moscow 1959.
4. Memoirs, as 2 above.
5, 6. Memoirs.
7. Memoirs; also Eisenstein: *Drawings*, Moscow 1961, page 20.
8. Memoirs.

9. Letter to Marie Seton, quoted in Seton: *Sergei M. Eisenstein*, London 1952, page 216.
10. Eisenstein: *The Film Sense*, trans. and ed. Jay Leyda, New York 1942, London 1943, page 180.
11. Eisenstein: *Que Viva Mexico!*, London 1951, page 27.
12. Geduld and Gottesman, as 1 above, page 66.
13. Geduld and Gottesman, page 69.
14. 'The Principle of Film Form', translated from the German by Ivor Montagu, first appeared in *Close-Up*, September 1931. An expanded version appeared as 'A Dialectic Approach to Film Form', translated by John Winge, in *Film Form*, ed. Jay Leyda, 1949.
15. Geduld and Gottesman, page 190.
16. Geduld and Gottesman, page 282; previously published in English in *Sight and Sound*, Autumn 1958, and by Salka Viertel in her autobiography: *The Kindness of Strangers*, New York 1969, pages 155–7. All English versions of this letter are less complete than the original German text, first published by Jay Leyda in *Sergei Eisenstein, Künstler der Revolution. Materialen der Berliner Eisenstein-Konferenz. lo. bis 18 April 1959*, which adds the following sentences: 'In situations like mine, people have shot themselves. I wonder that I don't do so! Who knows – it could still happen!'
17. Geduld and Gottesman, page 212.
18. Geduld and Gottesman, page 353: letter to Theodore Dreiser from Mary Craig Sinclair.
19. Geduld and Gottesman, page 319.
20. Geduld and Gottesman, page 393.
21. Geduld and Gottesman, page 33.
22. Seton, as 9 above, pages 226–7.
23. Seton, page 230.
24. Seton, page 233.
25. Geduld and Gottesman, page 341.
26. Seton, page 516.
27, 28. Geduld and Gottesman, page 309.
29. Seton, page 237.
30. Geduld and Gottesman, page 341.

ysis

31. Geduld and Gottesman, pages 130, 132–3.
32. Seton, page 280.
33. Seton, page 285.
34. Seton, page 256.
35. Geduld and Gottesman, page 343.
36. Memoirs.

9. 'Polemics Rage Around Me'

1. Ivan Anisimov: 'The Films of Eisenstein', *International Literature*, 3, Moscow 1931.
2, 3. *Voprosyi Kinodramaturgi*, 3, 1959.
4. Marie Seton: *Sergei M. Eisenstein*, London 1952, page 314.
5. Vladimir Nizhny: *Lessons with Eisenstein*, trans. and ed. Ivor Montagu and Jay Leyda, London 1962.
6. *Cahiers du Cinéma*, 125, 1961.
7. Jay Leyda: *Kino*, London 1960, page 302.
8. Ilya Weisfeld: *The Craft of Film Making*, Moscow 1961.
9. *Kino*, as 7 above, page 327.
10. *Kino*, pages 328–9.
11. *Kino*, page 11.
12. Seton, as 4 above, page 355.
13. Article in *Pravda*, Spring 1937, quoted by Seton, pages 368–9.
14. *Kino*, page 330.
15. Seton, page 359.
16. *Kino*, page 304.
17. Quoted by Weisfeld, as 8 above.
18. Seton, page 369.
19. Seton, page 366.
20. Esther Shub: *In Close-Up*, Moscow 1959.
21, 22. Eisenstein: Memoirs (MS. unpublished, in Eisenstein archive, Moscow).
23. Eisenstein: *Film Essays*, ed. Jay Leyda, London 1968, page 86.
24. Shub, as 20 above.

10. Pedagogic Respite

1. Eisenstein: *Film Essays*, ed. Jay Leyda, London 1968, page 86.
2. Eisenstein: Memoirs (MS. unpublished, in Eisenstein archive, Moscow).
3. Vladimir Nizhny: *Lessons with Eisenstein*, trans. and ed. by Ivor Montagu and Jay Leyda, London 1962, page 13.
4. Nizhny: page 1.
5. Eisenstein: *Film Form*, ed. and trans. Jay Leyda, New York 1949, London 1951, pages 90–1.
6. Quoted by Esther Shub: *In Close-Up*, Moscow 1959.

11. Alexander Nevsky

1. Eisenstein: *Notes of a Film Director*, trans. X. Danko, London 1959.
2. Eisenstein: Memoirs (MS. unpublished, in Eisenstein archive, Moscow).
3. Eisenstein: *Film Essays*, ed. Jay Leyda, London 1968, pages 48–65: 'The Dynamic Square'.
4. Eisenstein: 'Colour and Music. The Colour Genealogy of "Moscow 800"'. First published in the collection *Mosfilm: Articles* etc., Moscow 1961.
5. *Iskusstvo Kino*, 11, 1962.
6. 'Questions of the Historical Film', *Iz Istorii Kino*, 4, Moscow 1961.
7. 'Colour and Music', as 4 above.
8. *Notes*, as 1 above, page 37.
9. *Notes*, page 45.
10. Jay Leyda: *Kino*, London 1960, page 349.
11. *Kino*, page 350.
12. *Iskusstvo Kino*, 1, 1958.
13. Eisenstein: *Film Form*, ed. and trans. Jay Leyda, New York 1949, London 1951, pages 152–3.
14. For much of this see *Notes*, as 1 above, pages 149–67.
15. Ilya Ehrenburg: *Men, Years, Life*, London 1961–66. Vol. 3, *Eve of War 1933–41*, trans. Tatiana Shebunina and Yvonne Kapp, page 194.
16. S. S. Prokofiev: *Documents, Recollections*, Moscow 1956.
17. Eisenstein: Preface to *Sergei Prokofiev* by Israel Nestyev, New York 1946.
18. Eisenstein: *The Film Sense*, trans. and ed. Jay Leyda, New York 1942, London 1943, page 115.
19. *Voprosyi Kinodramaturgi*, 3, 1959.
20. *Documents, Recollections*, as 16 above.
21. *Iskusstvo Kino*, 1, 1958.
22. V. Nikolskaya: 'The Composition of the Film Alexander Nevsky' in *The Problems of the History of Cinema*, Moscow 1957.
23. See *The Film Sense*, as 18 above, pages 125–56.

24. *Notes*, as 1 above, page 108.
25. *Notes*, page 204.

12. The Path Towards Ivan
1. Letter to Jay Leyda, quoted by Marie Seton: *Sergei M. Eisenstein*, London 1952, page 388.
2. *Voprosyi Kinodramaturgi*, 3, 1959.
3. Eisenstein: *The Film Sense*, trans. and ed. Jay Leyda, New York 1942, London 1943, pages 186–7.
4. Ilya Weisfeld: 'Birth of an Idea' (on some of Eisenstein's unrealized scripts). *Iskusstvo Kino*, Moscow, January 1958.
5. Eisenstein: *Film Essays*, ed. Jay Leyda, London 1968, page 85.
6. *Film Essays*, page 89.
7. *Film Essays*, page 90.
8. Seton, as 1 above, page 406.
9, 10. *Sight and Sound*, Spring 1961, page 84.
11. Letter to Yuri Tynianov, quoted by Weisfeld, as 4 above.
12, 13. Eisenstein: 'Colour and Music. The Colour Genealogy of "Moscow 800"'. First published in the collection *Mosfilm: Articles* etc., Moscow 1961.
14, 15. Weisfeld, as 4 above; and Eisenstein's letter to Tynianov, as 11 above.
16. Esther Shub: *In Close-Up*, Moscow 1959.
17. Letter to Tynianov, as 11 above.

13. Ivan the Terrible
1. Eisenstein: *Film Form*, ed. and trans. Jay Leyda, New York 1949, London 1951, page 261.
2. Eisenstein: 'Ivan Grozny', *VOKS Bulletin*, 7–8, 1942.
3. Eisenstein: 'My Drawings', *Mosfilm: Articles*, etc., 1, 1959. Included in *Ivan the Terrible: a Screenplay*, trans. Ivor Montagu and Herbert Marshall, New York 1962, London 1963, page 302.
4. *Film Form*, as 1 above, pages 261–2.
5. *Ivan the Terrible*, as 3 above, page 225.
6. *Ivan the Terrible*, pages 226–8.
7. Letter to Yuri Tynianov, quoted by Ilya Weisfeld: 'Birth of an Idea' (on some of Eisenstein's unrealized scripts), *Iskusstvo Kino*, Moscow, January 1958.

8. *Film Form*, page 262.
9. *Film Form*, page 263.
10. Eisenstein: Memoirs (MS. unpublished, in Eisenstein archive, Moscow).
11. *Ivan the Terrible*, pages 120–4.
12. *Ivan the Terrible*, page 125.
13. *Ivan the Terrible*, pages 130–1.
14. Eisenstein: 'Nature is Not Indifferent', *Iskusstvo Kino*, November 1962.
15. *Film Form*, page 264.
16. N. Cherkasov: *Notes of a Soviet Actor*, Foreign Language Publishing House, Moscow.
17. *Iskusstvo Kino*, 11, 1962.
18, 19. Letter to Teleshova, 3 March 1942.
20. Eisenstein: 'People on a Film', *Izbranyie Statyi*, Iskusstvo, Moscow 1956.
21. *Film Form*, page 262.
22. Eisenstein: *Notes of a Film Director*, trans. X. Danko, London 1959, page 162.
23. Jay Leyda: *Kino*, London 1960, page 382.
24. Jean Mitry: *S. M. Eisenstein*, Paris 1961, page 165.
25. *Sight and Sound*, Spring 1961, page 86.

14. Years of Meditation
1. Related by Brooks Atkinson in article in *New York Times*, 11 March 1946.
2. Marie Seton: *Sergei M. Eisenstein*, London 1952, page 458.
3. Seton, page 460.
4. Jay Leyda: *Kino*, London 1960, page 394.
5. *Sight and Sound*, Spring 1961, page 86.
6. Eisenstein: 'Colour and Music. The Colour Genealogy of "Moscow 800"'. First published in the collection *Mosfilm: Articles*, etc., Moscow 1961.
7. Eisenstein: Memoirs (MS. unpublished, in Eisenstein archive, Moscow).
8. *Eisenstein: Künstler der Revolution*, Berlin 1960.
9. Eisenstein: *Notes of a Film Director*, trans. X. Danko, London 1959, page 7.

15. Requiem
1. Eisenstein: Memoirs (MS, unpublished, in Eisenstein archive, Moscow).

Bibliographical Note

Despite the phenomenal volume of commentary that Eisenstein, his life and work have inspired, surprisingly little of it has been in the form of a biography or critical monograph.

The voluminous biography by Marie Seton (The Bodley Head, London, 1952) is really the only work of this kind on Eisenstein. Comprehensive and extensively documented though it is, it nonetheless suffers from two major shortcomings: apart from the author's extremely subjective interpretation – in her simplistic, and therefore distorted, attempt at a Freudian analysis, as well as her conviction, unsupported by the facts, of a mystical side to the director's make-up – the biography contains certain errors of fact and judgement that throw a question-mark over the whole work. It is disputed from many points of view by other close acquaintances of Eisenstein. A lack of objectivity similarly detracts from the merits of the biography by the Swedish writer, Bengt Idestam-Almquist ('Robin Hood') (Stockholm, 1951).

Ivor Montagu, who collaborated with Eisenstein on the film scenarios written in Hollywood, recently published his fascinating memoirs of that period in *With Eisenstein in Hollywood* (Seven Seas Publishers, Berlin, 1968), which also includes their scenarios of *Sutter's Gold* and *An American Tragedy*.

The book edited by Harry M. Geduld and Ronald Gottesman, *Sergei Eisenstein and Upton Sinclair: The Making and Unmaking of Que Viva Mexico!* (Indiana University Press, Bloomington; Thames and Hudson, London, 1970), is a scrupulous and effective presentation of numerous previously unknown documents from the Sinclair archive, and clears up to a great extent the mystery surrounding Eisenstein's unfinished Mexican film. I hope that in due course the publication of the complete Eisenstein archive will answer those questions that remain.

Among the critical monographs on Eisenstein, the only one of outstanding merit is that by Jean Mitry (Classiques du Cinéma series, Editions Universitaires, Paris, 1961); it contains extremely interesting analyses of Eisenstein's films which make it mandatory reading for any student of the subject. There is also the monograph by Barthelémy Amengual (*Premier Plan*, No. 25, October 1962), which includes a number of original observations on Eisenstein's work. Léon Moussinac's contribution (published posthumously in *Cinéma d'Aujourd'hui*, Seghers, Paris, 1964) is a warm appraisal, particularly interesting for the documents and previously unpublished letters it contains.

Then there are: the brochure by Vsevolod Vishnevsky (Goskinozdat, Moscow, 1939), the first pamphlet on Eisenstein to be published, which is an essential inclusion in any bibliography on the subject; the volume by Paul Rotha and others (*Eisenstein, 1898–1948*; Society for Cultural Relations with the U.S.S.R., London, n.d.); the annotated transcripts of a number of Eisenstein's lectures, *Lessons with Eisenstein*, by V. Nizhny (Dennis Dobson, London, 1968); *Montaz w Tworezosci Eisenstein*, by Regina Dreyer-Sfard (Warsaw, 1964); *Battleship Potemkin*, by I. Rostovtsev (Iskusstvo, Moscow, 1962), a treatise on the film; the volume published by Peter Konlechner and Peter Kubelka of the Österreichisches Filmmuseum (Vienna, 1964).

Important chapters or passages devoted to Eisenstein appear in a number of books. *Kino: A History of the Russian and Soviet Film* (Allen & Unwin, London, 1960) by Jay Leyda, a former student and collaborator of Eisenstein, and the editor of his works in the U.S.A., constitutes an invaluable source of information, including as it does deep-searching analyses, much original data, and personal recollections about Eisenstein. *In Close-up* by Esther Shub (Iskusstvo, Moscow, 1969), one chapter of which is devoted to Eisenstein, is indispensable to the researcher. *The Director's Counterpoint*, by S. Yutkevich (Iskusstvo, Moscow, 1960) also has a valuable chapter, as has Victor Shklovsky's book *Once upon a Time* (Sovietsky Pisately, Moscow, 1966), while *Sergei Eisenstein – Künstler der Revolution* (Henschel-Verlag, Berlin, 1960) includes speeches by participants at a Berlin conference on the life and work of Eisenstein, as well as other important documents.

Numerous studies, recollections and other articles relating to Eisenstein written by friends, colleagues and acquaintances have appeared in a wide variety of publications all over the world. Among the more important of these are those by: Henri Agel, Grigori Alexandrov, Guido Aristarco, Pera Attasheva, Umberto Barbaro, Gaston Bounoure, Nikolai Cherkasov, Jean Domarchi, Theodore Dreiser, Regina Dreyer, K. Eliseyev, Louis Fischer, Charles Ford, Joseph Freeman, Hermann Herlinghaus, Béla Illés, René Jeanne, Naum Kleiman, Grigori Kozintsev, Leonid Kozlov, Yuri Krasovsky, Luigi Lanza, Nikolai Lebedev, Jay Leyda, Lubomir Linhart, Herbert Marshall, Vsevolod Meyerhold, Boris Mikhin, Ivor Montagu, Léon Moussinac, V. Nikolska, Francesco Pasinetti, Paul Rotha, Georges Sadoul, Victor Shklovsky, N. Sokolova, Maxim Strauch, Jerzy Toeplitz, Herman Weinberg, Ilya Weisfeld, Rostislav Yurenev, and Sergei Yutkevich.

Finally there are Eisenstein's own numerous writings. First and foremost, his three books, *Film Form*, *The Film Sense* and *Film Essays*, all edited by Jay Leyda, provide unparalleled source material. Then, apart from the scenarios for his films, *Battleship Potemkin*, *The General Line*, *Sutter's Gold*, *An American Tragedy*, *Que Viva Mexico!*, *Alexander Nevsky* and *Ivan the Terrible* that have been published in many countries, various other notes, articles, commentaries and memoirs have appeared in Soviet publications and in numerous translations, particularly in English and German, and have been published in book form in the U.S.A., England, Germany, Italy, Switzerland, Hungary, Portugal, Romania, the Argentine and elsewhere.

Gosfilmofond – the Soviet State Film Archive – has listed five films about Eisenstein apart from Jay Leyda's 'Project-film'. These are:

Eisenstein's Visit to Holland. Produced by Hispano Film, The Hague, 1930. 1 reel. Director: Henk Alsem. A documentary about Eisenstein's visit to Amsterdam;

Eisenstein in Mexico. Produced by Sol Lesser. 1932;

In Memory of Eisenstein. Produced by the Central Studio for Documentary Films, Moscow, 1948. 2 reels. Script and direction: Pera Attasheva. Including shots of Eisenstein's burial and of his apartment at Potylika;

Sergei Eisenstein. Produced by the Central Studio for Documentary Films, Moscow, 1958. 5 reels. Script: Rostislav Yurenev. Director: V. Katanian;

Eisenstein and Prokofiev. Produced by the Television Studio in Moscow, 1964. 7 reels. Script: Leonid Kozlov. Director: E. Kovylkina.

Not many years ago a start was made in the Soviet Union on editing and publishing Eisenstein's writings. Several volumes have materialized to date, but they are much less complete and free from shortcomings than was naturally expected. And of course there still remains a vast assortment of personal pages that have yet to see the light of print.

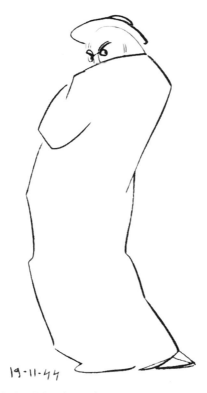

19·11·44

'Fear': sketch by Eisenstein

Index

Agadzhanova-Shutko, Nina
  Ferdinandovna, 91–2
Agitprop trains, 44
Aksyonov, Ivan, 54
Alexander Nevsky, 27, 33, 43, 58,
  82, 104, 106, 142, 206–21, 222,
  226, 227, 230, 232, 248, 249, 268,
  272
Alexandrinsky Theatre, 36
Alexandrov, Grigori, 50, 51–2, 62,
  64, 66, 71, 79, 88, 92, 101, 102,
  103, 119, 122–3, 130, 134, 136,
  137, 139, 144, 149, 153, 155, 156,
  161, 162, 181, 182, 183, 187, 190
All Union Conference of Cine-
  matographic Workers, 190
Alupka Palace, 96
Amengual, Barthelémy, 279
American Cinema, 84
American Tragedy, An, 44, 137, 151,
  152, 156, 157–60, 187, 232, 268
Amkino, 179
Andreyev, Leonid, 54
Anisimov, Ivan, 186
Antoine, André, 47
Antonioni, Michelangelo, 272
Antonov, Alexander, 92, 101
Appia, Adolphe, 47, 58
Aragon, Louis, 265
Arbatov, 49, 50
Architecture, 18, 20, 21–2, 34–5
Arms and the Man, 149
Aron, Robert, 139
Arsenal, 128
Association of Revolutionary Cine-
  matographic Workers (ARK), 83

Atkinson, William Walker *see* Yogi
  Ramacharaka
Attasheva, Pera, 16, 114, 131, 184,
  195, 281
Auriol, Jean-Georges, 140
Aussi Longue Absence, Une, 272
Averchenko, Arkady, 37
Avventura, L', 272

Babel, Isaac, 88, 93, 197, 199,
  205
Bach, J. S., 106
Bachman, J. G., 155
Balázs, Belá, 139–40
Ballet, classical, 17
Balzac, Honoré de, 14
Barbaro, Umberto, 272
Barbusse, Henri, 142
Barnet, Boris, 196
Bartenev, S., 103
Battleship Potemkin, The, 27, 36, 40,
  43, 55, 64, 67, 83, 85, 88, 90–113,
  117, 118, 121, 126, 132, 133, 134,
  143, 144, 147, 175, 189, 195, 207,
  224, 226, 242, 244–6, 266, 272,
  273
Bebyutov, Valeri, 54
Becker, John, 183
Beethoven, Ludwig van, 11, 133
Beilis, Mendel, 229
Bely, Andrei, 189, 229
Benia Krik, 93
Berliner Tageblatt, 110, 141
Bezhin Meadow, 27, 192–9, 201, 207,
  218, 272
Biomechanics, 55–6

Birman, Serafima, 251, 253, 256
Black Consul, The, 189, 201
Black Death, The, projected film
  about, 229
Black Majesty, 189, 268
Blue Bird, The, 34
Bogdanov, A. A., 49
Boitler, Mikhail, 70
Bolshoi Theatre, 68, 96, 101, 103,
  190, 227, 228, 238
Bonaparte, Napoléon, 32, 146
Borah, Senator, 165
Boris Godunov, 36, 230, 231
Bouissounouse, Janine, 139
Boule de Suif, 17
Bounoure, Gaston, 218
Brecht, Bertolt, 140
Brothers Karamazov, The, 32, 253
Bruno, Giordano, projected film about,
  229
Bryullov, 231
Budberg, Moura, 172
Bull-fighting, 170, 172

Callas, General, 181
Callot, Jacques, 39
Campanella, Tommaso, projected film
  about, 229
Carabiniers, Les, 272
Caricatures, 36–8, 72
Carroll, Lewis, 189
Cavalcanti, Alberto, 111
Cendrars, Blaise, 142
Censorship, 110–11, 144, 147
Chaliapin, Fyodor, 36, 142, 180
Chapayev, 222

Chaplin, Charles, 16, 18–19, 111, 131, 155, 161, 163, 165, 177, 233, 257
Charlot, Jean, 166, 172
Chekhov, Anton, 230
Chekhov, Mikhail, 49
Chelyuskin Expedition, projected film about, 188
Chemin de Buenos Aires, Le, 141
Cherkasov, Nikolai, 211, 220, 246, 251, 252–3, 265
Chiappe, Jean, 13, 147, 148
Cinderella (Prokofiev), 249
Cinéma Suisse, Le, 139
Circus, The, 33–4, 50, 64
City Lights, 161
Civil War, The, 38–45
Close-up, The, 26, 107
Clowns, 34
Cocteau, Jean, 142
Cocu Magnifique, Le, 58
Codine, 272
Colman, Ronald, 160–1
Colour, 58, 134, 226, 228, 229–33, 261–2, 266–7
Colpi, Henri, 272
Columbine's Garter, 59
Columbine's Scarf, 59
Commedia dell'Arte, 43, 50, -57, 76
Comoedia, 149
Comus, 146
Condition Humaine, La, 116, 188
Constant Prince, The, 36
Cooper, Fenimore, 24
Costa, Olga, 166
Covarrubias, Miguel, 166
Craig, Gordon, 48, 142
Cruze, James, 157
Cubism, 50, 54

Dana, H. W. L., 153, 180
Daughter of France, 188
Daumier, Honoré, 16, 17, 26, 124, 204
Death Day, 183, 184
Death of Werther, The, 170–2
Debussy, Claude, 133
Degas, H.-G. E., 26, 135
Deserto Rosso, Il, 272
Dessalines, J. J., 189
Devil's Disciple, The, 146
Dewey, John, 153
Diary of a Scoundrel see *Even a Wise Man Stumbles*
Dickens, Charles, 32, 74
Dietrich, Marlene, 154
Disney, Walt, 16, 154
Distler, V. V., 201
Dneprov, 42, 43
Dobb, Maurice, 146
Dr Mabuse, 71
Dohnanyi, Ernst von, 59
Don Juan (Molière), 36
Don Quixote, 142
Don't Drink Wet Water, 57
Dostoyevsky, Fyodor, 32, 135
Double, The, 41
Dovzhenko, Alexander, 17, 127–8, 190
Dreiser, Theodore, 137, 141, 151, 157, 158–9, 160

Dreyfus Affair, projected film about, 149
Dumas, Alexandre, 31
Duncan, Isadora, 47, 58
Dürer, Albrecht, 39

Eddington, Sir Arthur, 176
Ehrenburg, Ilya, 47, 114, 214, 249
Einstein, Albert, 132, 147, 163, 177
Eisenstein and Prokofiev, 281
Eisenstein Archive, 95
Eisenstein in Mexico, 184, 281
Eisenstein, Julia Ivanovna, 20–1, 22–3, 24, 25, 26–7
Eisenstein, Mikhail Osipovich, 20, 21–3, 24, 25, 32, 241
Eisenstein, Modest, 24
Eisenstein, Sergei, in the Red Army, 36, 38–44; in France, 23–4, 141–4, 146–9; in Germany, 109–11, 138–9, 140–1, 183; in England, 110, 144–6; in Switzerland, 139–40; in Belgium, 147; in Holland, 147; in the U.S.A., 149–61; in Mexico, 161, 162, 163–83
Eisenstein's Visit to Holland, 281
Eliseyev, K., 41, 42–3, 72
Elizabeth, Queen, 144–6
End of Saint Petersburg, The, 116–17, 119, 131
Engels, Herr, 24–5
Engineering, 35–6
Enough Stupidity in Every Wise Man see *Even a Wise Man Stumbles*
Ensor, James, 147
Epstein, Jean, 16
Ermler, Friedrich, 196, 250
Eugene Onegin, 230
Even a Wise Man Stumbles, 34, 59, 60, 62, 64–9, 72, 78, 79
Evreinov, Nikolai, 241

Factory of the Eccentric Actor (FEX), 58–9, 83
Fadeyev, 188, 201, 222
Fairbanks, Douglas, 111, 136, 149, 165
False Nero, The, 201
Faust (Murnau), 138
Feld, Hans, 140
Ferghana Canal, The, 33, 61, 223–7, 272
Feuchtwanger, Lion, 111, 197, 201, 257
Film Essays, 280
Film Form, 269, 280
Film Sense, The, 242, 253, 265, 280
First International Congress of Independent Cinematography, 139–40
First Sovkino Theatre, 103
Five Minutes, 117
Flaherty, Robert, 155, 161
Fledermaus, Die, 21
Foregger, Baron Foregger von Greiffenturn, 48, 49, 57, 58, 60
Fourteenth of July, The, 42
France, Anatole, 130
French Revolution, The, 31–2
Freud, Sigmund, 49
Frunze, General, 101, 222
Fuchs, George, 47
Futurism, 47

Gamblers, The, 41
Gamboa, Fernando, 166
Gance, Abel, 16, 142
Garbo, Greta, 154–5
Garland's Inheritance, 69
Gas Masks, 69–70, 85
Geduld, Harry M., 165, 179, 183, 184, 279
General Line, The, 33, 40–1, 116, 127, 128–36, 137, 138, 144, 147, 150, 176, 224, 226, 232, 272
Georges Dandin, 42
German Expressionism, 70, 75
Gilded Putrefaction see *Dr Mabuse*
Gillette, William King, 161
Giry, Mira, 144
Glass House, The, 155–6
Glizer, Judith, 205
Glumov's Diary, 66–7, 70
Godard, Jean-Luc, 244, 272
Goethe, J. W., 98
Gogol, Nikolai, 34, 41, 135, 189, 229–30
Goldwyn, Samuel, 160
Gomorov, Mikhail, 92, 101
Gorky, Maxim, 44, 189, 205
Gorunov, 252, 253
Goskino, 72, 79
Götterdämmerung, 141, 183
Gottesman, Ronald, 165, 179, 183, 184, 279
Götz von Berlichingen, 34
Goya, 39
Grand Hotel (Vicki Baum), 149
Greco, El, 26, 222, 239, 250, 252
Greene, Ernest, 180
Griffith, D. W., 71, 74–5, 107, 153, 158, 250
Grosz, Georg, 140
Guernica, 208
Guilbert, Yvette, 142

Hadji Murad, 224
Hairy Ape, The, 152
Hamlet, 48, 224
Hansel and Gretel, 34
Harlow, Jean, 154
Hays Organization, The, 160
Heartbreak House, 56, 60
Heir to Genghis Khan, The see *Storm over Asia*
Heroic-Experimental Workshop Theatre, 48
Hill, Steven P., 71
Hirschfeld, Magnus, 140
Hitler, Adolf, 183
Hoffmann, E. T. A., 41
Hogarth, William, 39
Hokusai, 26, 204
Holbein, Hans, 146
House of Culture, Veliky Luky, 41, 42
House of Peasants, 104
Human Attitude to Horses, A, 57

Ibsen, Henrik, 41
Idestam-Almquist, Bengt, 279
Illustration, L', 98
Immermann, Karl, 39
In Favour of a World Commune, 48
Inkhizhinov, Valeri, 166
In Memory of Eisenstein, 281
Inspector General, The, 55

Index

Institute of the History of the Arts, 269
Intolerance, 74
Iron Flood, The, 88–9, 117
Isaacs, Jack, 139
Ivan the Terrible, 22, 27, 34, 58, 72, 76, 83, 104, 106, 135, 142, 229, 230, 233, 234–63, 265, 267, 268, 269, 272
Izvestia, 83, 199

James, William, 52
Jannings, Emil, 138–9
Japanese language, 44, 108
Japanese woodcut artists, 39
Jazz Comedy, 187
Jeans, Sir James, 176
Joyce, James, 142–3

Kabalevsky, 257
Kabuki Theatre, 44, 132, 205
Kahle, Frida, 166
Kalotozov, Mikhail, 103
Kalinin, Mikhail, 101
Kamerny Theatre, 45, 48
Kapital, Das, 126
Kapitza, Peter, 249
Kartashov, Vitka, 193
Kazan, Elia, 272
Keaton, Buster, 131
Kerensky, Alexander, 36, 38
Khanum, Lola, 225
Khanum, Tamara, 225
Kholstomer, 224
Khudekhov, 37
Kidnapper, The (d'Ennery), 57
Kimbrough, Hunter, 165, 175, 177, 179, 180, 182
King Hunger, 54
Kino-Gazeta, 83
Kino-glaz, 88
Kino-Pravda, 66, 76, 88
Kisch, Egon Erwin, 111, 139
Kislovodsk Sanatorium, 184
Kleiman, Naum, 16, 198
Kleist, Heinrich von, 39
Knorre, F. F., 59
Koltsov, Mikhail, 83
Korda, Alexander, 253
Kozintsev, Grigori, 56, 58, 83
Krasovsky, Yuri, 95
Kremlin Hospital, 264
Kriyukov, Liyosha, 93
Krupskaya, 126
Kuleshov, Lev, 71, 76, 190, 196

LaFollette, Senator, 165
Lan-fang, Mei, 116, 188
Lang, Fritz, 71, 140
La Sarraz Congress, 139–40
Lasky, Jesse, 149, 157, 160
Lawrence, D. H., 189
League of Youth, The, 56
Lebedev, Nikolai, 76
Lef, 62, 76, 126
Léger, Fernand, 142
Leiva, Augustin Aragon, 179, 184
Lenin, 49, 119, 122–3, 125–6
Leonov, Leonid, 251
Lesser, Sol, 183, 281
Levitsky, Alexander, 92
Levshin, A., 92

Leyda, Jay, 10, 14, 57, 75, 85, 98, 130, 131, 132, 136, 175, 176, 190, 192, 193, 194, 197, 198, 210, 221, 228, 260, 265, 280
Life in Mexico, 161
Linder, Max, 66
Listen Moscow, 21, 69, 85
Litvinov, 189
Liveright, Horace, 155
Lomonosov, projected film about, 229
London Film Society, 144
London, Jack, 50
Londres, Albert, 141
Longfellow, Henry Wadsworth, 153
Lower Depths, The, 44
Lubitsch, Ernst, 154, 158
Lunacharsky, Anatoli, 49, 58, 62, 102, 103
Luria, A. R., 269

Macbeth, 58, 170–2
Madame Bovary, 67
Madame Sans-Gêne, 34, 42
Maeterlinck, Maurice, 34, 39, 41
Malraux, André, 116, 128, 188
Maly Theatre, 62
Mandrot, Hélène de, 139
Mann, Thomas, 10
Marinetti, F. T., 47, 142
Markish, Perets, 249
Marriage, The, 34, 59
Marset, Alfred de, 139
Martyrdom of the Jesuit Missionaries in North America, The, 152
Marx, Karl, 126
Masks, 57
Masquerade (Lermontov), 36
Mass, Vladimir, 57
Mathematics, 35, 80–1
Matushenko, 96
Maugard, Best, 166
Maupassant, Guy de, 17
Maxim Maximovich Maximov, 187
Mayakovsky, Vladimir, 47, 48, 49, 57, 62, 68, 76, 103, 125–6
Meisel, Edmund, 109–10, 113, 122, 123, 134, 138, 140, 207
Mélies, Georges, 23
M-G-M, 137
Mexican, The, 50–2, 58, 64
Meyerhold, Vsevolod, 18, 36, 48, 49, 54, 55–6, 58, 59, 60–1, 76, 125, 199
Michelangelo, 252
Michoels, Solomon, 249
Mignet, *History of the French Revolution*, 31
Mikhin, Boris, 72, 77, 78, 79–80, 82
Misérables, Les, 31
Mitry, Jean, 85, 130, 142, 144, 213, 218, 260–1, 279
Molière, 36, 42
Montage, 25, 31, 35, 44–5, 67, 71, 74–5, 77, 80, 81, 85, 104–8, 115, 124–5, 132–4, 213, 250
Montage of Attractions, 60, 62–3, 69, 78, 80, 85, 124, 132, 213, 272
Montagu, Ivor, 57, 110, 128, 141, 142, 146, 154, 155–6, 159, 160, 189, 279
Moreau le jeune, 38
Morozov, Pavlik, 192

Mosaic Hall, 57
Moscow, 187–8
Moscow Art Theatre, 34, 62
Moscow 800, 266–7
Moscow's Hand, 34
Moscow the Second, 188
Moscow University, 269
Mosfilm, 201, 227, 250, 256
Mother, 91, 115
Moussinac, Léon, 14, 114, 115, 121, 126, 139–40, 147, 148, 199, 279
Murnau, F. W., 140
Musée Grévin, 24, 117
Mystery-Bouffe, 48
Mystery-Play of Liberated Toil, The, 48

Napoleon's Tomb, 23
Nemirovich-Danchenko, V. I., 47, 57
Neuhaus, Heinrich, 214
Newton, Isaac, 209
New York Sun, 111
Nezlobin Theatre, 34
Nibelungen, Die (Hebbel), 34
Nielsen, Asta, 16, 110
Nikandrov, 119, 126
Ninth of January, 91
Nizhny, Vladimir, 203, 205, 280
Notre Dame de Paris, 23
Novy Lef, 126

October, 21–2, 24, 37, 56, 71, 117–26, 141, 143, 207, 241
Officers' Engineering School, 37, 106
Ogonyokh, 38
Old and New see *The General Line*
Oppenheim Family, The, 201
Or, L', 142, 152, 156
Orlov, Dmitri, 209
Orozco, José Clemente, 166
Ostrovsky, Alexander, 34

Pabst, G. W., 140, 142
Parallel montage, 75
Paramount Pictures, 149, 152, 154, 155, 156, 157, 159–60
Paris-Midi, 149
Patatra, 69
Pavlenko, Pyotr, 208, 209, 210–11, 223, 225, 226
Pavlov, Ivan, 49, 63, 80, 176
Payne, Frances, 177
Pease, Major Frank, 155, 163
People's Commissariat of Enlightenment, 49
Perekop, 222–3
Pereshvalsky, Father Nikolai, 130
Pere Tru (Peredvizhaniya Trupa), 62
Petersburgskava Gazeta, 37
Petrograd Institute of Civil Engineering, 35, 36, 38
Petrov, Yevgeni, 114
Peyich, 41, 42
Phèdre, 57
Picasso, Pablo, 54, 91
Pickford, Mary, 111, 136
Pirandello, Luigi, 140, 186–7
Piriyev, Ivan, 51
Piscator, Erwin, 140
Planck, Max Karl Ernst Ludwig, 176
Pletnyov, Valeri, 49, 53, 69, 72
Podvoysky, N. I., 117

Poe, Edgar Allan, 32, 135, 176
Poet's Love, The, 229–33, 272
Political Directorate for the Western Front (Puzap), 42, 44
Porter, Edwin S., 74, 75
Posada, 166
Potemkin, Prince, 139
Pravda, 83, 198, 257
Precipice, 53–4, 85
Prestige of an Empire, The, 229
Priestley, J. B., 224
Prince Igor, 210
Prokofiev, Sergei, 214–18, 220, 226, 231, 249, 250, 251–2, 256–7, 261, 264–5
Proletkino, 78
Proletkult Congress, 49
Proletkult Theatre, 47, 48–9, 56, 58, 62, 72, 76, 78, 79, 82, 83
Propper, 38
Pudovkin, Vsevolod, 75, 91, 115–16, 119, 127, 128, 131, 134, 190, 250, 253
Pushkin, Alexander, 19, 135, 225, 229–33
Puss in Boots (Tieck), 56, 60

Queen of Spades, The (Tchaikovsky), 58
Querschnitt, 181
Que Viva Mexico!, 10, 27, 32, 33, 135, 165, 166, 172–84, 187, 190, 194, 218, 222–3, 224, 226, 232, 262, 267

Rachmaninov, Sergei, 180
Ranevskaya, 251
Red Cavalry, 88–9
Red Pepper, 72
Reed, John, 56, 161
Reich, Zinayida, 60
Reinhardt, Max, 47, 110
Religion, 123–4, 130
Resnais, Alain, 244, 272
Revue du Cinéma, La, 140
Richter, Hans, 99, 139, 140, 144
Rin-Tin-Tin, 153
Rivera, Diego, 137, 161, 166
Road to Life, The, 189
Robeson, Paul, 16, 189–90, 201
Rolland, Romain, 11, 42
Romance Sentimentale, 144, 187, 207, 232
Romm, Mikhail, 17
Roosevelt, Franklin D., 221
Roshal, Grigori, 17
Rostotsky, 205
Rostovtsev, I., 98, 280
Rostropovich, Mtsislav, 214
R.S.F.S.R. Theatre No. 1, 48
Russ, 210
Russian Revolution, The, 31–2, 35–8, 75–6
Ruttmann, Walter, 143
Rzheshevsky, Alexander, 192, 193

Sachs, Hanns, 140
Saint-Simon, Claude, 41
Saldivar, Don Julio, 176
Satirikhon, 37
Savchenko, Igor, 196
Schenck, Joseph, 137, 138

Schopenhauer, Arthur, 41
Schulberg, B. P., 159, 160
Science of Shocks, 80
Scriabin, Alexander, 133
Selznick, David, 160
Semper Ante Theatre, 48
Sennett, Mack, 154
Serafimovich, Alexander, 88, 117
Sergei Eisenstein (V. Katanian), 281
Seton, Marie, 9, 51, 57, 80, 84, 166, 179, 182, 184, 188, 197, 241, 270, 279
Sevzapkino, 83
Shaw, G. B., 144, 146, 149, 163
Sheinin, Lev, 229
Shelley, Percy Bysshe, 146
Shklovsky's, Victor, 83, 104, 130, 141, 209, 214, 265, 270, 280
Shub, Esther, 16, 17, 71, 78, 101, 122, 130, 166, 196, 199, 232, 260, 280
Shumyatsky, Boris, 186, 187, 188, 194, 197, 198, 201
Simonov Monastery, 83
Sinclair, David, 183
Sinclair, Upton, 118, 161, 163, 165, 166, 173, 175, 177–84, 186
Siqueiros, David Alfaro, 166, 181
Sketches, 25–6 170–2, 182, 183, 234–5, 239–40
Slavinsky, Yevgeni, 92
Smishlayev, Valeri, 50, 53, 54
Sokhotsky, Professor, 35
Sound cinema, 104, 126, 134, 192, 194, 201
Sovietskoye Iskusstvo, 188
Sovkino, 103, 116, 122, 123, 136, 149, 175
Sozialistische Filmkritik, 141
Spinoza, Baruch, 176
Stage design, 42–3, 47, 50, 53–4, 57–8
Stalin, Joseph, 122–3, 136, 180, 186, 199, 214, 238, 265
Stanislavsky, Konstantin, 47, 48, 49, 60
State Institute of Cinematography, 41, 96, 189, 202–5, 252, 269
State School for State Direction, 54
Stern, Seymour, 177, 179, 180–1
Sternberg, Josef von, 140, 155, 160
Stevens, George, 160
Stokowski, Leopold, 177, 182, 253
Storm over Asia, 54
Strauch, Maxim, 21, 24, 25, 34, 36, 45, 47, 56, 62, 92, 94, 95, 96, 99, 119, 205, 270
Strauss, Sara Mildred, 183
Strick, Joseph, 143
Strike, 27, 33, 54, 72, 76, 77, 78–88, 103, 104, 117, 224, 246
Stroheim, Erich von, 17, 154
Stroyeva, Vera, 17
Stuart, Mary, 144–6
Studies for Eisenstein's Mexican Film, 10, 175, 176
Sutter's Gold, 155, 156–7

Tairov, Alexander, 48, 57, 59
Taking of the Winter Palace, The, 48

Teleshova, Elisabeta, 195, 211–13, 250, 251, 252
Television, 269
Ten Days That Shook the World, 117
Theatre, 34, 36, 37, 39, 41, 46–72
Théâtre Libre, 47
Theatre of the Four Masks, 48
Three Ages, The, 131
Three Sisters, The, 230
Thunder over Mexico, 183, 184, 269
Tikhonovich, V., 58
Time in the Sun, 184, 269
Tinyanov, Yuri, 230, 233, 253
Tisse, Edward, 79–80, 82, 92, 96, 100, 101, 102, 103, 119, 137, 139, 140, 144, 149, 153, 162, 181, 183, 195, 223, 270
Toeplitz, Jerzy, 113
Toland, Gregg, 135
Toller, Ernst, 111, 140
Tolstoy, Leo, 224, 227
Towards the Dictatorship, 72, 78, 117
Trauberg, Leonid, 58, 196
Trenker, Luis, 157
Tretyakov, Sergei, 69, 116, 117, 126, 199
Trotsky, Leon, 121
Tselikovskaya, Ludmila, 251
Turandot, 34, 36
Turgenev, Ivan, 192, 194
Typage, 57, 76, 94, 119, 125–6, 193, 253

Ugly Duchess, The, 201
Ulanova, Galina, 17, 251
Ulysses, 143
United Artists, 136

Vakhtangov Theatre, 193
Vasiliev, Dmitri, 211
Vasiliev Brothers, The (Georgi and Sergei), 190, 196, 205, 222, 250
Vertov, Dziga, 66, 67, 76, 88
Victoria, Queen, 146
Vidor, King, 154
Viertel, Salka, 179
Villa, Pancho, 173
Vinci, Leonardo da, 11, 80, 142, 146, 198
Vinogradov, A. K., 189
Vishnevsky, Vsevolod, 7, 17, 91, 190, 198, 201, 210, 257, 280
Viva Villa, 184
Voroshilov, Kliment, 122

Wagner, Richard, 141, 227–8, 230
Walküre, Die, 199, 227–9
Wallenstein, 34
War and Peace (Prokofiev), 228
War and Peace (Tolstoy), 253
War of the Worlds, The, 146, 149
Washington, George, 153
Weisfeld, Ilya, 16
Welles, Orson, 253, 272
Wells, H. G., 146, 189
We the Russian People, 201
Whitman, Walt, 271
Williams, Albert Rhys, 161
Wise Man, The see *Even a Wise Man Stumbles*

Index

Woman of Paris, A, 131
Wundt, Wilhelm, 105
Wyler, William, 135

Yakulov, Georgi, 58
Yaroslavsky, 122
Year 1905, 91–3, 94

Yogi Rāmacharaka (William Walker Atkinson), 49
Yutkevich, Sergei, 54–5, 56–7, 59, 187, 190, 280

Zaharoff, Basil, 141
Zakhava, Boris, 193

Zapata, Emiliano, 173
Zarkhi, Nathan, 188
Zhitnaya Street Studio, 82
Zhunguo, 116
Znamya, 210
Zola, Emile, 32, 149, 202
Zvenigora, 127

Acknowledgments

The author wishes to express his gratitude for their assistance in the preparation of this book to the following institutions and individuals:

The National Film Archive, Bucarest, and the Central Research Section of the Archive; the National Central Archive for Literature and Art, Moscow; the Museum of the Moscow Art Theatre; the Österreichisches Filmmuseum, Vienna.

Ioan Grigorescu, Ervin Voiculescu, Dumitru Fàrnoagà, Stela Kintescu, Domnica Stoicescu (Romania).

Lev Kuleshov, Grigori Kozintsev, Naum Kleiman, Leonid Kozlov, Ilya Weisfeld, Bella Epstein, Rostislav Yurenev, Bianca Tisse (Soviet Union).

Leopold Stokowski (U.S.A.), Professor Maurice Dobb (Cambridge, England), David J. Francis (The British Film Institute, England), Henri Colpi (France), Lic Xavier Campos Ponce and Señora de los Angeles Saldivar (Mexico).

I wish to thank Peter Konlechner and Peter Kubelka (Austria) for their friendly help in enabling me to view all the available films of Eisenstein.

I am indebted to Professors Ronald Gottesman and Harry A. Geduld (Indiana University, U.S.A.) for their kindness in making me acquainted with their researches; and to Professor Gottesman for his valued assistance in coordinating my chapter on *Que Viva Mexico!* and for allowing me to consult some of the unpublished material relating to Eisenstein's Mexican film in the Upton Sinclair archive.

My thanks also to Oliver Stallybrass who edited this English language edition with great understanding, sympathy and competence. Finally, I wish to extend my special gratitude to Jay Leyda for his inestimable help and friendly encouragement, without which this book could never have been written.

Y. B.

The publisher wishes to thank Faber and Faber for permission to use the extracts from *The Film Sense*, and Dennis Dobson for the extracts from *Film Form*. The author has supplied most of the stills used in the book; for the remainder, the publisher wishes to thank the National Film Archive.